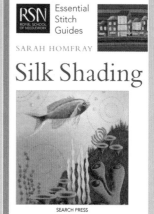

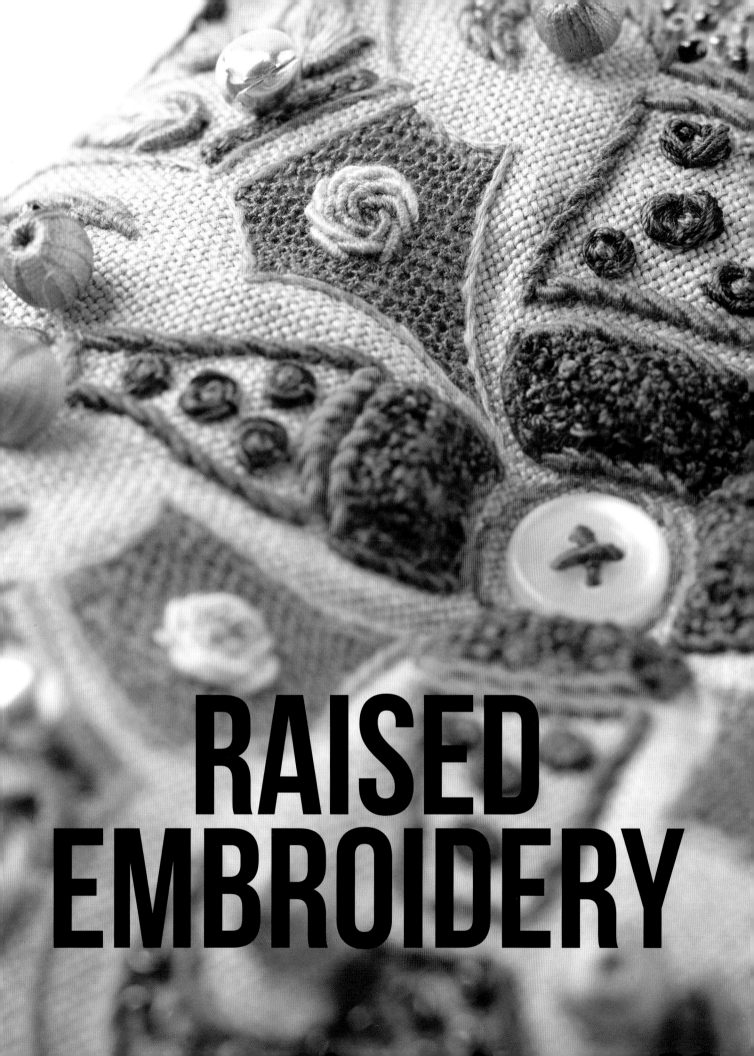

RAISED
EMBROIDERY

DEDICATION

For family and friends, but especially for Mummy.

ACKNOWLEDGEMENTS

I would like to thank the RSN for the adventure of creating this book – thanks to all my teachers, colleagues and students, past and present, for inspiring me and putting up with me; to Deb for being there and of course to Edd for his patience.

The following artists kindly supplied work to be featured in this book, for which they have my gratitude: Jenny Adin-Christie, Kate Barlow, Laura Baverstock, Angela Bishop, Stella Davies, Margaret Dier, Lisa Bilby, Jennifer Goodwin, Jessica Grimm, Victoria Laine, Jacqui McDonald, Hattie McGill, Helen Richman, and Elena Thornton.

First published in 2017

Search Press Limited
Wellwood, North Farm Road,
Tunbridge Wells, Kent TN2 3DR

Text copyright © Kelley Aldridge 2017

Photographs by Paul Bricknell at Search Press Studios, except for pages 7 and 80 © The Royal School of Needlework, and as noted throughout

Photographs and design copyright © Search Press Ltd 2017

ISBN 978 1 78221 189 1

The Publishers and author can accept no responsibility for any consequences arising from the information, advice or instructions given in this publication.

Suppliers
If you have difficulty in obtaining any of the materials and equipment mentioned in this book, then please visit the Search Press website for details of suppliers:
www.searchpress.com

For more information about the RSN, its courses, studio, shop and exhibitions, visit:
www.royal-needlework.org.uk

For information about the RSN degree programme, visit:
www.rsndegree.uk

Printed in China through Asia Pacific Offset

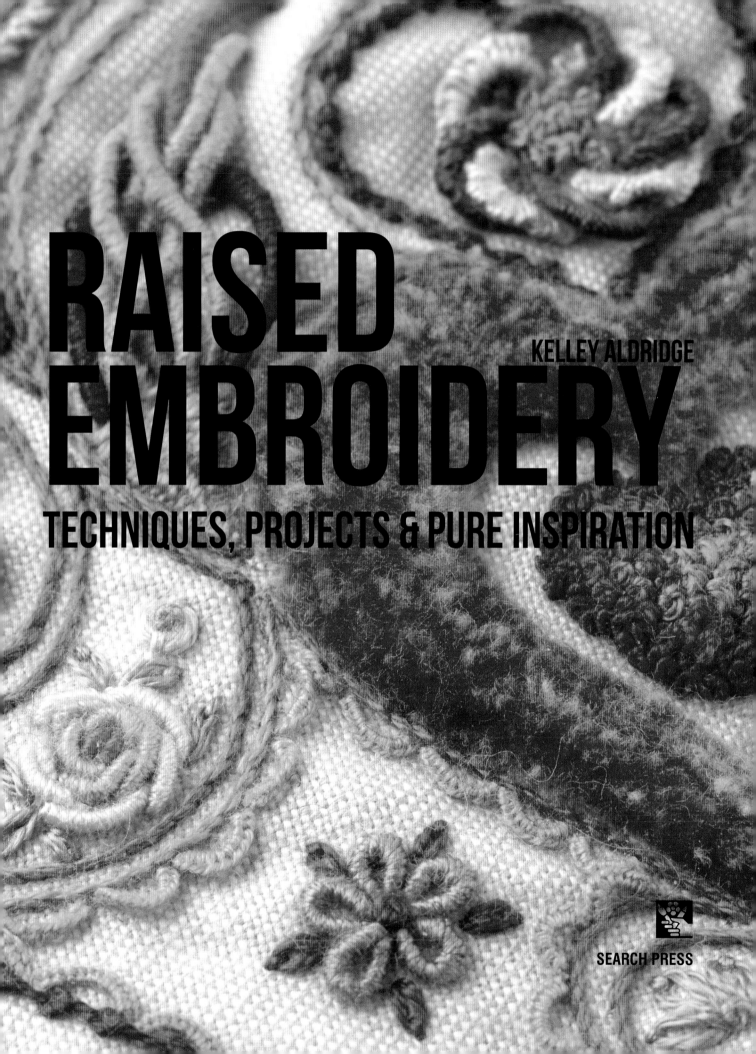

RAISED EMBROIDERY

KELLEY ALDRIDGE

TECHNIQUES, PROJECTS & PURE INSPIRATION

SEARCH PRESS

The Royal School of Needlework 6

Introduction to raised embroidery 8

History of raised embroidery 10

Materials 12

Inspiration and design 18

Basic techniques for
raised embroidery 22

Padding techniques 34

Attaching stitches 38

Raised stitches 42

Needlelace stitches 56

Wired shape techniques 58

PROJECTS 62

Wearable raised embroidery 64

66 Brooch

Other wearables 80

Useable raised embroidery 86

88 Phone sleeve

Other useables 102

Collectible raised embroidery 108

110 Biscornu

Other collectibles 126

Further inspiration 132

Index 144

CONTENTS

RSN THE ROYAL SCHOOL OF NEEDLEWORK

Founded in 1872, the Royal School of Needlework (RSN) is the international centre of excellence for the art of hand embroidery. It is based at Hampton Court Palace in west London but also offers courses across the UK, in the USA and Japan. Today it is a thriving, dynamic centre of teaching and learning, and believes that hand embroidery is a vital art form that impacts on many aspects of our lives from clothes to ceremonial outfits, and from home furnishings to textile art.

To enable and encourage people to learn the skill of hand embroidery the RSN offers courses from beginner to degree level. The wide range of short courses includes introductions to each of the stitch techniques the RSN uses, beginning with Introduction to Embroidery. The RSN's Certificate and Diploma in Technical Hand Embroidery offers students the opportunity to learn a range of techniques to a very high technical standard. The Future Tutors course is specifically designed for those pursuing a career in teaching technical hand embroidery. The RSN's BA (Hons) Degree course is the only UK degree course solely focussed on hand embroidery and offers students opportunities to learn core stitch techniques, which they are then encouraged to apply in contemporary and conceptual directions. Graduates can go on to find careers in embroidery relating to fashion, couture and costume; to interiors and soft furnishings or in the area of textile art including jewellery and millinery.

At its Hampton Court headquarters, the RSN welcomes people for all kind of events from private lessons to bespoke stitching holidays, intensive Certificate and Diploma studies, tours around our exhibitions, which comprise either pieces from our own textile collections or students' work, or study days looking at particular pieces or techniques from our Collection. Work by students and from the Collection also forms the core of a series of lectures and presentations available to those who cannot get to the RSN.

The RSN Collection of textiles comprises more than 2,000 pieces, all of which have been donated, because as a charity the RSN cannot afford to purchase additions. The pieces were given so that they would have a home for the future and to be used as a resource for students and researchers. The Collection comes from all over the world, illustrating many different techniques and approaches to stitch and embellishment.

The RSN Studio undertakes new commissions and conservation work for many different clients, including public institutions, places of worship, stately homes and private individuals, again illustrating the wide variety of roles embroidery can play, from altar frontals and vestments for churches to curtains, hangings and chair covers for homes and embroidered pictures as works of art.

Over the last few years the RSN has worked with a number of prestigious names including Sarah Burton OBE for Alexander McQueen, Vivienne Westwood's Studio for Red Carpet Green Dress, Patrick Grant's E Tautz, the late L'Wren Scott, Nicholas Oakwell Couture for the GREAT Britain Exhibition, the Jane Austen House Museum, Liberty London, the V&A Museum of Childhood and M&S and Oxfam for Shwopping.

For more information about the RSN, its courses, studio, shop and exhibitions, see www.royal-needlework.org.uk, and for its degree programme see www.rsndegree.uk.

Hampton Court Palace, Surrey, home of
the Royal School of Needlework

INTRODUCTION TO RAISED EMBROIDERY

I adore embroidered objects, and am always seeking new ways of incorporating stitch in three-dimensional items. There are already a number of excellent books available on this subject, written by some very talented embroidery artists, but this book is about exploring new possibilities. Many of you will know the craft of raised embroidery as 'stumpwork', but this is a Victorian term for a broader craft that incorporates three-dimensional, padded, raised, and partially free-standing stitching. In this book we take a fresh look at some traditional raised embroidery techniques. New and experienced stitchers alike will find information and inspiration in these pages – and I hope that the projects and images I have included here will persuade you to see this form of embroidery in a new way.

WHAT EXACTLY IS RAISED EMBROIDERY?

Essentially, raised work is a three-dimensional form of embroidery that uses padding and other forms such as wire, wood and card, to support flat and raised stitches, needlelace and other embellishments. Raised embroidery is the technique of texture – ridges and domes, grit and grains, looping spirals and, of course, layers upon layers. It is also about being more than the sum of its parts. Most raised embroidery pieces are assembled from a number of components or objects, which are stitched separately, then attached to a base fabric. This gives the first hint of how endless the opportunities for imagination and creativity in raised embroidery are. Above all, raised embroidery is fun – it can be whimsical, bold, classy or zany, whatever appeals to you!

Once upon a time, a person would announce their status in society by the level of decoration on their clothes or by the sumptuousness of their home furnishings. This form of display lives on today, having developed into owning the latest technical gadget in the hand (or on the wrist), driving the most expensive vehicle, or having the most elite fashion label on display.

Where does embroidered finery fit in a world of downloads, social media, mass-produced kits and flat-packed furniture? At heart we are no different from our fellow stitchers at any time in history – we are driven to embellish, enliven and enhance our surroundings, which includes our own personal image. In a world that is getting ever more streamlined and same-looking, we can create personal sparkle by stitching something completely unique. In this book, I show you how this sparkle can extend to all areas of your life, not just the walls of your home. Come with me on a journey of colour and texture, history and modernity, and wrap yourself in raised embroidery!

Opposite
Detail of Sweetie Dress
Kate Barlow

This charming half-scale gown's focal point is the delightful embroidered 'sweets', which have been worked in various stitches including long and short shading, couching and wrapped beads. The full piece can be seen on page 109.

8

HISTORY OF RAISED EMBROIDERY

Raised work, or embossed work (it was not known as 'stumpwork' until the Victorians renewed its popularity) was a status symbol in the second half of the seventeenth century, as it was expensive to create, time-consuming and fragile. It represented the best of a lady's skill with needle and thread.

These historical pieces are usually richly decorated, without scale or perspective (much like Jacobean crewelwork) and based around moral or religious themes. Biblical stories such as Moses in the river, and the subject of Faith, Hope and Charity, were often depicted, reflecting the trends and fashions of the time. Once completed, the embroidery was usually sent away to be made up professionally into ornate boxes or frames for mirrors or paintings. Such items were highly prized and cherished by succeeding generations of the family and, if they became damaged or worn, the embroidery would often be recycled into pictures or smaller decorative panels, which can be seen today in many museums and stately homes.

Seeing the quality of these older pieces today, it is almost impossible to believe that these 'ladies' were in fact very young girls, often no more than ten years old. The raised work objects each lady produced was usually the final piece she worked as it combined many elements learned throughout her education.

Girls from less wealthy families were also taught various forms of needlework, but with a more domestic focus, such as plain stitching and monogramming. Whether rich or poor, embroiderers throughout history enjoyed the idea of 'mixed media' as much as their modern counterparts – they used a wide variety of items in addition to their silk and metal threads: beads, glass, recycled pieces of broken jewellery and natural objects such as small shells were included in these fantastical pieces, and the great exuberance of the stitcher is often evident.

10

Barbara and Roy Hirst did much to renew interest in this fascinating form of embroidery from the 1980s onward, and their Millennium Casket (now in the Embroiderer's Guild Collection) was a tour de force in raised work.

Today new embroiderers have emerged to take the technique even further: Jane Nicholas, Alison Cole and Di van Niekerk take inspiration from historical examples to create fresh designs whilst artists such as Jane Hall, Sue Newhouse and Annemieke Mein pursue a more experimental approach. Today, popular themes revolve around flora and fauna, with flowers and insects commonly incorporated into the design.

Whether your stitching style is based in history or modernity, raised work has as much scope for your imagination today as it ever has – enjoy!

MATERIALS

The great thing about raised embroidery is that it uses such a diverse collection of materials, much of which you probably already have. The following pages look in a little more detail at the tools and materials you can use, along with any special considerations.

NEEDLES

A good variety of needles is recommended for the many different techniques involved in raised embroidery. Generally speaking, the higher the size number, the finer the gauge of the needle. They can be divided into the following broad types:

Embroidery needles These have long eyes and sharp tips.

Tapestry needles These are blunt-tipped.

Curved needles These needles are really useful for working stitches onto fabric which has been stretched over a hard backing (as in box-making). In my view, the finer the needle, the better.

Milliner's needles Also called straw needles, this type of needle has a small round eye that is the same thickness as the shaft. This makes them ideal for bullion knots and cast-on stitches.

A selection of the needles detailed above.

FABRICS

This is such a huge subject that the best advice I can give is to make sure your fabrics are 'fit for purpose' – you want your project to look good and give pleasure for years to come, so using appropriate fabrics for embellishment and backing is essential. If you are new to the intoxicating world of textiles, I suggest you make yourself familiar with the characteristics and care requirements of anything you are tempted to use before you commit yourself!

Fabrics for embellishment should be strong enough to cope with the techniques and threads that you are intending to use. Fabrics with a higher thread count, such as cotton, work well, as do some kinds of silk and linen. Stretchy fabrics are difficult to embroider upon, so I would not recommend them for a beginner. The same holds true for any fabric worked on the bias (i.e. at a slant) for the same reasons.

Whichever fabric you use, always support it with a backing layer of either calico or cotton and work your stitches through both layers, just to be on the safe side.

THREADS

As with fabrics, there are many types of threads on the market today, so consider the purpose of the piece you are stitching in order to make the best thread choice. When choosing a thread, take into consideration its strength, colour-fastness (if the item is to be washed at any stage) and whether it will allow you to achieve the effect you want.

Stranded cotton A popular all-round type of thread that consists of six strands. These can be used together for a bulky effect, or individually for a very fine finish. This type of thread is usually bought in 8m (8¾yd) skeins.

Silk Used in much the same way as stranded cotton, silk threads come in a variety of thicknesses and an array of jewel-like colours.

Cotton perlé Generally a bulkier thread, although it is available in a variety of thicknesses. It is known for its highly twisted appearance and slight lustre.

Quilting cotton Often overlooked, there are some lovely variegated hand-quilting cottons that are good value for money and can be used in all forms of decorative stitching. They are bought on reels.

Crewel wool Fine, two-ply wool usually used in Jacobean crewelwork. Most surface stitches can be worked in this thread and it gives a nice chunky effect.

Synthetic metallic This type of thread comes in many forms, but usually resembles version of gold, silver and copper. Metallic thread adds a lovely sparkle and richness to your work, but it can seem temperamental and prone to snapping. Taking particular care and using shorter lengths in the needle is recommended for the best results.

Rayon As with synthetic metallic threads, rayon thread can seem temperamental, but the results are worth the extra effort owing to the amazing colours in which this thread is available.

Metallic Available from specialist suppliers, this is the 'real stuff'. It is not designed to go through the eye of a needle, and as a result is usually attached to the fabric with couching stitches (see page 38).

Ribbon Fine silk ribbon works beautifully in surface embroidery stitches. The colours can be extraordinarily rich and variegated, while the flatness of the ribbon creates interesting effects when stitched like an ordinary thread.

SCISSORS, FRAMES AND OTHER TOOLS

We stitchers love our gadgets, and for such an all-encompassing technique as raised embroidery, the list of possible tools could be endless! However, before you invest large sums in lots of new toys, here is a list of what you should have readily to hand:

Fabric scissors A pair of scissors with long, sharp blades is essential. These are to be used only on fabric: scissors blunted on paper will cause fabric to fray.

Embroidery scissors Small scissors with fine tips, these are better able to work accurately in tight spaces.

Rough scissors Keep a pair of scissors to use on paper or fine wires – essentially, anything other than fabric and thread – in order to keep your other pairs in the best possible condition.

Hoop frame A pair of hoops, one of which fits snugly inside the other. These are to hold your fabric taut. Available in various sizes, I recommend using them attached to a seat paddle, a table clamp or a floor stand in order that you can work hands-free.

Tweezers Fine-tipped jeweller's tweezers allow greater control over thread, wires and beads. Have both a straight and a curved set to work in tight spaces.

Square slate frame For bigger projects, where you must keep the entire design flat, use a large slate frame rather than a hoop frame.

Pins Fine pins with glass heads will save your fingers.

Thimble I use one on each hand to protect my fingers.

Curved-tipped pliers These angled pliers are used to draw needles through fabric when they get tightly wedged.

Fabric paints and applicators These can be used to add colour to the background of your work. Make sure they are waterproof.

Needlelace forms These are specialist tools, usually made out of wood, to create three-dimensional shapes to work needlelace over.

Needle case Useful for storing your needles safely and ensuring none are left behind in your piece!

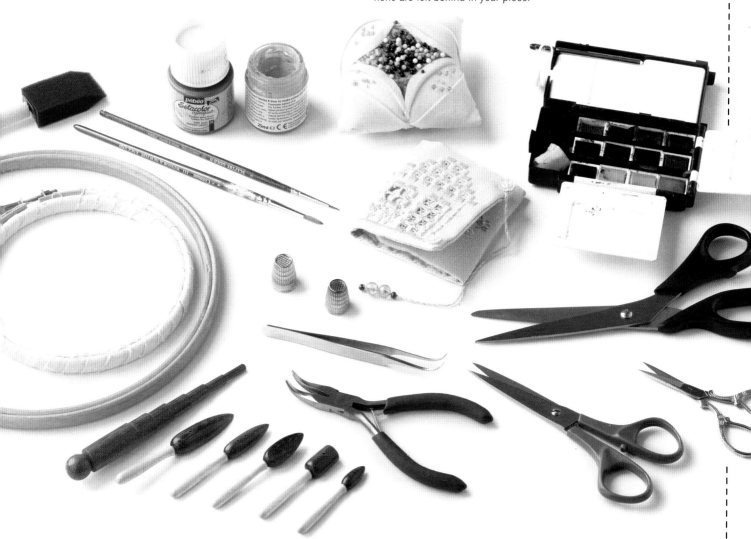

EMBELLISHMENTS

This is a general term for things like beads, charms, shisha mirrors and anything else you can attach to your fabric as decoration. Have fun shopping!

Buttons These are available in a huge variety of shapes, sizes and materials. Often sold individually, they can be mini works of art in themselves and can be used as accents or even as the central motif in a piece.

Beads Just as varied as buttons, beads can be used as scattered elements in a background or provide focus on another element, such as a piece of jewellery.

Charms Usually made out of metal, these are often grouped together and sold by theme such as 'baby' or 'seaside'. They can add a touch of whimsy to a piece.

Scrapbooking embellishments Scrapbooking is a craft which involves creating beautifully decorated pages to display mementoes and photographs. The huge range of embellishments and add-ons created for scrapbooking is ideal for use with your embroidery as well. Small paper flowers and miniature clothes pegs are just two examples of suitable items you can find in scrapbooking shops.

Jewellery findings Findings are the fastenings and attachments on brooches, necklaces, earrings and bracelets that hold the piece in place. While not strictly embellishments, as they are rarely decorative, they are essential for your finished pieces.

REPURPOSED MATERIALS

Some people refer to this category as 'found objects' or 'upcycling'. Essentially, this means anything that originally had a different purpose, but which you would like to use in your project. It can include shells, coins, bits of broken jewellery, mirrors, stamps, and even old sewing tools.

I like reusing bits and pieces in my raised embroidery as it gives the object a personal meaning. Just remember the 'fit for purpose' rule, and think carefully before you cut your great-grandmother's wedding dress into strips to use as an embellishment – be sure you really want to!

Feather

The tip of this quill has been secured at the base of the embroidered and wired organdie leaf, using several fine couching stitches (see page 38) in invisible thread.

Beetle's wing case

A fine copper thread was couched (see page 38) in a zig-zagging fashion along the length of the wing case in order to secure it to the fabric and provide decorative colour contrast.

Coin

Variegated cotton perlé thread and a traditional shisha stitch (see page 40) was used to secure this coin to the fabric in a sampler.

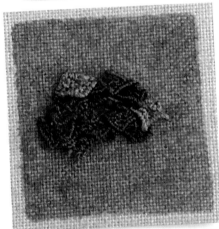

INSPIRATION AND DESIGN

CREATIVITY

Many people would hesitate at calling themselves artistic, but I believe everyone is naturally creative – it's something we're all born with. Do you sometimes vary what you eat for breakfast? Do you wear something different each day? Do you see a beautiful picture or photograph and stop for a moment to appreciate it? These are all expressions of personal taste, and that is another way of saying you are a creative being. Once you recognise this – and that there is no pressure to do anything but suit your own taste with your raised embroidery – your confidence will grow.

Being creative is about combining ideas, building on what has gone before, and throwing in a dash of your own personal style. Once you realise that everything has already been done in some form or other, and that all you are doing is adopting an idea to tweak and alter and make your own, you will feel 'off the hook'. Without self-imposed pressure, you can start without any preconceptions of having to be born creative.

FINDING YOUR INSPIRATION

I am an 'image magpie' and I am sure that I am not alone – many of you will have files full of pictures torn out of magazines, boxes of photocopied patterns, drawers and baskets and shelves full of fabric, threads, and beads. Many of you, like me, will have incorporated digital sources into your physical folders and scrapbooks and shoeboxes. Sites like Pinterest are my virtual, searchable filing cabinet of pictures. From here I can see all my saved images, as well as those saved by others around the world! If you've not been introduced to this website, I strongly encourage you to make friends with it at your earliest convenience.

This is where I start my designing journey – once I've decided what I want to make, and pondered any specific details I want to include, I can then start looking for relevant pictures. If, for example, I want to create a commemorative cushion that suggests a couple's mutual interest in sailing, as a golden wedding anniversary gift, I will look for images of boats, anchors, hearts, rings and so on. I will start to fill a Pinterest board with inspiring images that I can look at again and again, letting them soak into my brain. Whilst I am at it, I go and search different colour palettes, both online and in favourite fabrics from my collection.

Keep an open mind

With the wonders of the planet on your computer and tablet and smartphone, it can be easy to forget that there are wonders of a different sort outside your door. Go for a walk and look at all the textures, colours, shapes and patterns that are everywhere around you.

Skies never fail to put on an amazing colour show, and your surroundings will be full of exciting or interesting sights. The area where I live is bursting with amazing old stone walls – both upright and falling down!

Small children are endlessly pocketing treasures like pinecones, feathers, acorn caps and knobbly twigs – not to mention pebbles, chestnuts, seedheads, shells, and so on. Be a child again, and go for a wander – take it all in and be inspired!

DESIGNING YOUR RAISED EMBROIDERY

The design of a three-dimensional piece of embroidery differs from that of a flat 'picture' embroidery. In a three-dimensional piece, the form takes precedence, and the decorative elements must work within it.

CHOOSING THE SIZE AND SHAPE

You may already have a rough idea of what motifs you wish to include, and what colours you like, but before you commit to anything, you should confirm the size and shape of the object that the embroidery will go on. The easiest way to do this is to create a mock-up of the finished item.

This rough piece can be drafted on paper or on scrap calico – suitable for a simple project like a tote bag – or you can make a model from card for more complex shapes; such as a compartmental box, for example. Putting form first will very quickly show you how many sides, panels, edges, tops and bottoms there are to consider, and it can help to fire your imagination further.

I usually draw out or make my rough design ideas on a much bigger scale than the final piece as this makes it easier to see. You can reduce your design on a photocopier or scanner later once you have confirmed that it will work.

CONSIDERING THE FUNCTION

Once you have checked the form of a piece will work, you must also consider the function, which will influence the choice of stitches and techniques used. A delicately-wired dragonfly wing would work beautifully on a box lid, for example, but would be a disaster on a garment! Similarly, scratchy metallic threads that are really effective on a decorative cushion would drive you crazy if they were used in a necklace. You need to modify either the materials and techniques you use in order to fit with the piece's intended use, or instead alter the piece itself to accommodate the materials and techniques you do not want to compromise.

SELECTING THE MATERIALS

Before you make a final decision, play around with your materials. Threads can be combined, fabrics can be dyed and manipulated, and you might consider cross-crafting: scrapbooking, painting, calligraphy, and even dressmaking offer endless possibilities for the embroiderer.

This is your opportunity to sample any stitches or techniques you think you might like to use. Stitches can look completely different depending on the thread and scale you use, so try several and experiment. You will undoubtedly prefer the look of some over others, and this will help you to choose what will go on your final piece.

Once this is done, you are nearly there! You have decided what the object is going to be, and have confirmed its size and shape. You have developed a design to embellish it with, and have picked out the threads, fabrics and additional elements that you are going to use. You have collected all your supplies and equipment together, and you're just itching to start...

Hunting Scene
75cm (29½in) high
Part of the RSN collection

These fragments are most likely from a seventeenth-century casket. The hunt was a typical subject matter. Here, the huntsman, supported by his two dogs, is blowing his horn to flush the stag through the forest. The scene is particularly colourful – especially the huntsman himself – and the colours have stayed very strong.

The trees are made with a combination of techniques including silk wrapped purl and silk shading slips. Some of the oak leaves have been worked in couched silk gimp. Some of the hillocks, one of the dogs and deer are in needlelace. One hillock is worked in cut looped stitches and another is in over twisted threads.

BEFORE YOU BEGIN

Regardless of how different your projects are from one to the next, and despite how roundabout your creative process may be, once your design is ready, following the following routine will prove useful:

Gather your materials There is nothing so frustrating as not having the right thread or bead to hand when it is needed. Equally, it can be disappointing to learn of a wonderful product that would have been perfect for your project when it is too late. Take your time and make an effort to source and obtain the best that you can afford to create your raised work piece – stitching it will require hours of your time, and you want it to look just right when it is finished.

Create an order of work As tempting as it is to dive in and get stitching, make sure you have figured out the steps you will need to take, and the order in which to take them, before you thread a single needle. The old saying 'plan the work and work the plan' applies here! If there are any unforeseen problems to your project, it is likely you will spot them at this stage and be able to adjust accordingly. A few moments spent working methodically through exactly what you need to do from start to finish will act as a final check to make sure you have not forgotten anything obvious, and can sometimes flag up a potential problem – or an opportunity.

Framing Raised work really should be worked on fabric that is held at a good, firm tension, so make sure you have the appropriate frame to support your work in progress. See pages 24–31 for framing techniques.

Transfer the design Copy the design from your paper plan onto the fabric. Make sure the design on the fabric is identical to the one you worked hard to get right on paper. This is the stage where you can unintentionally spoil your efforts if you are not careful and precise; take your time and draw slowly. See pages 32–33 for techniques on transferring your design.

Padding If your project involves padding of any kind, now's the time to do it; it will probably be a bit messy, and it's best to get it over with and the work surface tidied up again before commencing on any more stitching. See pages 34–37 for padding techniques.

Now, you are ready to begin!

The order of work
Consider this to be your final read-through before handing in the essay, or the technical rehearsal of a play where all the gremlins are worked out before opening night. As the old saying goes: 'measure twice, cut once'!

MOODBOARDS

I have never built the habit of using a sketchbook to develop my ideas into raised embroidery pieces. I think sketchbooks can be beautiful, but I would be so busy trying to make them look good, that I would not be focussing on designing what I wanted to stitch! Instead, I use a moodboard to structure my thoughts. A moodboard is simply a large corkboard, with lots of clear-headed pins (coloured pins can interfere with the images they're pinning) that I use to secure favourite images – either torn from magazines or printed out from the computer – onto the cork. I also pin up a colour palette, either printed from online or a swatch of fabric that is inspiring me, along with a few 'keywords' which sum up what I am trying to communicate.

Above: a blank moodboard, empty of materials but full of potential!

Gradually the board fills with doodles, swatches of colour-matched threads, beads, suitable fabrics, and more and more developed designs that have been retraced and traced again, until I have enough to start. By this time the moodboard is usually a total mess, so I spend a bit of time tidying it up to tell the 'story' of the piece, gather all my materials into one project bag or box, and away I go. If you have never designed your own work before, try creating a moodboard – you will create more mess along the way, but you will also surprise yourself at how much you like the process, and the end result.

Below: A more developed moodboard, absolutely covered with threads, sketches, notes and colour scheme ideas.

BASIC TECHNIQUES FOR RAISED EMBROIDERY

These basic techniques are required for all raised embroidery, regardless of what direction your project ends up going. They may not be the most glamorous or attractive techniques, but forming good habits here will give the best foundation for successful results.

Hiding securing stitches

It is important that your securing stitches are invisible: they need to be worked in an area which will eventually be covered with embroidery. When in doubt, keep to the drawn design lines on the fabric, as these must always be covered anyway.

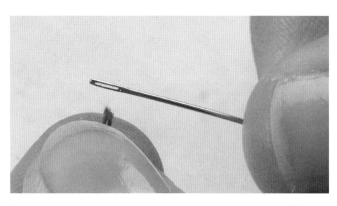

THREADING A NEEDLE

Take your thread between your thumb and index finger so that less than 2mm (1/16in) of the thread is showing. Holding the needle with your dominant hand, push the needle onto the thread.

TYING A KNOT

It is crucial to knot your thread and then start stitching in a secure way, to ensure that your stitches do not come undone in the future. This is the easiest way to put a knot into the end of your thread.

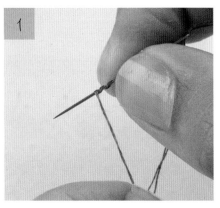

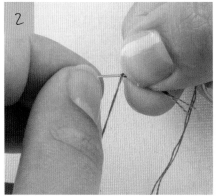

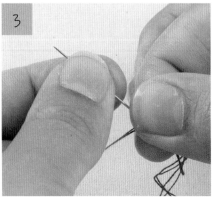

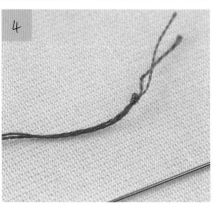

1 Thread your needle. Using your thumb and index finger, hold the tail onto the shaft of the needle so that the tail is at the eye end. Wrap the thread two or three times around the needle towards the sharp end of the needle.

2 Hold the wrapped loops on the needle with your dominant thumb.

3 Pull the needle through.

4 You have a knotted thread.

Pulling through

If you are struggling to pull your needle through at step 3, don't hold the loops around the needle quite so tightly. Having a softer tension should allow you to pull the needle through with less resistance.

22

CASTING ON

This is one of the most fundamental rules of embroidery: when working professionally, casting on and casting off is always done on the front of the frame and waste knots are cut off so that they do not get in the way of subsequent stitches.

You should always cast on and cast off near to your first or last stitch so that there is not a long stitch on the reverse of the frame, as this can affect the fabric tension.

Casting off

To cast off the thread, do so just as you cast on: make two small backstitches next to each other and then cut off the thread on the fabric's surface.

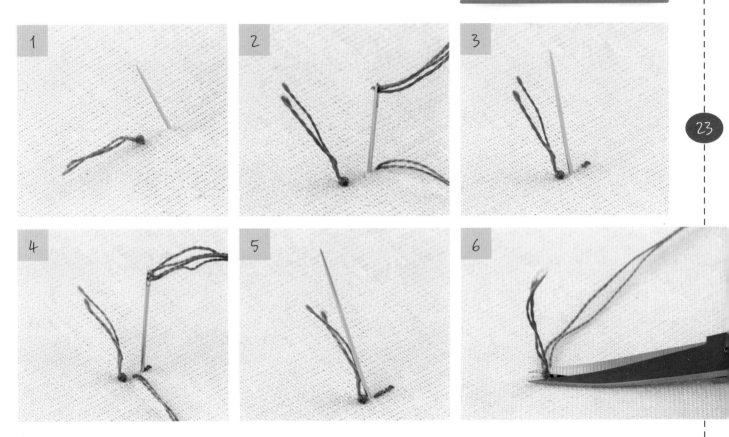

1 Make a knot in the end of the thread. Take the needle down through the fabric and then bring it up in front of the knot.

2 Work a small backstitch that is roughly 1mm (¹/₁₆in) long.

3 Bring up the needle between the first stitch and the knot.

4 Create another 1mm (¹/₁₆in) backstitch that goes back down into the hole of the first stitch created.

5 Come up at the starting point of your second stitch.

6 Cut off the waste knot on the surface of the fabric.

23

FRAMING UP A HOOP FRAME

A 'hands free' hoop frame will make your embroidery much easier to handle, once you get accustomed to using it. The important thing to remember is that your fabric must be at a very firm tension.

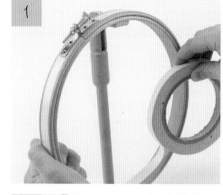

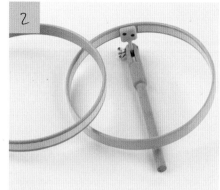

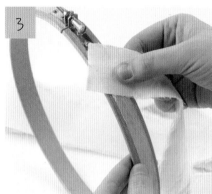

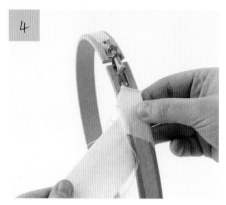

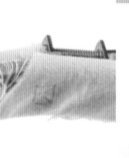

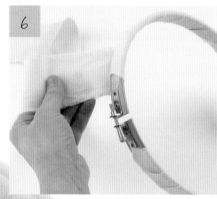

Securing the strip

To make your job easier, use a curved needle when securing the end of the fabric strip next to the frame's hard surface in step 3.

1 Attach a strip of double-sided sticky tape around the outside of the hoop frame, then repeat on the inside.

2 Separate the hoops.

3 Cut or tear a long strip of calico, 2.5–5cm (1–2in) wide. Peel off the backing from the double-sided sticky tape, then place one end of the calico strip on the sticky tape at an angle, starting at the screw of the outer frame.

4 Take the strip underneath to begin wrapping the hoop.

5 Wrap the strip around again, overlapping the previous edge as shown.

6 Continue wrapping all the way round the hoop.

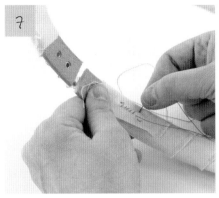

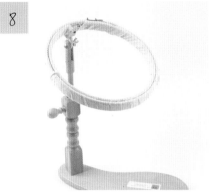

7 Trim away any excess calico, then secure the strip by oversewing half a dozen or so stitches at the end.

8 Repeat on the inner frame, then temporarily sit the smaller frame within the larger until you are ready to work. I recommend the use of a seat frame as shown here, which has a stem you can secure within a seat part, leaving your hands free to work. Floor stands and table clamps are also available to fit these kinds of hoops.

9 Unscrew the outer hoop to make it as large as possible, then cut your fabric to the size of your outer hoop, plus 5cm (2in) on every side.

10 Place the fabric over the inner hoop, then place the outer hoop over the top.

11 Gradually make the fabric taut, by alternately tightening the screw on the outer hoop (see inset) and pulling the excess fabric outside of the hoop away from the centre. Pull evenly on all sides to avoid distorting the fabric.

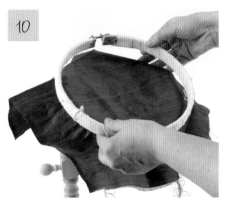

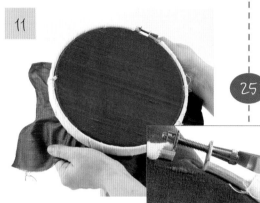

The completed hoop frame, ready to be worked upon.

FRAMING UP A SLATE FRAME

Here I will show you how to successfully frame up a slate frame. Once your fabric is secured to the calico (muslin) background, you can adjust the tension on the fabric by moving the frame's pins into different holes on the arms.

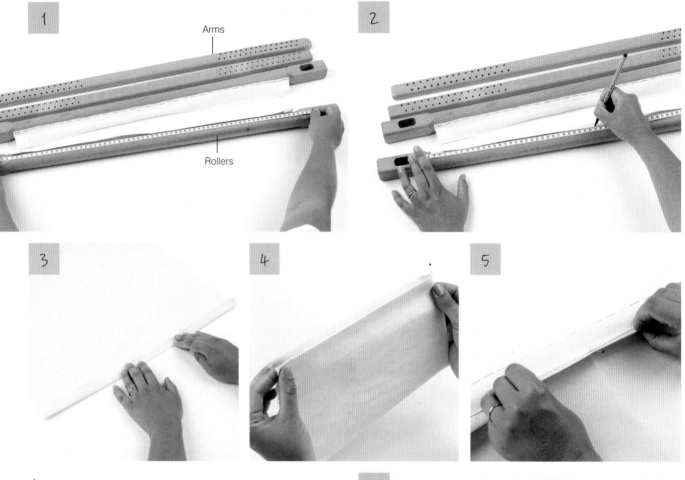

Arms

Rollers

1 Slate frames are handmade, so it is not guaranteed that each roller will be the same length. Check the length of both with a tape measure before you start. Measure the distance between the two large holes.

2 Mark each roller's mid-point on the webbing using a pencil.

3 Fold over the top and bottom of the calico (muslin) backing, on the grain of the fabric, by 1.5cm (²/₃in).

4 To find the centre of the fabric, fold it in half and insert a glass-headed pin at this point.

5 Match the glass-headed pin to the mid-point marked on the roller, and pin the calico (muslin) to the webbing so that the folded edge sits directly underneath the webbing.

6 Pin the folded calico (muslin) edge and webbing together. Do so by working outwards from the middle of the webbing to the right-hand edge, spacing the pins 2.5cm (1in) apart, smoothing the fabric at a slight tension against the webbing.

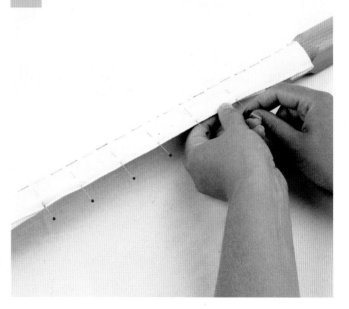

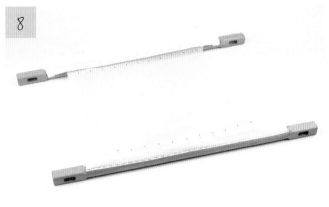

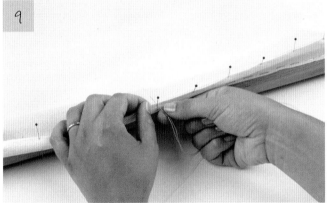

7 Return to the mid-point and then pin outwards to the left-hand edge, again spacing the pins about 2.5cm (1in) apart, attaching the calico (muslin) all the way along its length.

8 Repeat steps 4–7 on the opposite side of the roller so that each end of the calico (muslin) is pinned in place.

9 Thread a size 7 or 9 embroidery needle, or a large sharps needle, with buttonhole thread and tie a knot in the end. Starting at the mid-point, cast on the thread by making two overcast stitches, then continue the overcast stitches along towards the right-hand edge, locking both the calico (muslin) and webbing together.

10 The overcast stitches should be 3mm ($\frac{1}{8}$in) apart; alternate the lengths so that the tension is distributed evenly across the webbing. Varying the stitch size prevents the fabric ripping when the frame is tightened. Remove the glass-headed pins as you sew.

11 To finish off the thread at the edge of the calico (muslin), work several stitches overlapping those you have already done and then cut off the buttonhole thread.

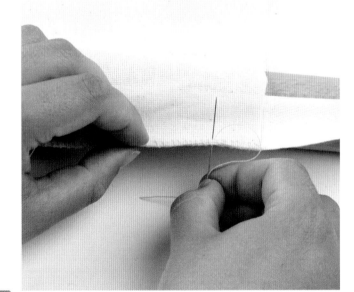

Cutting your background fabric

Make sure you cut on the grain of the fabric so that the length and width are the same at both ends of the fabric. This will ensure an even tension to work on across your frame.

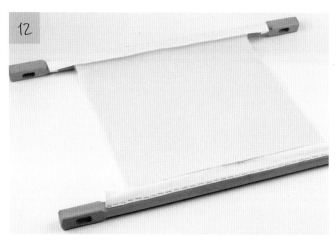

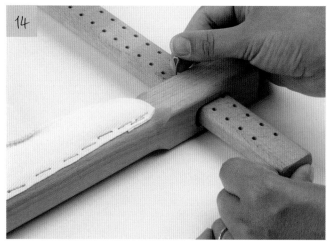

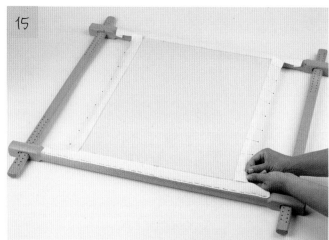

12 Return to the mid-point and sew outwards to the left-hand edge this time, using overcast stitch and buttonhole thread. Repeat steps 9–11 on the opposite roller; the calico (muslin) is now securely attached.

13 Slot the arms into the frame. Make sure each arm is a mirror image to each other so that the holes in the arms are in the same place.

14 Insert the split pins or pegs into the holes to hold the rollers away from each other and to tighten the calico (muslin). The fabric should be tight but not drum-tight at this stage.

15 Pin a strip of cotton webbing, otherwise known as herringbone tape, to both unstitched edges of the calico (muslin) so that it sits evenly along the grain of the fabric. Two-thirds of the webbing should be on the fabric and the other one-third should be off the fabric.

16 Thread a size 7–9 embroidery needle, or large sharps needle, with buttonhole thread and knot the end. Make two stitches through the calico (muslin) and webbing at the top of the frame, then cut off the knot. Work a diagonal stitch that is roughly 2cm (¾in) long through the webbing and up under the edge of the calico (muslin), pulling it firm as you go so that the webbing folds over the edge of the calico (muslin). When you reach the other end of the frame, cast off the buttonhole thread with two additional stitches. Repeat this process on the other side of the calico (muslin) so that both pieces of webbing are attached.

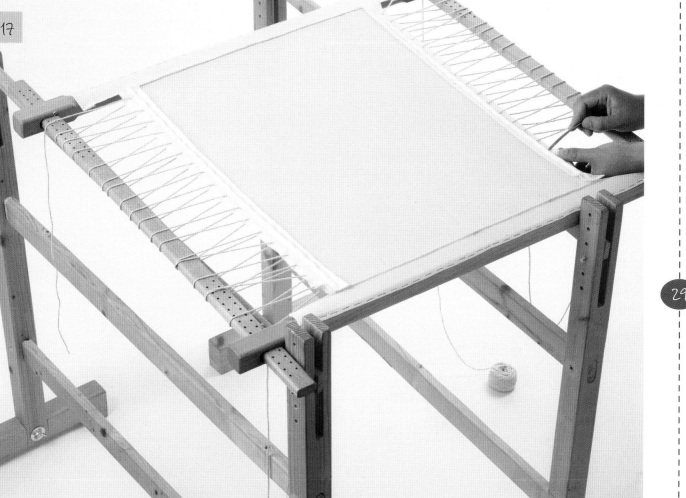

17 With your fabric secured, place the frame onto a trestle so that you can string it. Thread the end of a ball of string into an upholstery bracing needle. Starting at the top of one edge, take the needle down into the edge of the webbing – being careful not to insert it through the calico (muslin). Create stitches by coming up around the arm of the frame with the string every 2.5cm (1in). Once completed, cut the string leaving a 50cm (20in) tail on each end. Repeat this process on the other side of the frame.

18 Slacken off the frame by taking the split pins out of the arms and placing them in holes further towards the middle of the frame. Take your background fabric – here I have used purple silk – and lay this onto the calico (muslin) so that it sits in the same direction with the grains of both fabrics matching.

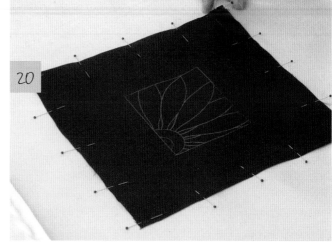

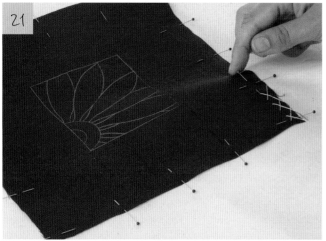

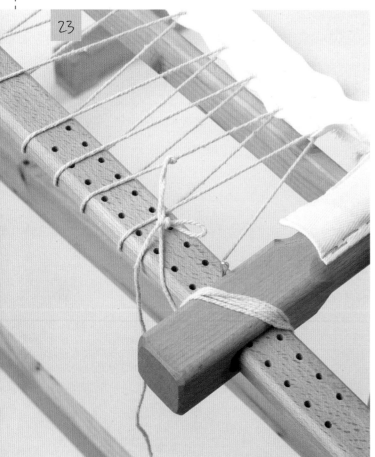

19 Place a pin through both layers of fabric, in the middle of each side, first pinning one side, then the opposite side, then repeating for the remaining two sides.

20 Continue placing pins roughly 2.5cm (1in) apart, working from the middle out, pinning one side in place and then turning the fabric around to ease the opposite side out.

21 Thread a needle with a doubled length of machine thread. Cast on at the edge of the calico (muslin) with a knot and two waste stitches, then cut the knot off. Scoop the needle through the purple silk for the first part of the herringbone stitch, then return to the calico (muslin) for the next stitch.

22 Continue to work this stitch around all four edges of the purple silk fabric. Remove the pins once the fabric is stitched.

23 Apply some more tension to the frame by moving the split pins further out from the middle of the frame; move them one by one, to increase the tension evenly.

Pinning out fabric

Both fabrics should lie flat and at the same tension.
If puckers form in the fabric you are applying, you are
pinning too tightly against the calico (muslin).

24 You now need to tighten the tension on the string. Starting from the centre of the right-hand strip of webbing, work towards one edge, pulling the string tight and adjusting all the loops. Secure the string with a slip knot at one end and then return to the middle of the webbing and work back in the opposite direction. You are aiming for the webbing edge to sit perpendicular to the arm of the frame so that the calico (muslin) is evenly stretched. Once one side of the frame is tensioned, tighten the opposite side using the same method.

25 To tension the frame so that it is drum-tight, stand the base of the frame upright on the floor and use the sole of your foot to push down the end of the bottom roller so that the split pin can be pulled out. Push down again to move the pin into a lower hole so that the tension on the fabric is increased. Repeat on the opposite side so that both split pins sit within the same corresponding holes, to give even tension across the frame. To doublecheck that the frame is at a consistent tension, measure the distance between the rollers at each side of the frame.

Take the pressure off

When tightening the string (as in step 24), pull the string against the arm part of the frame, as this takes pressure off your hands.

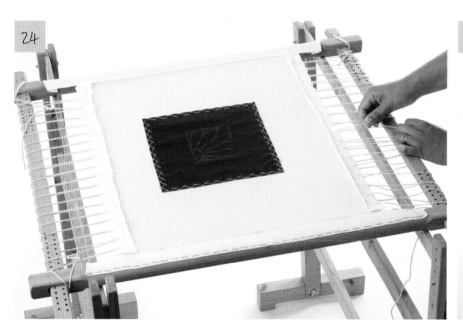

The framed-up fabric.

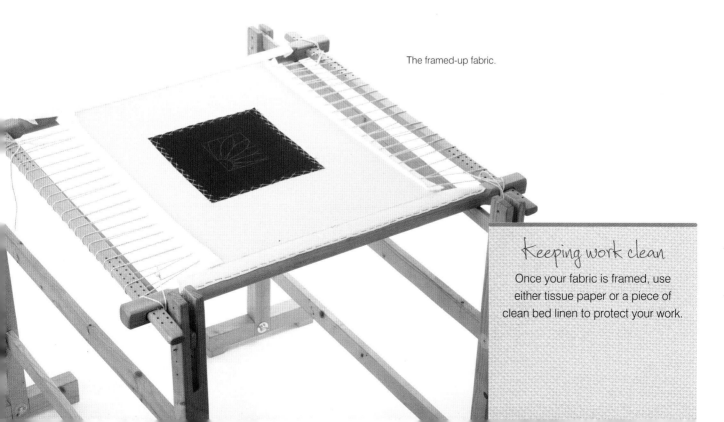

Keeping work clean

Once your fabric is framed, use either tissue paper or a piece of clean bed linen to protect your work.

TRANSFERRING A DESIGN

Even the most abstract, contemporary piece of embroidery benefits from some sort of design outline on the base fabric. The design lines will need to be completely hidden by stitch at some point during the construction, so the rules of thumb are to be very precise and steady in all your line drawing and to transfer only what you need; small fiddly dots and flourishes are better worked freehand in stitch.

TRACING

The simplest method is to trace your design from paper to fabric.

1 Work the design on paper fairly strongly, using a black pen. Lay the fabric flat over the paper, and make sure you can see the design in the centre of the fabric, and square with the grain (if present).

2 Use an HB pencil to carefully trace the design onto the fabric. Use fine lines that are just visible – there is no need to work too darkly or strongly, as this makes it harder to hide the lines under your stitching later.

3 Make sure you transfer every element of the design to the fabric; you may find it helpful to compare the paper original to the fabric before you move on.

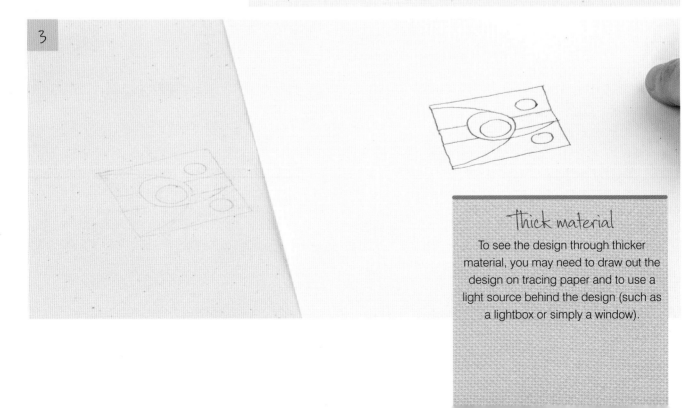

Thick material

To see the design through thicker material, you may need to draw out the design on tracing paper and to use a light source behind the design (such as a lightbox or simply a window).

PRICK AND POUNCE

Sometimes your fabric will be too thick or too textured to be able to use the tracing method for transferring your design; in these instances, the prick and pounce method is your best option.

Pounce is a powder, and can either be black or white. Black pounce is made from charcoal, while white pounce is finely ground cuttlefish. A mid-tone grey can be made by blending the two together.

Making your own brush

A pounce brush – used to apply pounce – can be made from rolled soft felt or a domette fabric.

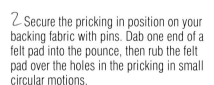

1 Place your tracing on some padding such as thick felt or a folded piece of fabric. Insert a needle into a pricker and pierce the tracing paper along the design lines at 5mm (¼in) intervals.

2 Secure the pricking in position on your backing fabric with pins. Dab one end of a felt pad into the pounce, then rub the felt pad over the holes in the pricking in small circular motions.

3 Carefully remove the pins and lift the pricking away, ensuring you do not spill any excess pounce. Pull the pins away vertically to avoid flicking the paper.

4 Before the pounce blows off the linen or becomes smudged, make the design outline permanent by painting over it with a small paintbrush and grey watercolour paint.

5 Once the paint has dried, remove any excess pounce by brushing it away with a soft brush.

PADDING TECHNIQUES

Padding gives your work a variety of levels, which in turn supports the textured stitches and gives interesting structure to your embroidery. You can use almost any soft material to 'stuff' a shape – before toy stuffing was readily available, bunches of recycled threads called 'orts' were often used – and any thread that will fit into a needle's eye to work padding stitches.

Part of the charm of raised embroidery is thanks to various levels of padding. There are a surprisingly wide variety of padding approaches; here I am showing you my favourites. Whichever technique you use, it is always better to apply padding after the fabric is framed up and at the proper tension.

CHAIN STITCH PADDING

Working layers of chain stitches on top of each other is a super way of squeezing padding into the thinnest and most awkwardly shaped areas in your design. I use several strands or a thick thread to make the process quicker.

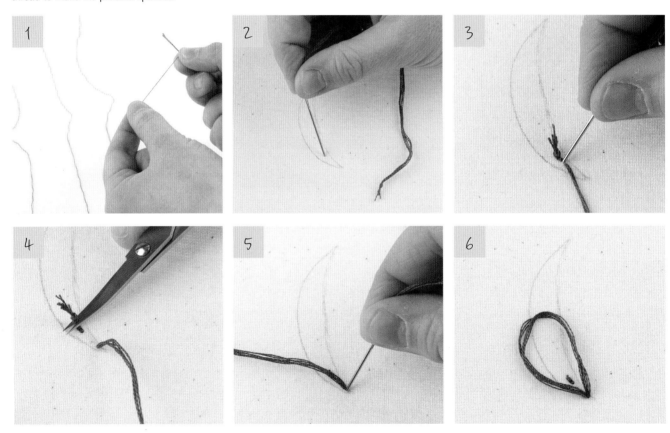

1 Ensure the area to be padded is clearly outlined on the fabric for your main design. Pinch the end of a skein of stranded cotton, and take it to your elbow. Cut this length off to use. Tease away each strand of the cotton, then place them back together (this reduces the risk of them tangling).

2 Thread a large-eyed chenille needle with all six strands of the cotton. Tie a knot in the end of the thread and take the needle down through the surface from the front within the design.

3 Draw the thread through so the knot sits on the surface and then make two small backstitches next to it.

4 Bring the needle back up inside the design line where you intend to start stitching (in this case, at the bottom of the shape), then cut away the surface knot using embroidery scissors.

5 Take the needle back down through the same hole as you started.

6 Draw the thread through, leaving a small loop.

7 Bring the needle up inside the loop, approximately 2–3mm (⅛in) above the original hole.

8 Draw the needle through and pull the thread tight. This completes one chain stitch and begins the second.

9 Repeat steps 6–7, using the new hole as the starting point.

10 Continue making chain stitches, working up the centre of your shape. Use a simple stab stitch to secure the final chain, coming up inside the loop and then down just outside it.

11 Work parallel lines of chain stitch on either side of the first line until the shape is completely filled. This shape uses five rows of chain stitch.

12 Repeat the process, starting from the centre with a new line of chain stitch on top of the previous layer.

13 Once the first row on the second layer is complete, work outwards. Do not work right to the edge of the shape – leave off the outermost rows. Here I have worked just three rows.

14 Continue working and reducing the number of rows until you have built up a definite raised area in the centre.

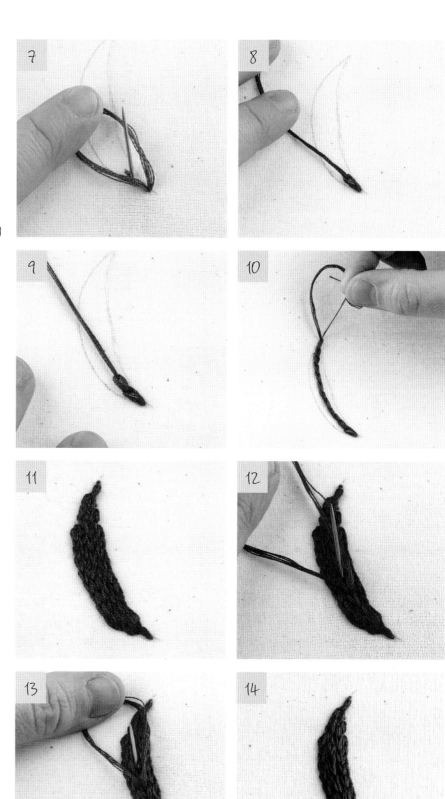

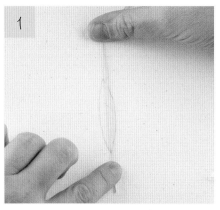
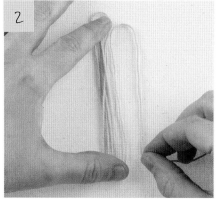
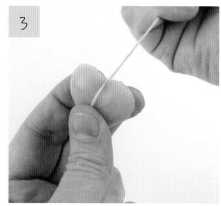
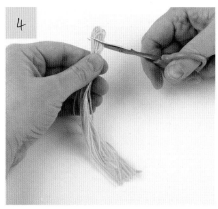
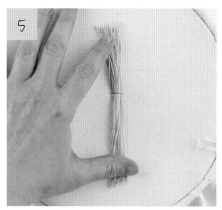
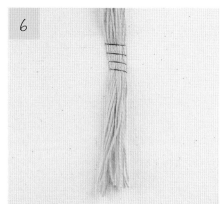

SOFT STRING PADDING

This technique creates hard, durable support for such effects as metal thread cutwork, applied leather or other fabrics, as well as providing a rigid shape to cover in ribbons and or beads. Note that the string would normally be the same colour as the stuffing in order to help hide it within the design. It is shown in a different colour here for the purposes of clarity.

1 Transfer the design and frame up the fabric. Measure a length of soft string against the longest part of the design, adding an extra 2.5cm (1in) at either end.

2 Fold the string back and forth to build up a 'tube' of string that will fill the shape at its widest point.

3 Unfold the string and draw it over a block of beeswax. This makes the string slightly tacky, so that it is easier to shape and stitch over later.

4 Refold the string into the tube and use embroidery scissors to cut the loops at both ends.

5 Carefully place the string tube over the design, so that it fits within the width of the shape and extends slightly beyond both ends. Thread an embroidery needle with fine sewing thread and secure it as normal. Bring the needle up on the edge of the widest part of the design and take it down over the tube of string, again through the design line. Draw the thread through tightly.

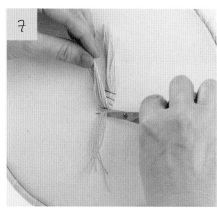

6 Work away from the centre of the shape, adding further stitches over the tube. Work down to the point where the design starts to taper.

7 Lift up the bottom of the tube and use the point of the embroidery scissors to draw out a few strands of soft string from the core of the tube as shown. Trim them away as tightly to the last stitch as possible.

8 Lay the tube back down and reshape it with your fingers (the beeswax will help it keep its shape), then continue working down.

 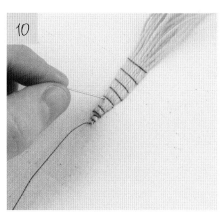 

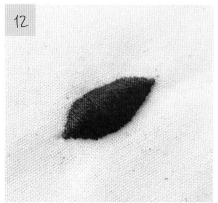

9 Continue folding back and trimming out (see inset) strands of the string as the shape tapers.

10 Work down to a single piece of soft string, then cut it off. Bring the needle up at the tip and make a bridging stitch by taking the needle down at an angle into the shape a little further up.

11 Work satin stitch (a series of long flat stitches that zigzag across the area) from the point back up towards the widest part of the shape.

12 Work up and over the widest part and then repeat the process towards the other point until the shape is completely covered.

> Tip
> Beeswax makes embroidery scissors quite mucky – run them under a hot tap and wipe clean if necessary

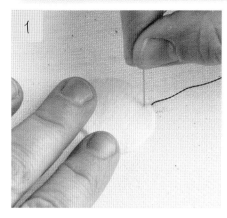 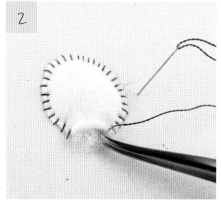 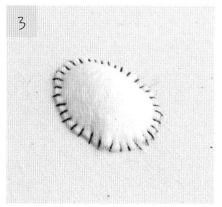

FELT AND STUFFING PADDING

This technique allows you to 'sculpt' the padding with strategically placed stab stitches before you cover it with stitches or fabric – or both.

1 Ensure the area to be padded is clearly outlined on the fabric for your main design. Cut a slightly smaller version of the shape from felt and place it just within the drawn outline. Thread an embroidery needle with fine sewing thread, and start to secure the felt shape in place using small stab stitches: secure the thread as described earlier (see page 23), bring the needle up just outside the felt, then take it down through the felt.

2 Work nearly all the way round the felt shape with the stab stitches, then push a small amount of toy stuffing into the remaining gap until the felt bulges a little. You may find using tweezers helpful for small areas of padding.

3 Stitch up the remaining gap using stab stitches.

ATTACHING STITCHES

The most common method of attaching elements such as threads and embellishments to your fabric is couching, but this doesn't do justice to the possibilities, so I have included a separate section here. Whether you are attaching a secondary thread or an object (such as a bead or other embellishment), remember that the job of attaching can be every bit as decorative as the thing being attached. Here is an opportunity for you to use your funky, 'novelty' fibres that will not go through a needle – attach them on the surface of the fabric with a more user-friendly thread instead!

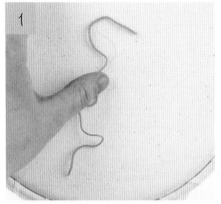
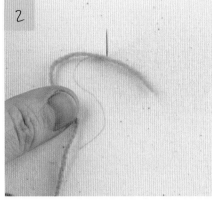
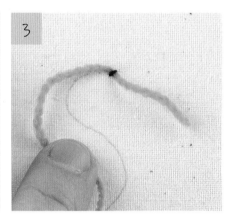

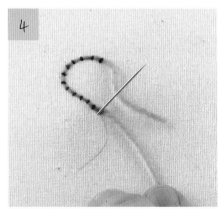

COUCHING

1 Lay the thread to be couched onto the design line on the framed fabric. In this example I will be couching a length of rose crewel wool. Cut enough thread so that you can leave a 'tail' at both ends.

2 Secure the thread as normal, then thread an embroidery needle with your couching thread (here I am using red crewel wool). Bring the needle up at one end of the design just to the side of the thread to be couched.

3 Take the needle over the thread and down on the other side. Draw it through to hold the thread in place firmly.

4 Continue couching the thread in this way, following the design line. Leave roughly 2–3mm (⅛in) between stitches and always work perpendicular to the thread being couched. This not only helps hold the thread securely, but is visually pleasing.

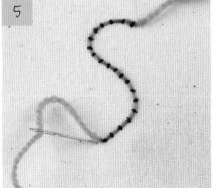

5 Continue couching to the end of the thread. Trim off the ends using embroidery scissors, unless the thread you have used is likely to fray. If the thread will fray, the ends will need to be plunged by threading the tail onto a needle, drawing it through and securing the thread on the back of the work.

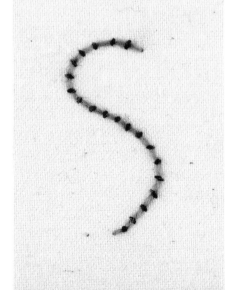

The completed couched thread.

Couching variations

Trailing couching (left) and couched goldwork (right).

 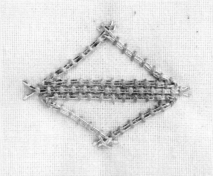

Couched vermicelli

I have based this example on a form of machine quilting. Here the line 'squiggles' in all directions, just like the pasta from which it takes its name. I have couched a sparkling green variegated thread with an invisible thread, encouraging it to change direction wildly within the square.

Experimental couching

Here I have used a fine green thread to attach a bulkier blue thread to the fabric, but have been intentionally irregular in the spacing and density of the couching stitches. This gives a looser, freer, more random effect.

SHISHA

Buttons and beads are easy to attach: they have holes for thread to pass through! But shisha mirrors, coins, shells, beetle wings and the like need a special stitch to fix them into place. A fine but strong thread is best, and remember to hold the object in place whilst you are stitching.

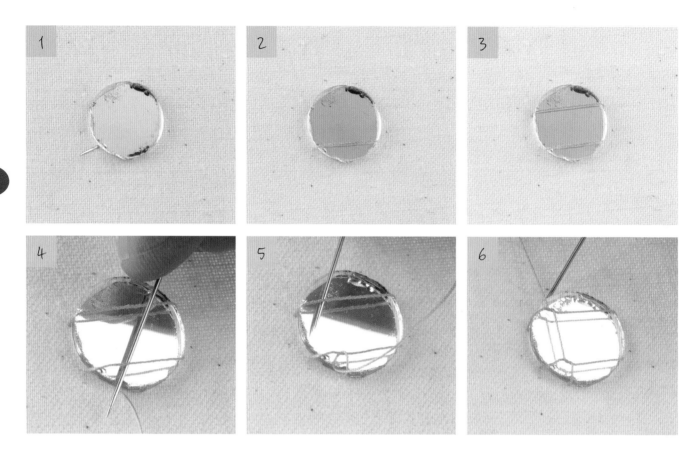

1 Frame up the fabric and place the shisha where you want it to sit on the surface. Thread and secure the needle as usual and bring it up close to the edge of the mirror at the 8 o'clock position.

2 Take the needle down at the 4 o'clock position and draw the thread through, creating a horizontal stitch.

3 Bring the needle up at 2 o'clock and take it down at 10 o'clock.

4 Bring the needle up at the 7 o'clock position, then take the needle over and under the lower horizontal stitch as shown.

5 Draw the thread through and repeat on the upper horizontal stitch.

6 Draw the thread through and take the needle down at the 11 o'clock position.

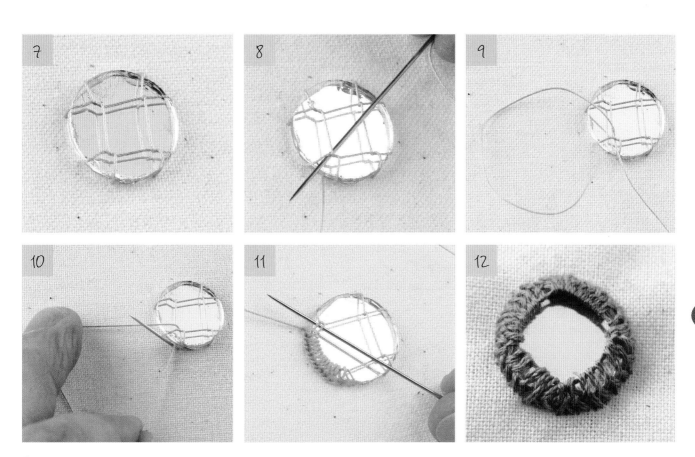

7 Bring the needle up at the 1 o'clock position and take it down at the 5 o'clock position, looping round the horizontal stitches as before. This completes the holding stitches.

8 Bring the needle up at one corner, between the start of two holding stitches. Take the thread under the intersection as shown.

9 Draw the thread through, but not tightly – leave a loop.

10 Take the needle down outside the loop, then up inside the loop. Work closely to the edge of the shisha.

11 Working clockwise round the edge of the shisha, make similar stitches to loop round the holding stitches and draw them away from the centre. Be careful not to pull the loops so tightly that you pull them off the mirror entirely. This process works a little like a buttonhole stitch, leaving a nearly circular piece of mirror showing in the middle.

12 Work all the way round and secure to finish.

RAISED STITCHES

Part of raised embroidery's charm is its highly textured and dimensional stitches. Traditional and contemporary raised embroidery pieces include a huge variety of flat and raised stitches but I'm going to focus on the latter here. I encourage you to try all sorts of materials in your work, but generally speaking these stitches work best with simple, smooth threads – the texture is in the stitch itself!

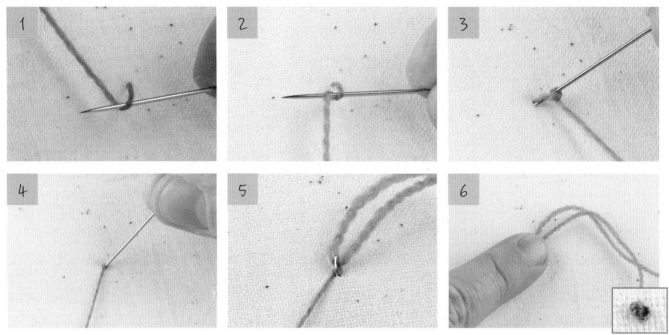

FRENCH KNOT

This versatile stitch looks like a little 'bobble' on the fabric. It can be made larger or smaller depending on the thickness of thread you use and the number of times you wrap it around the needle.

1 Frame up the fabric and thread your embroidery needle. Bring your needle up where you want the French knot to finish. Draw the thread through, then hold your needle above the surface near where you came up. Bring the thread round the needle.

2 Loop it round the thread.

3 Push the point of the needle into the fabric a thread's width away from where you initially brought it up.

4 Pull your thread taut so the knot is closed and sitting on top of the fabric.

5 Push your needle through the fabric until only a tiny part of the eye is showing.

6 Place your finger over the top of the eye as you take the needle through, holding the knot in place. Draw the thread through to finish (see inset).

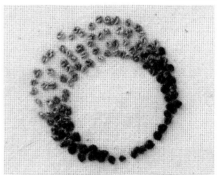

Examples of French knots.

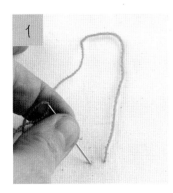 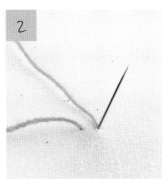  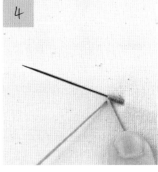

BULLION KNOT

Rather than bulging out at the eye, milliner's needles stay the same width all the way along, which makes them useful for bullion knots.

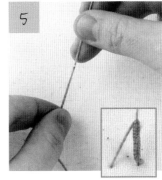 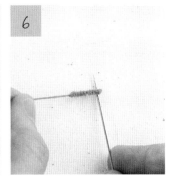

1 Frame up the fabric and thread your milliner's needle. Bring your needle up where you want the bullion knot to start, and take it down where you want it to end.

2 Draw the needle through a little, leaving approximately 10cm (4in) of thread on the surface. Bring your needle partially back up through the first hole.

3 Hold the needle firmly and wrap the thread round the needle several times.

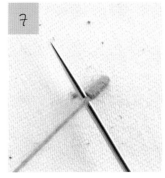 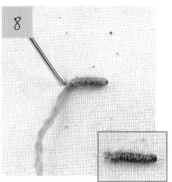

4 Slide the wrapped thread down the needle towards the surface, then lay the needle flat and make sure the wrapped thread reaches the second hole. Add or remove wraps to get the required length.

5 Lightly pinch the wrapped thread between thumb and forefinger and gently draw the needle through until you feel resistance. Relax your pinching fingers to reveal the knot (see inset).

6 Lay the knot down towards the second hole. Pull the slack out by moving the needle back and forth inside the loop underneath the knot, 'polishing' the knot.

7 Put the needle underneath the thread outside the loop and gently push the knot together.

8 Take the needle back down through the second hole, then draw the thread through and secure to complete the bullion knot (see inset).

43

Bullion knot variations

Clockwise from top right: looped bullion knot, long bullion knot, bullion knot rose (see page 114).

Curved bullion knots

The number of wraps you make on the needle, along with the distance between the start and end points on the base fabric can significantly alter the appearance of the resultant knot. You can make a bullion knot curve simply by winding too many wraps on the needle to fit between the start and end points. This is how bullion knot roses and the twining, looping knots used in Brazilian embroidery (see page 46) are achieved.

CAST-ON STITCH

This stitch, often used in Brazilian embroidery (see page 46), is usually worked in rayon, but here I am using crewel wool for visual clarity. Any strong, non-textured thread will work well. Just like the bullion knot (see page 43), cast-on stitch benefits from using a milliner's needle.

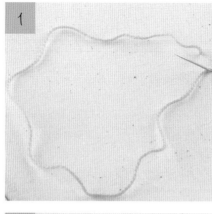

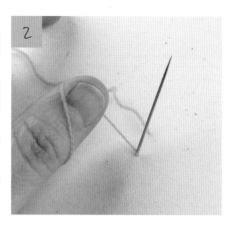

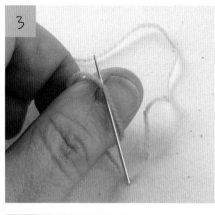

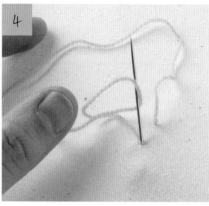

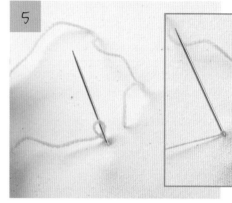

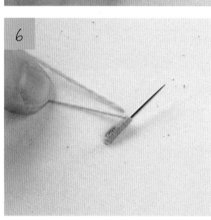

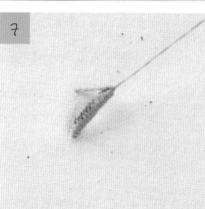

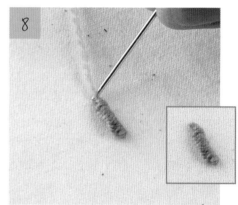

1 Frame the fabric. Thread a milliner's needle, secure it as normal, then bring it up where you want the cast-on stitch to start, and take it down where you want it to end. Draw the needle through, leaving a tail of thread, approximately 10cm (4in) long, on the surface. Bring your needle partially back up through the first hole.

2 Hook your thumb underneath the loop near the needle.

3 Take the needle underneath the loop on your thumb.

4 Draw your thumb out, leaving the loop on the needle.

5 Draw the thread to close the loop on the needle. Draw it tight (see inset). This 'casts on' the thread.

6 Repeat the process several times to increase the length of the overall stitch on the needle until it is long enough to reach the hole at which you first took the needle down.

7 Hold the cast-on stitches between your finger and thumb and draw your needle all the way through.

8 As with the bullion knot (see page 43) 'polish' the back of the knot by moving the side of the needle back and forth beneath the knot, then gently push the knot together before taking the thread down through the hole. Draw the thread through and secure it on the back to complete the stitch (see inset).

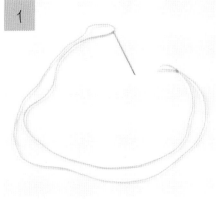

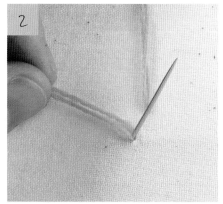

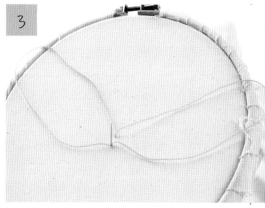

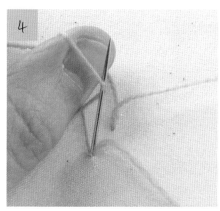

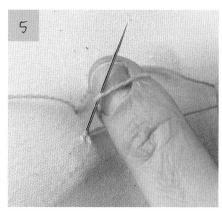

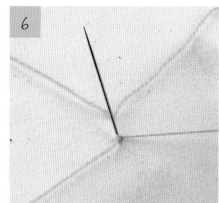

DOUBLE CAST-ON STITCH

This stitch creates a 'domed' or padded effect; it can be worked in a wide variety of shapes and can also be shaded from one side to the other.

1 Thread a milliner's needle with a length of thread and tie a small knot at the end to make a sealed loop.

2 Frame the fabric, then bring the needle up where you want the stitch to start. Take the needle down where you want it to end, then bring it back up through the starting hole.

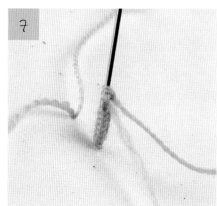

3 Before you draw the needle through, split the loop by taking one side of the thread over the needle.

4 Cast on by following steps 3–5 of cast-on stitch (see opposite).

5 Draw the thread through to pull the loop tight, then cast on from the other side, using the second loop of the thread and your other thumb.

6 Draw the thread through to tighten the loop.

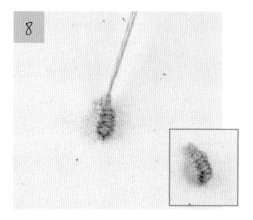

7 Repeat steps 4–6, using alternate loops of the thread, until you have cast on sufficient stitches to reach the end point.

8 Pinch the knot and draw the thread through, then polish and push the knot together (see step 6 of the bullion knot instructions on page 43) before taking the needle down through the end point, and securing the thread (see inset).

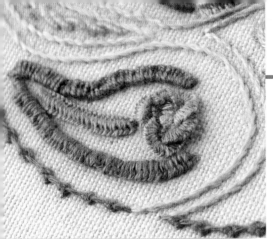

Brazilian embroidery

The distinctive shiny appearance of rayon thread, widely produced in Brazil, gives the cast-on stitch technique its other popular name of 'Brazilian embroidery'. The two cast-on stitches shown on the following pages are often combined beautifully with bullion knots in lovely floral displays.

Raised Heart in Lime
Kelley Aldridge

This 10 x 10cm (4 x 4in) sample of raised stitches includes bullion knots, velvet work, cast-on stitches, French knots, rosette stitches and whipped wheels.

Raised Heart in Rose

Kelley Aldridge

An alternative colourway of the *Raised Heart in Lime*
opposite, the piece has been shaped into a heart to
follow the design, and made into a lavender pillow.

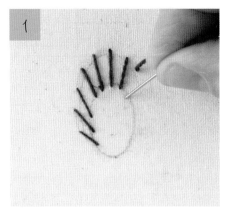
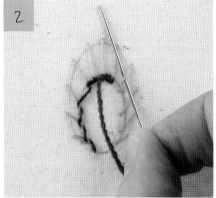
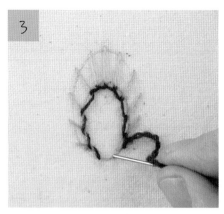
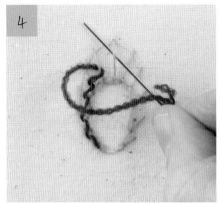
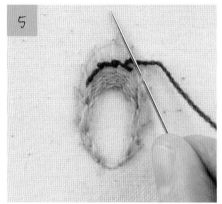
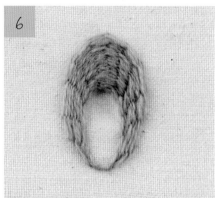

RAISED STEM

The working stitches are shown in red at every stage, then replaced with blue to make it easier to distinguish the two.

1 Transfer the design and frame the fabric, then thread the needle and secure your thread as normal. Work evenly spaced stitches – approximately 5mm (¼in) apart – to form a 'ladder' filling your shape. If the ladder is straight, start at one end and work to the other. If it is a curved ladder, as with this example, start in the middle and work one side of the shape, then start again at the middle to work the other side. Secure the thread.

2 With the ladder in place, thread a tapestry needle and whip the first stitch by taking the needle over the stitch, then underneath the stitch, and back over, looping around it once. Whip all of the stitches in turn in this way. For straight ladders, work from the rightmost stitch to the leftmost. For curved ladders, start working from the inside edge.

3 Take the needle down through the fabric and secure the thread at the end of the ladder. This completes the first row.

4 Create the next row in the same way, working round the ladder outside the first row.

5 Irregularly shaped ladders may require partial rows. To make these, simply start further round the shape.

6 Continue adding rows until the shape is filled.

Raised stem stitch

In this example, taken from part of a sampler, raised stem stitch has been worked in a straight band in variegated thread. It has been embellished with thread-wrapped fine wires which have been twisted around a fine knitting needle to get their shape.

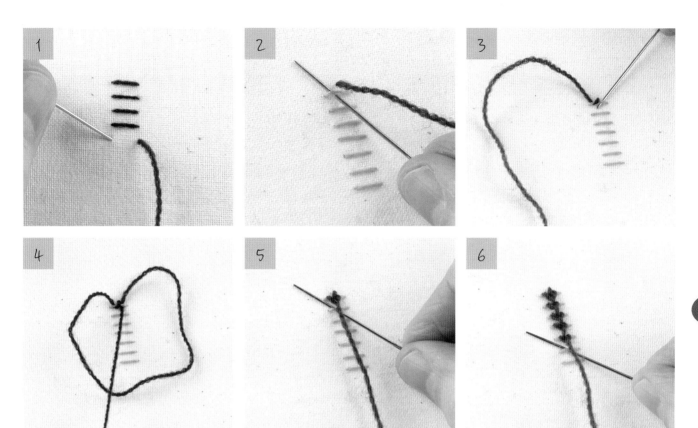

RAISED CHAIN

When worked in a line, this stitch produces a result that resembles a braid. This stitch can also be worked as a single, textured 'dot'.

1 Frame the fabric and thread an embroidery needle. Use this to make a short ladder of straight stitches. Secure the thread.

2 Swap to a tapestry needle and bring the needle up slightly above the first straight stitch. Draw the thread through and slip the needle under the first straight stitch.

3 Draw the thread through and to the left, then bring the needle round and under the same straight stitch on the right, working downwards.

4 Draw the thread through, making sure the thread comes over the top of the loop that this creates.

5 Take the needle under the second straight stitch.

6 Repeat steps 3 and 4 to create the next chain stitch, then continue working down the length of the ladder.

7 At the end of the last chain stitch, take the needle down through the fabric and secure to finish.

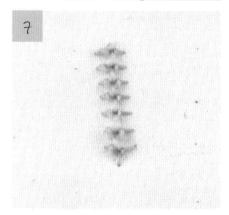

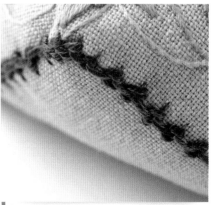

Biscornu detail

Raised chain stitch is ideal for hiding seam lines, as in this example.

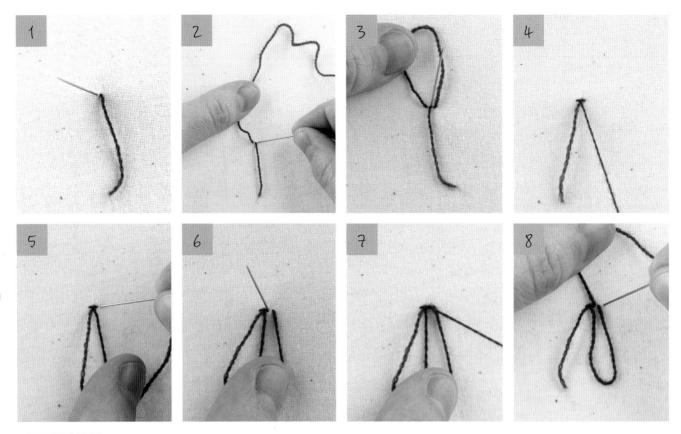

TURKEY RUG

Also known as 'velvet work', this stitch creates a tuft of thread which can be shaded. When it is trimmed back and shaped, the results can be breathtaking.

1 Frame the fabric and thread an embroidery needle. Do not secure the thread or knot the end. Start by taking the thread through from the front. Draw it through so a little tail remains on the front, then bring the needle up slightly to the left of where you first went down.

2 Draw the needle through, being careful not to pull through the tail. Hold the thread in a loop above the working area, then take the needle back down slightly to the right of the starting hole.

3 Take the needle through, leaving a small loop, and bring the needle back up through the starting hole.

4 Draw the needle through to tighten the loop.

5 Hold the thread out of the way below the stitch and take your needle down just to the right of the completed stitch.

6 Draw the thread through, leaving the loop on the surface and bring it back up through the same hole as the end of the last stitch.

7 Draw the thread through but keep the loop in place.

8 Hold the thread in a loop above the working area, then take the needle back down slightly to the right of the hole where you started this second stitch.

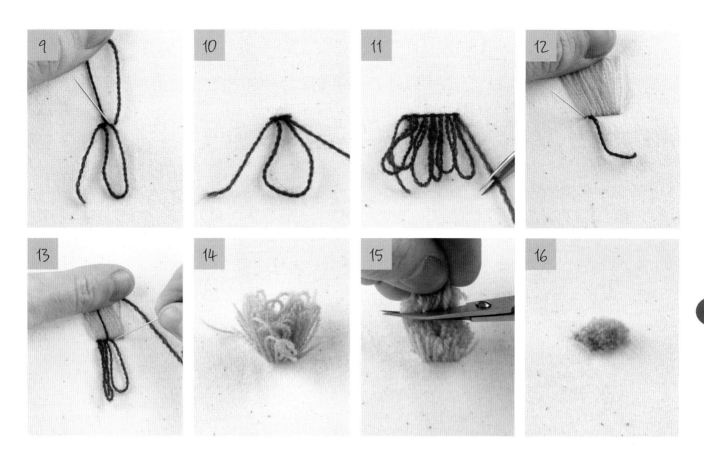

9 Take the needle through, leaving a small loop, and bring the needle back up through the starting hole of this stitch.

10 Draw the needle through to tighten the loop and complete the second stitch.

11 Continue to the end of the row. Remove the needle and trim any excess to the same length as the preceding loops.

12 Hold the completed row (marked in blue) out of the way and start the next row underneath the first, at the leftmost point.

13 Work the second row below the first, continuing to hold the preceding row (or rows) out of the way.

14 Continue working rows below the previous ones, working from left to right each time, until you have filled the area you want. Secure the thread as normal.

15 Lift the stitches up, then use embroidery scissors to cut away the ends of the loops.

16 Trim the loops to the desired length.

Building up quickly
Using more than one strand of thread in your needle at once will help to build up the stitch more quickly.

WOVEN WHEEL

Woven wheel stitch requires an odd number of 'spokes'. This stitch is thread-hungry, so thread your needle with a more generous amount of thread than normal before you begin. This will save you from having to rethread so often.

1 Frame up the fabric and use a pencil to draw a circle of the size you want the finished wheel to be. Thread a tapestry needle with your thread and secure as normal. Bring the needle up just outside the edge of the circle and down through the centre to create a straight 'spoke'.

2 Continue placing evenly spaced stitches around the circle to create an odd number of spokes.

3 With the wheel complete (marked in green), bring the needle up at the centre. Be careful not to undo your last stitch.

4 Draw the thread through. Working clockwise, take the needle alternately under and over the spokes.

5 Work all the way round the wheel, pulling the thread firmly so that it pulls in to the centre.

6 Continue working round the needle. Because you have an odd number of spokes, you will now take the needle over the ones you worked under on the first circuit, and under the ones you worked over.

7 Continue working round the wheel, alternating working over and under the spokes.

8 For a flatter wheel, simply work to the edge of the pencilled circle, then take the needle down at the edge of the wheel and secure the thread.

9 For a thicker wheel, continue working further rows round the outer edge of the circle to overfill the wheel until it becomes difficult to continue. The thread will crowd and gradually build up into an attractive raised shape.

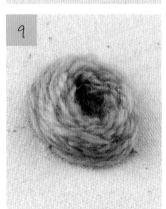

Paired spokes

As a variation, you can also use fly stitches, anchored at the centre, to create pairs of spokes for your woven wheel.

WHIPPED WHEEL

Unlike woven wheel, you can use an odd or even number of spokes for this stitch. The number of spokes you use will change the finished result. Using more spokes works better for particularly large wheels.

1 Follow steps 1–3 of the woven wheel (see opposite) to create a spoked circle.

2 Draw the thread through, then take the needle under the first spoke.

3 Draw the thread through, then take the needle back round and under the first spoke again. When you draw this through it whips the thread.

4 Whip the next spoke in the same way and continue working in the same direction.

5 Working back to the first spoke completes the row. Start again on the first spoke.

6 Continue building up rows until you reach the edge of the wheel. To speed things along, you can take the needle under the next spoke along on the second part of the whipping.

7 Continue building up until you reach the edge of the circle, then take the needle through to the back to finish the wheel.

8 You can use a different number of spokes (including an even number). You can also overfill the wheel for a more raised effect.

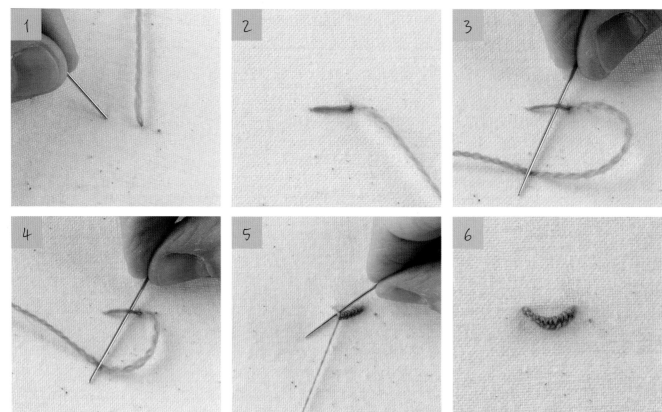

DETACHED BUTTONHOLE

This stitch is used to create a 'bar' of thread which is most often seen as the loop to catch a pearl button on wedding dresses; it can be used single or in a line to create scalloped edging and is best worked with a fine thread.

1 Frame the fabric. Thread a tapestry needle, secure it as normal, then bring it up where you want the stitch to start, and take it down where you want it to end.

2 Draw the thread through, then bring the needle back up at the start. Draw the thread through and loop it round the stitch.

3 Take the needle under the stitch and over the loop.

4 Draw the thread through, then take the needle back round and repeat.

5 Continue working along the stitch, taking the needle under the stitch, over the loop and round. As you work along, the tension will gradually draw out the initial stitch.

6 Work to the end, then take the needle through the end hole and secure the thread. The tension will have created an attractive little loop.

Using detached buttonhole stitch

The pink scalloped edge here is worked using detached buttonhole stitch to form a neat border.

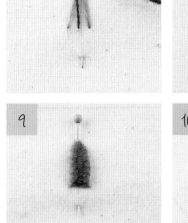
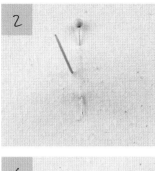
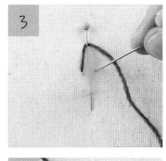
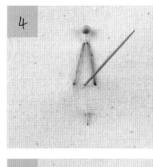
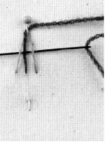

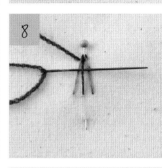
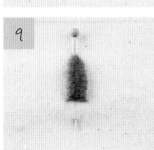

NEEDLE-WOVEN PICOTS

This stitch creates a faintly textured, freestanding elongated triangle which is often used to depict leaves, petals or similar shapes. Fine thread works best.

1 Frame up the fabric. Insert a pin where you would like the tip of the picot to end. Bring it back through the fabric below the base of where the picot will be – they are typically 1.5cm (½in) in length, so bring the needle out 2.5cm (1in) below.

2 Thread a tapestry needle. Secure the thread and bring the needle up slightly above and to the left of where the pin emerges. This is the left point of the picot base.

3 Take the thread round the pinhead, then back down on the right in line with the left point of the base. This is the right point of the base.

4 Draw the thread through and bring the needle up between the two points. This completes the picot base (marked in purple).

5 Draw the thread through and loop it round the pinhead.

6 Take the needle under the right-hand leg of the picot base, over the emerging thread, then under the left-hand leg of the picot base.

7 Draw the thread through while easing it towards the tip of the picot.

8 Take the needle over the left-hand leg of the picot base, under the emerging thread, then over the right-hand leg of the picot base.

9 Draw the thread through, then repeat from step 6, alternating the direction of working each time until you reach the base. Keep the tension consistent for an even finish. At the base, take the thread through to the back and secure, then grasp the pinhead.

10 Draw the pin out to reveal the finished picot.

11 If you want to secure the picot in a permanent position, use a stab stitch to attach the tip to the fabric surface.

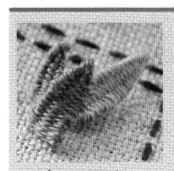

Neat finish
Push the thread up towards the tip with the side of your needle to ensure a neat finish.

Using needle-woven picots
This stitch is commonly used for leaves in decorative raised embroidery, as it gives an effective and resilient result.

NEEDLELACE STITCHES

Depending on which pattern you use, and how densely you work it, needlelace can look
as sturdy as a knitted jumper or as delicate as a dragonfly's wing. Most fine, smooth
threads will work, and the more you practise, the better you will be!

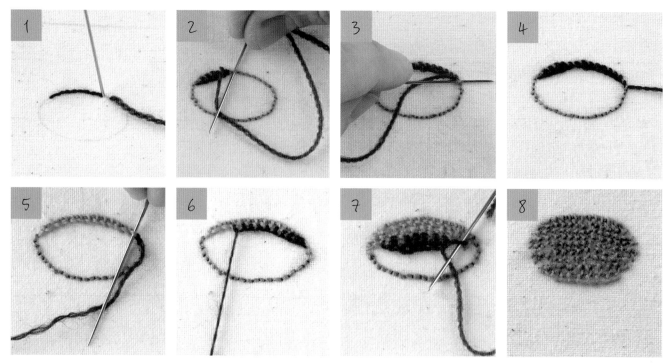

BRUSSELS

This is the basis of the majority of needlelace stitches. It can be doubled,
trebled, corded and worked in patterns, but ultimately they are all a version of
the single Brussels stitch, which in fact is a type of detached buttonhole stitch.

1 Transfer your design to the surface, frame the fabric and thread an
embroidery needle. Secure the thread, then work a series of small
(approximately 2mm or 1/16in) backstitches around the outline of the
shape to be filled. Backstitch is worked simply by bringing the needle
up a little further along the design line, then back down through the
hole where the previous stitch ends. Secure the thread.

2 Thread a fine tapestry needle and bring your thread up at the top
left of your shape, just inside the back-stitched outline. Work a row
of buttonhole stitches (see page 54) from left to right, anchoring the
stitches by taking the needle through the backstitches of the outline
and over the loop as shown.

3 Work all the way over to the opposite side of your design. Anchor
the end of the row by sliding the needle under the backstitch which is
just underneath the row you have just worked.

4 Repeat this step on the next backstitch down to firmly secure
the thread and finish the first row. This brings you down level to the
bottom of the next row to be worked.

5 Start the next row by working a buttonhole stitch through the
rightmost stitch of the previous row and over the loop.

6 Work right to left back along the row.

7 Anchor the thread in the same way on the left-hand side, then
continue working back and forth. If the shape you are working is an
irregular one (as in this example), you may need to work partial rows
of stitches. Because you are not working to the outline, anchor these
in the nearest stitch to whichever side you need.

8 Continue working down until you fill the shape. To seal the shape
in the final row, take the needle under the backstitches beneath as
you make each buttonhole stitch. Anchor the thread as normal.

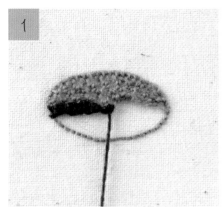

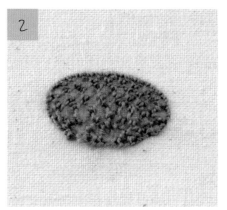

Using needlelace

Traditional raised embroidery pieces often have quite a large amount of needlelace worked on clothed figures. Contemporary work often uses fabric slips instead and reserves the lace effect for flowers, insects and similar details.

DOUBLE BRUSSELS

This variation gives a more open, lacy effect than Brussels stitch.

1 Work the stitch in the same way as Brussels stitch, but work a pair of buttonhole stitches, instead of just one, in each stitch of the previous row.

2 Fill the shape down to the bottom, then secure as for buttonhole stitch.

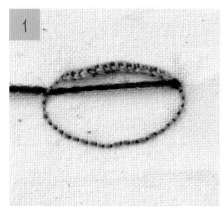

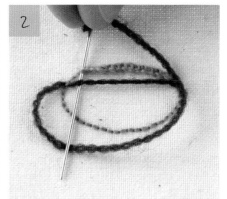

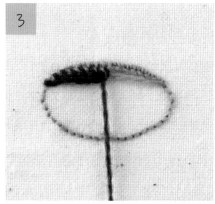

CORDED BRUSSELS

This variation results in a slightly denser appearance than other forms of Brussels stitch. It is less suited to very irregular shapes.

1 Work as for steps 1–4 of Brussels stitch (see opposite). Having anchored the thread, throw the thread back to the left-hand side. Take the needle under the backstitch on the left-hand side to secure the core.

2 Start the next row by working two buttonhole stitches through the rightmost stitch of the previous row; continue working two buttonhole stitches into every other stitch in the previous row until you reach the other side of the shape.

3 Work remaining rows back and forth, putting two buttonhole stitches into each two-buttonhole gap of the previous row.

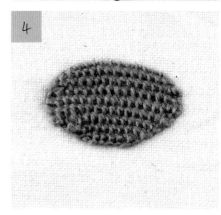

4 Fill the shape down to the bottom, then secure as for step 8 of Brussels stitch.

WIRED SHAPE TECHNIQUES

Take your stitches into the air! Whether it's a snippet of fabric, a fragment of embroidery, or a lovely little needlelace detail, the use of wire to form shapes that 'float' above the background is the true hallmark of traditional stumpwork.

In the majority of surviving historical stumpwork embroidery, wires are used to depict hands and to support three-dimensional embroidered fragments (such as long and short shaded leaves worked on fine linen). Today we can use sheer organzas, patterned cottons, and of course needlelace. Wire work on your embroidery lifts it into the magical, but beware! The price you pay is fragility – handle such pieces with extra care.

Brooches
6cm (2¹/₄in) high
Margaret Dier

Both pieces were made with long and short shading on fine cotton. The pansy petals were outlined with wire from behind, while the leaf was outlined with metal thread (silver pearl purl).

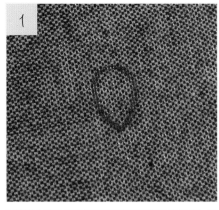

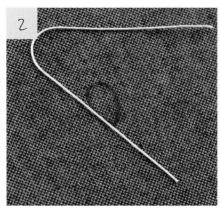

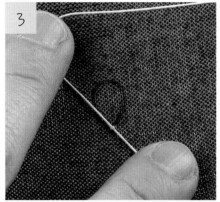

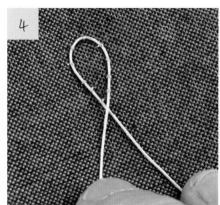

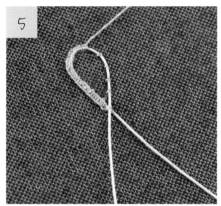

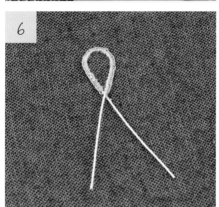

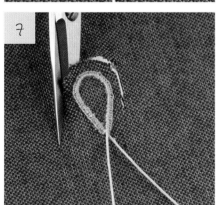

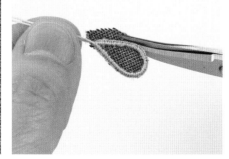

MAKING A WIRED SHAPE

At the heart of stumpwork are wired shapes, made as follows.

1 Frame up your fabric and use a soft pencil to draw your design.

2 Cut a length of fine paper-wrapped cake decorating wire sufficient to go completely round the shape plus an additional 5cm (2in). Lay the wire down on the design, leaving an inch spare at the start.

3 Thread an embroidery needle with a strand of complementary-coloured embroidery cotton. Secure the thread near the base of the design, then begin to secure the wire by making a stab stitch over the wire at the base.

4 Add additional stab stitches every 5mm (¼in) or so to anchor the wire. As you work, bend the wire to follow the design line.

5 Work closely-spaced buttonhole stitches all the way around the design, bringing the needle up on the outside of the wire and down inside the wire for every stitch.

6 Once you have worked buttonhole stitch all the way round the shape, secure the thread at the base of the design.

7 Use sharp embroidery scissors to cut out the shape, leaving a small border around the edges of the couched wire.

8 Neatly trim away the excess border, working carefully and closely to the buttonhole stitches.

The finished wired shape.

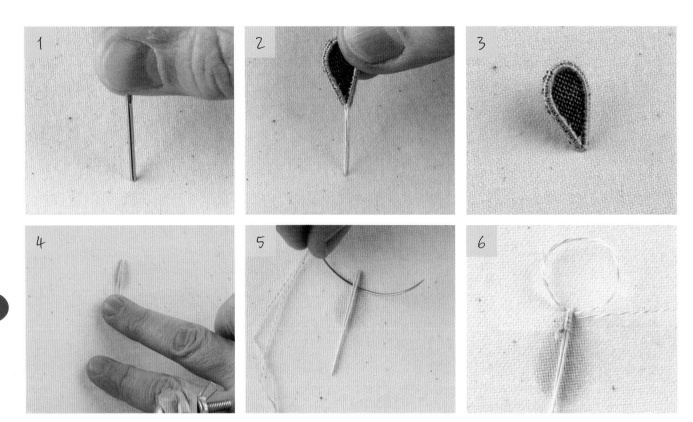

SECURING A WIRED SHAPE TO YOUR PIECE

The wired shape can be secured to backing fabric.

1 Using a large needle, such as a size 18 chenille needle, make a hole in the fabric of your piece where you want the wired piece to sit.

2 Pinch the two tails of the wired piece together and take them both down the hole.

3 Pull the tails so the wired piece sits on the fabric surface.

4 On the back of the piece, fold the wires down beneath the shape. This ensures the securing stitches will be hidden.

5 Thread a curved needle with an embroidery cotton in a similar colour to the surface fabric and knot the end of the thread. Beginning approximately 5mm (¼in) from the plunge point, take the needle

under the wires. Catch as little of the fabric as possible so less shows on the surface.

6 Draw the thread through so the knot catches against the wire. Working back towards the plunge point, begin oversewing the wire tails to the back of the fabric.

7 Work to the plunge point. Tie a knot in the thread at the back to secure it and trim the excess.

8 Trim away any excess wire to finish, cutting back so none shows beyond the surface shape.

9 With the wire secured, you can now gently shape the wired shape into its final form.

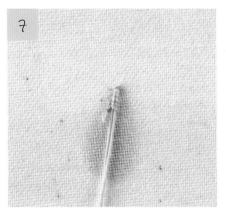

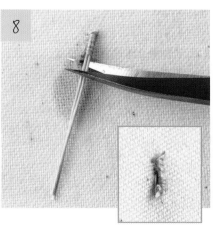

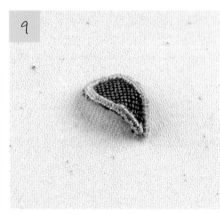

Bracelet

6.5cm (2¾in) high
Lisa Bilby

For this wearable piece, small flowers made from wired organza shapes were attached together at the centre, with small beads hiding the join. Delicately shaded beads in greens and golds are wired and anchored around the main bracelet frame to complete the look.

PROJECTS

I really do love 'off-the-wall' embroidery – and I mean that quite literally; whether they are practical pieces to pick up and use, decorative objects simply to enjoy looking at, or even pieces to wear, I love the pieces I make. So wide are the possibilities, in fact, that the main stumbling block can be working out where to start and what to make!

As a result, in this book I have looked at three broad categories of raised embroidery – wearable, useable and collectible – in order to give you some inspiration and guidance, and to get your own creativity turning over. In each section you will find a project that illustrates new techniques and how to use and combine the stitches in the earlier part of the book, along with a gallery of inspirational pieces both from my own collection and from those of other very talented artists at the Royal School of Needlework.

Feel free to follow the step-by-step instructions for these projects, but there is no need to recreate an exact replica – this is your creation, after all, so enjoy adding your own flourishes, designs and stitch choices to make a piece very personal to you.

Projects to try with me: a wearable brooch, a useable smartphone sleeve, and a purely decorative collectible 'biscornu'.

WEARABLE RAISED EMBROIDERY

Hand embroidery is incredibly time-consuming, labour-intensive, and usually on the small side, which makes it perfect for creating beautiful, one-of-a-kind accessories. Seen at close quarters from different angles, this is an opportunity to use the texture and levels of raised work to great effect.

Brooches or pendants are amongst the best objects to make if you are starting out with raised embroidery, as you can focus on the design without the added complication and pressure of a lengthy construction process. Similarly, making a necklace can be as simple as attaching a ribbon to an embroidered charm and tying it around your neck. Why not use a safety pin to attach a little embroidered scrap of vintage silk to add a quirky bit of decoration to a shirt? All of these are quick and simple ways to turn a piece of raised embroidery into something you can wear.

Another great thing about wearable embroidery is that it is always in motion. It catches and reflects light as well as casting shadows, so consider incorporating sparkly threads, shiny beads and padded layers along with raised stitches to make the most of this quality.

Considerations for making wearable raised embroidery

The context I am working in for this section is wearable accessories, rather than garments that are far more susceptible to wear and tear. Nevertheless, accessories have their own challenges, and there are certain things you need to remember when your designing and stitching your own piece. Consider how you will wear your embroidery: nothing too heavy around the neck or pulling on a top (or on ears), no sharp points to catch on clothing or skin, and everything secured firmly to avoid upsetting losses! Use materials that are able to cope with being lightly handled, and if you believe your accessory is likely to become a bit 'grubby' now and then, try to incorporate a way of carefully cleaning it.

Felt bead necklace

Kelley Aldridge

To make this necklace, I strung hand-felted beads onto a ribbon, spacing them with smaller glass beads. The felted beads were each partially covered with whipped wheels, beads and various corded threads.

Brooch

5 x 5cm (2 x 2in)

I'm a fan of 'statement' accessories – unusual pieces paired with very simple outfits are my favourite. As with the other projects in this book, the small size involved means you can make a feature of fine stitching and sumptuous materials without having to commit to a large project. Even better, it's portable to make as well as to wear! The important thing to remember is that the design needs to be very simple, and bold.

The piece is worked in a small frame as an embroidered panel, which is then stretched gently over either card or pelmet vilene, then lined on the back to hide the construction stitches. Given that it exists as a single item, and isn't attached in any way to anything else except the jewellery findings, it can be whatever shape you like. Start with your favourite colour and build out from there! Remember – be bold with your materials and simple with your design!

YOU WILL NEED

Orange silk dupion fabric

2mm (¹⁄₁₆in) wide green silk ribbon, preferably variegated

A selection of green seed beads

Soft string for padding

Stranded embroidery cotton in orange, lime green and two shades of blue-green

Fine variegated orange perlé cotton

Orange felt

Sewing thread

Backing fabric

Red felt

Brooch back jewellery finding

Basic sewing kit

Opposite:
The finished brooch

I like the idea that you can turn this piece into either a brooch or a necklace, depending on the jewellery findings (see page 16) you use. You could also turn a pair of them into earrings, but I think I would want to make a slightly smaller version myself.

DESIGNING THE PIECE

From the start, I wanted this piece to be eye-catching, in fact I wanted it to be eye-popping! The colours needed to be very bright, and I knew there would be at least one shisha mirror to catch and reflect back the light. Whether worn as a brooch or a necklace (or earrings), this little piece of embroidery would often shift and move with the wearer, so reflective and shiny materials would really flash and sparkle. Silk fabric and ribbons would help add rich colour and sheen, which would be counter-balanced with some interesting texture.

The size of this piece is relatively small – brooches generally are not too large for practical reasons. A pendant could be bigger, but only slightly. If you are familiar with the term 'inchie' – a tiny piece of textile-art sampling which measures no more than one square inch – you will have an idea of what I was envisaging, though the final piece is slightly larger than this to give more space for the decorative embroidery.

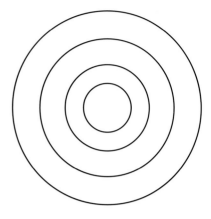

Template

This template is reproduced at actual size.

MOODBOARD

I love the work of artist Dave Galchutt, who is known for his use of vibrant colours. Inspired by the colours in one of his pieces, I began my moodboard by pinning colour sketches to the cork, then finding matching threads that would allow me to incorporate the same bold hues in my piece. I also came across a series of large ceramic titles by artist Christopher Gryder and was immediately struck with how lovely they would be in raised stitches.

I spent some time working out possible combinations of techniques and colour, making notes to myself and pinning them to the board, too.

ORDER OF WORK

The shisha mirror is attached first, as you need a lot of elbow room for this complex stitch. The ribbon and beadwork are worked last as they are very raised, which makes them liable to being damaged from working nearby stitches if you add them earlier.

A Secure the fabric to the hoop, then transfer the design (see pages 32–33) and secure the shisha (see pages 40–41). This stage is shown to the right.

B Work the stem stitch (see pages 70–71) areas.

C Work vermicelli (see pages 72–73) – the green areas first, then the red areas.

D Work the bullion knots (see page 43) and cast-on stitches.

E Add the ribbon and bead embellishment.

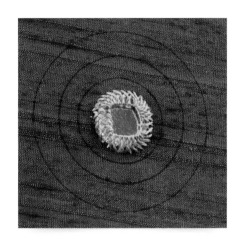

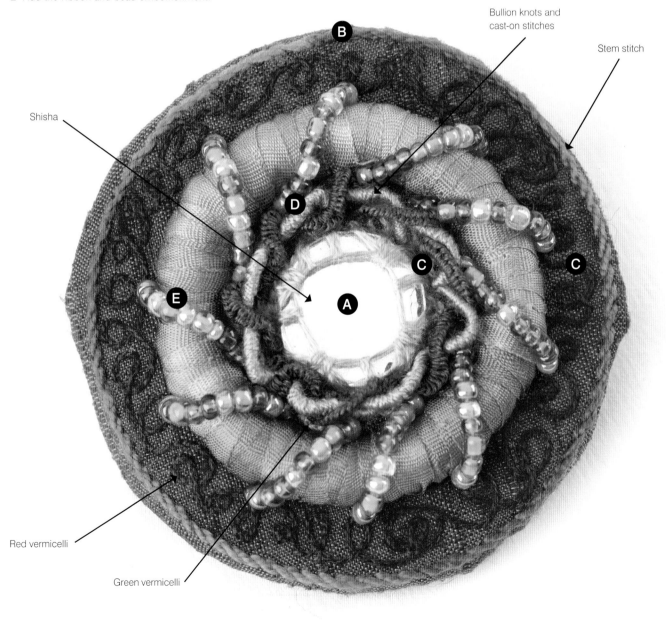

Bullion knots and cast-on stitches

Stem stitch

Shisha

Red vermicelli

Green vermicelli

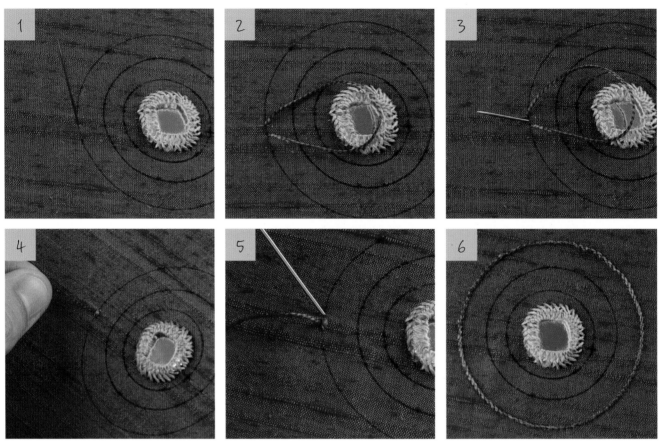

STEM STITCH

This is a 'workhorse' of a stitch, providing lines that are straight, curved, thick, thin, shaded and plain.

1 Using a semi-fine variegated thread in an embroidery needle and the cast-on securing method (see page 23), begin your stem stitch on the outer line shown on the template, bringing your needle up through the line itself.

2 Take your needle down about 2mm (1/16in) away from its starting point, pulling most of the thread through but leaving a loop on the surface of the fabric.

3 Holding the loop of thread to the inside of the border line, bring your needle up again, on the line, halfway between the start and end of the previous stitch.

4 Pull the working thread through completely, thereby tightening the first stitch.

5 Take the needle down 2mm (1/16in) further round the circle to start the next stitch.

6 Repeat all the way round until the border line is complete.

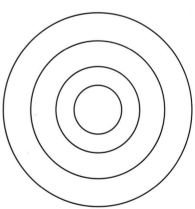

Tip

To turn a sharp angle in stem stitch, the first stitch in the line must be worked backwards to avoid bringing the needle up where it has just gone down.

Stem stitch

Stem stitch makes an excellent neat, understated and
subtle border. In this detail from the finished piece,
note how the variegated thread adds a little interest.

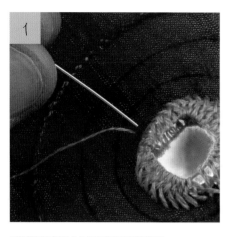
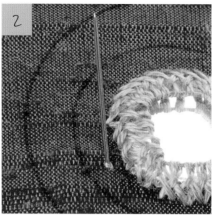
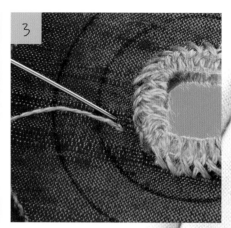

VERMICELLI BACKSTITCH

Named after the spiralling pasta, this creates an all-over background pattern.

1 Secure a fine embroidery thread in the area next to the shisha using the cast on method (see page 23). Ensure you cover your securing stitches as you work. Bring your needle up at the starting point of your stitch, and take it down about 2mm (1/16in) further on.

2 Pull all the thread through firmly. Start the next stitch by bringing your needle up through the middle of the previous stitch, splitting the thread as you go.

3 Take it down about 2mm (1/16in) further on, pulling thread firmly.

4 Repeat step 3, keeping lengths consistent and gradually curving around and about in a wandering 'squiggle' effect.

5 Fill the entirety of the inner circle with green vermicelli, then cast off the working thread so that it is hidden by the final split stitches (see page 23).

6 Fill the outer circle with red vermicelli stitch in the same way.

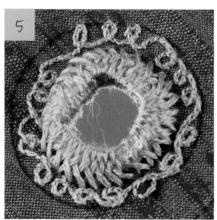

72

The brooch at the end of this stage.

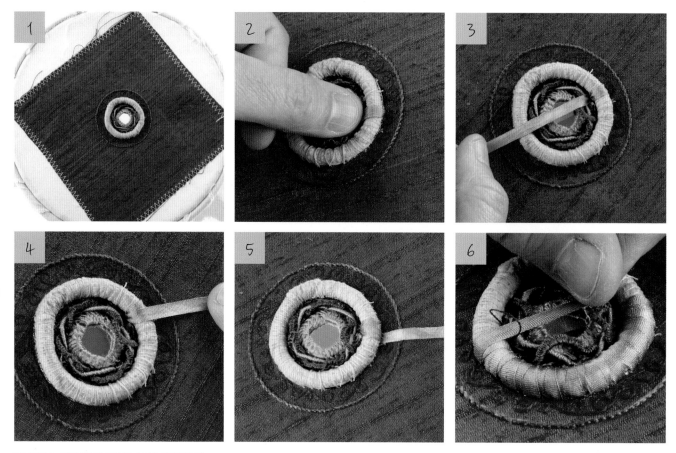

BEADS AND RIBBON 'CUTWORK'

Inspired by the goldwork embroidery technique, this creates a raised roundel of colour and sparkle.

1 Use soft string padding (see pages 36–37) to create a doughnut shape with neatly fitting ends on the surface as shown.

2 Thread a length of silk ribbon into a large-eyed embroidery needle and secure the end at the outer edge of the padding, via the cast-on method (see page 23). Take the ribbon over the padding at a slight angle.

3 Cast a fine red thread onto an embroidery needle and add a couching stitch to hold the ribbon down tightly on the inside of the padding.

4 Take the ribbon back over the padding, overlapping the previous section slightly.

5 Secure the ribbon on the outside.

6 Continue to secure the ribbon, 'zig-zagging' back and forth over the padding as you work.

7 Once you have worked all the way round, thread a fine embroidery needle with matching thread. Bring it up on one side of the padding and thread on ten or so beads.

8 Take the needle over the padding and down close to the padding on the other side, slightly further around. Draw through to pull the beads tightly against the padding.

9 Repeat all the way around.

The brooch at the end of this stage.

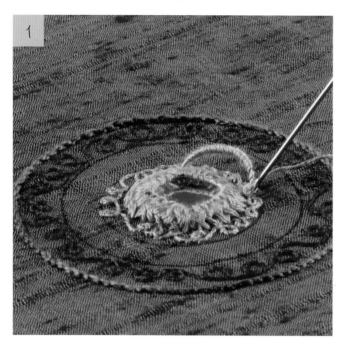

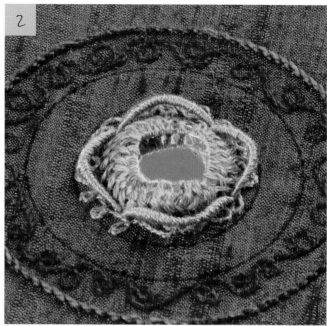

BULLION KNOT AND CAST-ON FLOWER

Inspired by Brazilian embroidery (see page 46), this motif combines three well-known raised stitches.

1 Work a long curved bullion knot quarter of the way round the shisha, starting at the 12 o'clock position and working round to the 3 o'clock position.

2 Work round the rest of the shisha with three more long curved bullion knots; the first from 3 o'clock to 6 o'clock, the second from 6 o'clock to 9 o'clock, and the third from 9 o'clock to 12 o'clock.

3 Just like bullion knots, cast-on stitches can be made curved by adding too many wraps to comfortably sit between the start and end points of the stitch. Use this to make a curved cast-on stitch over the first loop, bringing the needle up on the inside of the loop (i.e. nearer the shisha) and down on the outside of the next loop.

4 Repeat on the other three bullion knots, starting each overfilled cast-on stitch inside one bullion knot loop and taking it over the next loop.

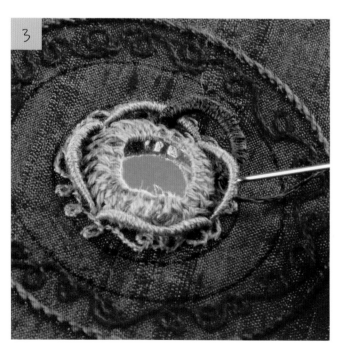

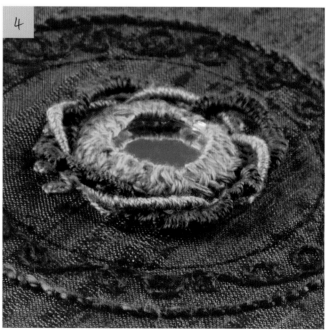

Overlapping bullion knots

Twisting and turning, the intertwined bullion knots and cast-on stitches are echoed by the orange vermicelli split stitches and the rows of beads going over the padded ribbon roundel.

CONSTRUCTION

1 Use scissors to trim your fabric into a circle, leaving a border of 2.5cm (1in) around the outer line (see template on page 68). Pin this to a piece of stiffened fabric cut to the same size as the template.

2 Use a strong thread and a curved needle to begin firmly lacing the fabric across the back of the roundel. Start by securing your thread then taking a small stitch through the seam allowance of the fabric on one side of the roundel.

3 Take a second small stitch directly opposite, so that the thread travels straight across the back of the roundel.

4 Make your next stitch a little way clockwise round the shape, then repeat steps 2 and 3, folding in the fabric seam allowance as you work. Your roundel will begin to resemble a wheel with criss-crossing strokes.

5 Continue working all the way round until all the fabric seam allowance has been secured, then secure and cast off your working thread. Using a single strand of embroidery cotton, work a line of detached buttonhole bar 'scallops' (see page 54) into the very edge of the fabric as a decorative finish, taking care not to damage the surface embroidery.

6 Cut a piece of red felt to 3–5mm (⅛–¼in) smaller than the piece and position it on the back of the roundel. Use a matching thread and a curved needle to secure the felt to the piece using small, neat stitches.

7 Use the matching thread and a curved needle to attach a brooch finding to the felt to finish.

Necklace variation

If you prefer, you can attach a necklace finding in place of the brooch back, then thread a chain or ribbon through to make a necklace.

The finished brooch.

OTHER WEARABLES

Delicate accessories for special occasions are the perfect opportunity to showcase your skills. I am so inspired by the work of my friends and colleagues who also trained at the Royal School of Needlework. Many of them are busy teachers and designer-makers, but only a few have branched out into wearable embroidery. Some examples of their, and my, work are shown on the following pages. I hope you are as motivated by their work as I am.

Queen's 90th birthday brooch

Helen Stevens, Marg Dier, Kate Nolan, Alena Chenevix Trench, Masako Newton, Becky Quine, Deborah Wilding, and Kate Barlow, with advisory input from other members of the studio team.

This exquisite brooch was worked by many of the Royal School of Needlework's staff in order to celebrate our patron Queen Elizabeth II's ninetieth birthday. As can be seen from the list of makers, this was a truly collaborative project, an approach often adopted by the RSN studio staff. Made from a mix of silk and cotton fabric and threads, the brooch measures 10 x 8cm (4 x 3¼in) at its widest and tallest points. Each of the four countries of the United Kingdom is symbolised by its national flower.

The English rose is made from wired long and short stitch petals, with yellow detailing worked in French knots and citrine gem stones added to the centre. The Welsh daffodil is a wired shape with each individual petal worked separately in double and triple Brussels stitch in a very fine variegated perlé thread. The trumpet of the flower is in double Brussels

stitch and also in fine perlé thread. The thistle of Scotland is a covered painted cotton ball with Turkey rug stitch to form the top. A wrapped wire was placed around the Turkey work in order to keep it upright and a string of tourmaline gem stones were added as a finishing touch. The cotton ball was then covered in detached buttonhole stitch to create the appropriate thistle markings. The leaves for the thistle were in green silk fabric with wired buttonhole edge. The Irish shamrock leaves are fabric with wired edges, with a gold pearl purl added as a final touch.

The elements were all plunged together through a piece of fabric where the wires could be finished off and a stable base formed. To this stable base we attached a bespoke silver brooch back made by Helen Stevens.

Shell necklace
Lisa Bilby

Wired satin petals with bead centres were secured to wired shells and ribbons to make this timelessly elegant piece. Marrying the neutral tones of the flowers to a clean white ribbon gives a clean but not antiseptic result.

Flower brooches

Lisa Bilby

These three small flowers measure just 3–5cm (1¼–2in) across. They are made from wired organdie, wired needlelace and incorporate embellished fabric petals wired with metal pearl purl.

Cuff

Kelley Aldridge

Designed to be wrapped around the wrist, this has been laid flat to show the detail of the stitches I used – namely bullion knots for the roses, raised stem band, raised leaves and basketweave ribbonwork. The central heart includes a padded whipped wheel that measures 2.5cm (1in). The whole piece is worked on vintage linen, which gives a wonderful warm neutral backdrop to the piece.

Corsage

Helen Richman

Made from wired silk and satin, this corsage has been embellished with complementary beads and metal threads. It was assembled with additional ribbons and wired beads before being secured to a backing pin attachment, a type of jewellery finding.

Fascinators

Jennifer Goodwin

Made as a set, these pieces are all wired silk embellished with silver thread. The largest measures 8cm (3¼in) across, while the smallest is just 3cm (1¼in), showing that size isn't everything!

Two of the fascinators are secured to hair pins, while the third is attached to a hair comb. Note how feathers have been incorporated into the designs, showing how found objects can add to the beauty of a piece.

Fascinator

Lisa Bilby

This is constructed from wired organza petals twisted onto a beaded and wired frame, which was in turn secured to a clear hair comb. Delicate stones have been wired in place to add interest and texture to the whole piece, which was worked by Lisa as a 'creative metal' piece for her Apprenticeship at the Royal School of Needlework.

USEABLE RAISED EMBROIDERY

Mediaeval raised work may have been a sumptuous pasttime of wealthy titled ladies, but it was functional, make no mistake! The finished embroidery was most often made into picture and mirror frames, or complex, multi-sectioned boxes, also called caskets. We find very old, delicately framed pictures or panels today because the original item became worn or damaged and was recycled into separate objects to preserve what remained. I'm glad and grateful that these pieces were loved enough to be kept in some form for us to enjoy today.

Modern versions of frames and caskets are still worked today, and can be great fun to make. However, raised embroidery can also be used to personalise your sewing accessories such as needle cases, tape measure covers, beanbag weights and pincushions; as well as bookmarks, key fobs, spectacles and phone cases. In fact, why stop there? You could use raised embroidery to update your napkin rings, place mats ... almost anything!

Considerations for making useable raised embroidery

Embroidery that is used is embroidery that is at risk of damage; your choice of stitches and materials must take this into account otherwise you will not be able to enjoy your finished piece for long. Unlike wearable embroidery which can be kept fairly protected if it is the right sort of item, by definition useable embroidery is destined to be handled in many ways on many occasions.

Give careful thought to what your project's purpose will be; whether it will need to be cleaned occasionally, where it will be stored, how it will be handled and so on. Make sure that the design works with these requirements, and that the stitches, techniques and materials support the design in the same way.

For example, a bookmark can be made with finer fabric and longer, looping stitches that can be flattened; but not with bulky padding as this would not allow the book to lie flat when closed. Conversely, a spectacle case that is kept in a bag should have low-level, short and tightly worked stitches that will not get pulled out of shape or damaged when pressing against other items in transit.

A note on cleaning: most raised embroidery cannot be cleaned very effectively and you do so at your own risk – so handle your pieces with care in the first place. If you must clean an object that has raised embroidery on it and you know the materials are colourfast, you can clean it by hand using warm water with mild detergent. Reshape it while damp then allow it to dry naturally. Needless to say, if the item is of sentimental, personal or historical value, you may need to learn to love the character that a little 'weathering' brings to the piece!

Needle case

7 x 7cm (3 x 3in)
Jacqui McDonald

This sampler of various raised stitches – including a wrapped bead, a needlelace-covered bead, French knots and needle-woven picots – provides a jaunty cover to a needle case. All of the elements are themed around the garden, and the neat borders give the impression of a charming, whimsical allotment.

More haste, less speed

Ideas rarely come in a single step! Absorb lots of ideas without judging them at first, and really think about what it was you want to make. Rushing to get going with a project before you are truly in love with the design can lead to dissatisfaction and frustration when it is too late to make important changes. Walk away from the design for a day or so before committing to anything. Keep thinking about it, and don't be tempted by that awful phrase 'that will do'!

Phone sleeve

Hand-embroidered projects are usually small, because the stitching takes so long to complete. The idea for a sleeve for my smartphone came from looking at historical pieces. Many were small bags designed to contain necessaries when out and about. Thinking about this, I nearly sat on my new smartphone, which lives in my back pocket. I had a lightbulb moment – what a great idea for a truly modern kind of 'bag'!

Having a 'pocket' that is separate from your clothing may seem a novel idea, but this phone sleeve is more traditional than it might seem. Pockets were not originally part of a garment, but separate items that were tied about the waist under the outer garments, with discreet slits in side-seams to allow access.

In keeping with tradition, here is a piece of raised embroidery that is to be used. Like the mirror frames and elaborate caskets of the seventeenth century, this project will allow you to display your skills with needle and thread to everyone around you.

YOU WILL NEED
Linen twill for the base fabric
Thin cotton fabric for the lining
Stranded cotton embroidery thread
4mm (⅛in) wide space-dyed
    silk ribbon
Metallic embroidery thread
String
Sewing thread
Fine cord (optional)
Basic sewing kit

Inspiration
For several years now I have put together a personalised colouring book 'calendar' for my sister who lives overseas. The process behind that indirectly led to the design of this piece. Keep your eyes and mind open – it is surprising where inspiration can come from.

Opposite:
The finished phone sleeve
The template on page 90 is designed for my smartphone, but you can easily adjust the patten by altering the blue dotted outline border – try drawing round your phone for an easy size adjustment.

DESIGNING THE PIECE

When I was designing this project, my mind was very much on bold floral shapes, repeating motifs and mandalas, as well as bold blocks of colour. Without much conscious thought, I began to doodle such ideas on a scrap piece of paper, which gradually became a rather nice stylised colouring page. It was roughly rectangular in shape and, although it was a bit too complicated to stitch at a smaller size, most of what I doodled remained in place when it was shrunk down on the photocopier to a more suitable scale.

The compact size of the project suggested the use of linen twill – a tough and hard-wearing fabric, often used in Jacobean crewelwork embroidery – absolutely ideal, as I would need only a small scrap or offcut of the expensive material. I wanted to have some fun with the sculpted velvet work technique (also known as Turkey knot stitch) and incorporate lots of bold colours and other textures. I am a fan of 1950s and 1960s graphic design, and started looking for ideas and colourways reminiscent of the period by searching through fabrics and threads.

This project started as a doodle and evolved into the piece you can see on the following pages. I hope you are encouraged to play with doodling and scribbling yourself, to see what you end up with – perhaps you will be tempted to work it up in stitches!

90

Template

This template is reproduced at actual size.

MOODBOARD

I found a lovely subtle colour palette which I printed out at best quality in order to get a good match in materials. There is quite a bit of sampling on this board, alongside historical images, ideas for constructions and the original large-scale drawing (see *Designing the piece* above) in the background.

ORDER OF WORK

The flower motifs are worked 'back-to-front' – the lower layers are worked first, and additional techniques are subsequently worked on top.

A Secure the fabric to the hoop, then transfer the design (see pages 32–33).

B Work the areas of Bokhara couching (see pages 92–93).

C Work fly stitch areas (see page 94).

D Work the stem stitch areas (see pages 70–71).

E Work the bullion knot outline (see page 43).

F Add the woven wheels (see page 52).

G Add the whipped wheels (see page 53).

H Fill the centres with French knots (see page 42).

I Work the Turkey rug area (see pages 50–51).

J Work the long and short stitch area (see page 98–99).

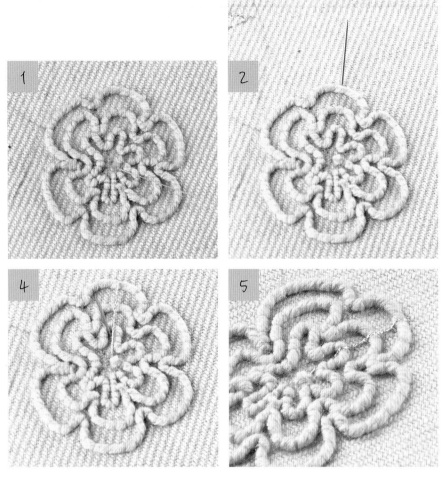

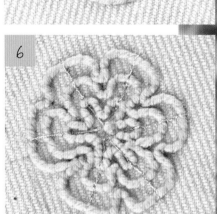

BOKHARA COUCHING OVER HARD STRING PADDING

This technique uses one thread to couch over itself; here I have created a ridged effect with some regular string underneath.

1 Using a standard sewing thread and a fine embroidery needle, couch (see pages 36–37) ordinary string to the background fabric, creating a flower-within-a-flower pattern on the bottom right of the design.

2 Using a metallic embroidery thread, bring your needle up just outside the couched string, at the middle of one of the petals.

3 Working from the outer edge of the petal towards the centre of the flower, take your needle down at the base of the petal and pull the thread completely through.

4 Bring the needle up right next to the inner edge of the first piece of string.

5 Couch over the metallic thread, pulling firmly so the thread 'hugs' the inner edge of the string. Repeat the process on the other side of the string, remembering always to pull the working thread firmly. Couch the middle piece of string and the inside edge of the outer piece of string in the same way to complete the first line of Bokhara couching.

6 Repeat steps 2–5 on all the other petals.

7 Working outwards from these initial lines, repeat steps 2 through 6, starting with a light shade of embroidery cotton at the centre of the petals and gradually working to a darker shade at the edges. Repeat for each of the petals.

Ridged flower detail

Traditionally used in goldwork, this hard-string padding gives the embroidery threads added dimension and a pleasing pattern that 'echoes' from the centre outwards.

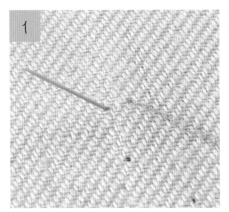
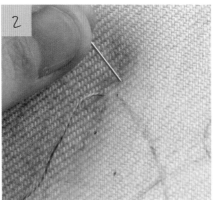
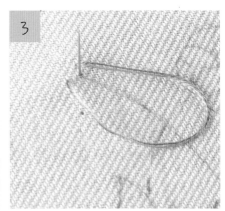

FLY STITCH

This useful stitch looks like a V or a Y depending on where you place the base of the stitch. It can be made to resemble the petals of a flower, a flock of birds, or a fern! In this project I worked close, vertical lines of Y-shaped fly stitches in embroidery cotton.

1 Secure your thread via the cast on method (see page 23) and bring your needle up at the start of the design line, slightly above and to the left of the start point.

2 Take your needle down slightly above and to the right of the start point of the design.

3 Pull most of the thread through, leaving a short loop. Holding the loop of thread flat against the fabric's surface, bring your needle up at the start point of the design – this will be the stem, or base stitch.

4 Pull the thread through firmly, taking up any slack thread.

5 Take your needle down a little way along the design line. This forms the Y and complete the first fly stitch. The length of this base stitch can be varied.

6 Continue making stitches in the same way along the design line, overlapping stitches so that the bottom of one fly stitch stem shares the same hole as the top of the stem of the following stitch, thus ensuring a solid line of stitches.

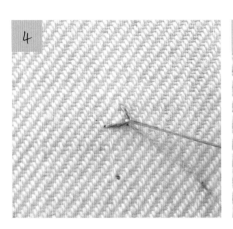
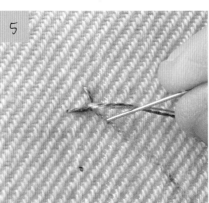
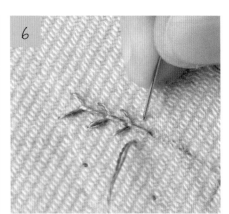

Fly stitch stem detail

A line of connected fly stitches in gradually changing shades of green thread provides an anchoring 'stem' down the centre of the piece.

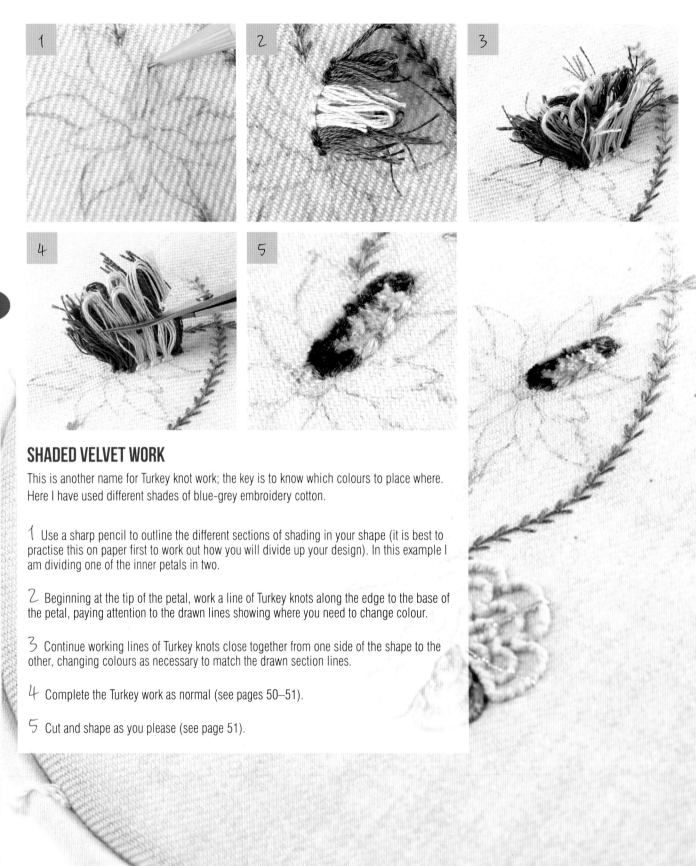

SHADED VELVET WORK

This is another name for Turkey knot work; the key is to know which colours to place where. Here I have used different shades of blue-grey embroidery cotton.

1 Use a sharp pencil to outline the different sections of shading in your shape (it is best to practise this on paper first to work out how you will divide up your design). In this example I am dividing one of the inner petals in two.

2 Beginning at the tip of the petal, work a line of Turkey knots along the edge to the base of the petal, paying attention to the drawn lines showing where you need to change colour.

3 Continue working lines of Turkey knots close together from one side of the shape to the other, changing colours as necessary to match the drawn section lines.

4 Complete the Turkey work as normal (see pages 50–51).

5 Cut and shape as you please (see page 51).

Velvet work petals detail

Three shades of blue-grey are used to add interest to the texture. Extremely close – and careful – trimming at the outer edges helps to create a domed effect to the petal.

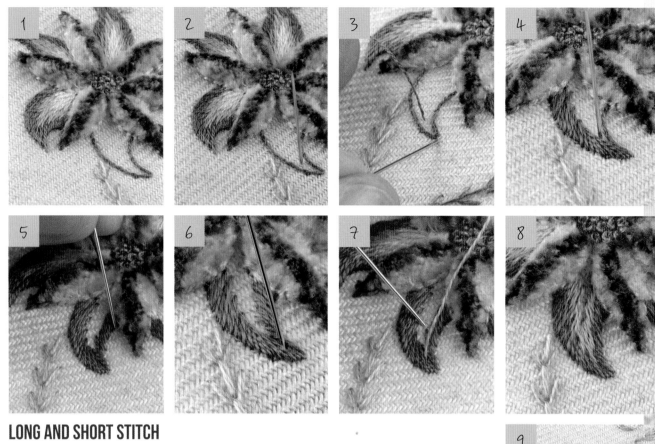

LONG AND SHORT STITCH

Long and short stitch is often referred to as thread painting or silk shading. This technique can be very intricate, or quite simple, as in this example, where the petals are each worked in three tones. The first four have been completed, and the sixth is shown part-worked to help illustrate the technique.

1 Outline the stitch with split stitch, using the darkest-toned embroidery cotton and a size 10 embroidery needle.

2 Secure the thread and bring the needle up inside the split stitch outline, approximately 5mm (¼in) from the tip of the leaf.

3 Draw the thread through and take the needle down just outside the split stitch outline.

4 Work stitches of varying lengths within the shape, down one side of the petal. They should all come up inside the shape and go down neatly just outside the split stitch outline. Bring the needle back up at the point.

5 Work down the other side of the petal, covering the split stitch outline completely. This completes the first row.

6 Secure the darkest-toned thread and thread the needle with the middle tone. Bring the needle up through the central stitch of the first row, approximately halfway along the stitch itself. Ensure you pierce the stitch as shown.

7 Take the needle down into the backing fabric, further within the shape.

8 As with the first row, work along each side of the petal in turn. For each stitch, bring the needle up within a stitch in the previous row, and take it down further within the shape. Vary how far into the first row stitch you pierce each time to blend the colours together.

9 Secure the thread, then thread the needle with the lightest-toned thread. Work your final row within the centre of the petal, covering the remaining surface fabric. As before, vary how far into the previous row you bring the needle up each time to create a soft gradated effect. This finishes the petal; so move on to complete the others in the same way.

Long and short stitch petal detail

A complete contrast to the three-dimensional velvet work petals, the long and short stitch petals were worked completely flat in bold orange threads with a silky sheen that makes the blue 'pop'.

CONSTRUCTION

1 Use large fabric scissors to trim the fabric for the front and back panels to the outline (see the blue dotted lines on the template on page 90), then mark and cut out two rectangles of the same size for the lining from orange lining fabric.

2 Place the front panel and one piece of lining fabric right sides together and pin. Machine stitch three of the four sides together, leaving one of the small sides open.

3 Repeat the process for the back panel, using the other piece of orange lining fabric. Use the fabric scissors to carefully trim away the corners as shown, as near the stitching as possible, on both pieces.

4 Turn both pieces right side out and use a blunt pointed object, such as a paintbrush handle, to push the corners fully out.

5 Use small neat stitches to sew up the open ends on each piece. Pin the panels together with lining sides facing, then use small neat stitches to sew the sides and base seams together to make a pocket.

6 Attach a cord to disguise the seam lines to finish.

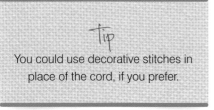

Tip
You could use decorative stitches in place of the cord, if you prefer.

The back cover

There is no need to decorate the back cover of the phone sleeve, but it provides a great canvas for your creativity and an opportunity for further personalisation. I decorated the back of mine with an enlarged version of the smallest flower motif, worked in raised stem band petals and surrounded by two rows of overlapping bullion knots. I also worked my initials in two strands of embroidery cotton below the flower to add a final personal touch.

The finished phone sleeve.

OTHER USEABLES

Practical items include book covers, bags and, of course, sewing paraphernalia such as pincushions, storage boxes and needle cases. These need to be fairly sturdy to survive their intended purpose, but that doesn't mean they need to look brutalist. As long as you pick stitches and materials that are appropriate, your useable items will remain beautiful and in good condition for a long time.

The most popular form of useable raised embroidery is still hard-backed – that is to say, mounted over card as a book cover or as box panels. I like to think that the pieces in this gallery will become heirlooms of the future, just as the mirror frames and caskets of the seventeenth century are today.

Hansel and Gretel
Jessica Grimm

Measuring 24cm (9½in) in height, this fabric-covered box has been decorated in the style of a fairytale gingerbread cottage. The roof opens at the top to reveal a partitioned interior, used for storage. Several techniques have been used including needlelace, appliqué, and long and short shading. Note the use of novelty buttons. This is a good example of how decorative you can make a practical piece like this storage box.

Bird etui
Jenny Adin-Christie

Several forms of needlelace have been combined here to create a delightful container for sewing tools. The techniques used include couching, long and short shading, Turkey work, French knots, various types of padding and wired shapes. A wide variety of materials have been used including silk, metal, cotton and felt. The piece measures 14cm (5½in) in height.

The Owl & the Pussycat book cover

Jenny Adin-Christie

Making a panel to attach to a book cover is a wonderful way of turning a favourite book into a decorative keepsake, or personalising a gift. This edition of *The Owl & and The Pussycat*, by Edward Lear, has had a front panel added that illustrates the two at sea in their 'beautiful pea-green boat'. The piece measures 14cm (5½in); just large enough to cover the front of the book.

Several forms of needlelace combined with couching were used here, alongside long and short shading, Turkey knot work and French knots. There are also various padded areas and wired shapes that utilise a variety of silks, metals, cotton and felt.

Note that the backing fabric has been chosen to match the fabric cover of the book – you might choose a contrasting or complementary colour if that better suits your design.

Etui cottage box

Kelley Aldridge

This delightful little box started its life not long after I completed my Royal School of Needlework Apprenticeship. Each of the panels shows my idea of an idyllic cottage garden, complete with birdhouse, vegetable patch, rambling roses and – of course – somewhere shady to enjoy a summer's evening.

   As well as being decorative, the piece opens up (see opposite, bottom) to reveal my embroidery kit. It thus forms a neat storage solution, and a handy way to keep my tools close to hand. The object of an evening class, it was designed to be a stitch sampler, and it incorporates over thirty different flat and raised stitches. The final two classes saw the participants assembling their samplers into their own personal cottage. Worked in stranded embroidery cotton on evenweave linen, I included a variety of bullion knots, rosette stitches, French knots, needle-woven picots and raised stem band on the four panels. Note that the stitches all lie fairly flat to the surface to avoid them snagging or becoming damaged during use.

COLLECTIBLE RAISED EMBROIDERY

I am a firm advocate of William Morris' rule: 'Have nothing in your houses that you do not know to be useful or believe to be beautiful.' Generally speaking, I like the 'less is more' approach to home decor, so any decoration has to either be very beautiful, very meaningful – or both – for me to have to dust it! The other projects in this book are intended to be both beautiful and useful, but the pieces in this final part of the book are purely decorative.

Framed pictures, of course, fall into this category and the following pages show some charming examples. However, I believe beauty can be as much in the hand of the beholder as their eye – three-dimensional stitches are best experienced up close, not held behind glass. You might fill large bowls with small embroidered cushions, working each one using different embroidery techniques to make it unique. Another example of embroidered collectibles are Christmas tree decorations – I myself have an ongoing project to cover my Christmas tree in all things stitch-related.

These projects help to explain why collectibles can be considered the purest form of raised embroidery. You need make no concessions for practicality or wearability in the materials and techniques you use; you are instead utterly free to exercise your imagination. The purpose of these projects is entirely aesthetic – each ornament is a tiny work of art in itself, made purely for pleasure and enjoyment.

Considerations for making collectible raised embroidery

Like the wearable and useable projects, some 'off-the-wall' collectible embroidery will need to be fairly robust, as it will be handled when it is admired! However, if the piece you are planning is intended to be viewed only at a distance, such as a hanging ornament, then you can include more fragile elements. Silk dupion, organza and other sheer fabrics can be used in these sort of pieces, as can fine silk threads and metals such as those used in goldwork embroidery. As always, make sure it is protected from damage when it is stored, and try to get your initials and date worked into it somewhere, so future generations will have a clue as to its origins!

Sweetie Dress
75cm (29½in) high
Katie Barlow

A half-scale model dress that features a variety of individually hand-embroidered old-fashioned sweets. Bright colours and clean details lend themselves perfectly to the various textures and shapes of the various sweeties. The techniques used include wrapped beads, stem stitch, couching and long and short shading – the trick is to find a technique that is appropriate to the specific look you are after.

Biscornu

Most people think of biscornus as the fifteen-sided canvas work pincushions which have become more and more popular with stitchers. However, the word *biscornu* is simply a French word meaning 'oddly shaped'.

The key construction feature of this piece, apart from the odd shape, is the central 'dip', which is formed by stitching through the centre of both sides of the cushion and pulling together. Incorporating this feature, I opted for a design which flowed outwards from the centre, rather than circling it. Although oddly shaped, the biscornu isn't actually irregular, and I felt I wanted repeating shapes throughout.

This project is a wonderful opportunity to squeeze in as much texture, padding and surface stitches as possible. It's time to get out your novelty threads, your beads, buttons and anything else you've been saving in your stash – they'll all fit in somewhere on a lovely, oddly shaped and encrusted biscornu. Make several and put them in a big wooden bowl!

YOU WILL NEED

Evenweave linen, natural colour, to use as the base fabric
Cotton calico for the backing
Fine twisted silk
4mm (⅛in) wide space-dyed silk ribbon
Small wooden beads
Vintage mother-of-pearl buttons, 1cm (½in) in diameter
Selection of small beads
Miniature bells
Sewing thread
Small piece of cardboard
Two small buttons
Felt
Toy stuffing
Fine cord (optional)
Basic sewing kit

DESIGNING THE PIECE

This 'collectible' item is intended to be picked up, turned over, and of course, touched frequently. A very light colour scheme would get grubby too quickly, and delicate materials would soon wear down and become damaged. I still stayed with a muted and limited palette to allow the texture and the stitches themselves to really stand out, but opted for more robust materials and techniques to withstand the inevitable handling.

MOODBOARD

Much of my initial inspiration for this project came from examples of encrusted calico – a style of embroidery designed to resemble coral, barnacles and other shell-like objects. With this in mind, I researched and gathered pictures of pale pink and mauve sea creatures, then found threads and textures that matched these hues.

Template

This template is reproduced at actual size.

ORDER OF WORK

You will find it easiest to work all of the design outlines first. This will allow you to see the layout as a whole as you proceed to fill the outlines with the other techniques.

A Secure the fabric to the hoop, then transfer the design (see pages 32–33).

B Pad these areas (see pages 34–37).

C Work the bullion knot outlines (see page 43).

D Work the stem stitch areas (see pages 70–71).

E Add the shisha (see pages 40–41).

F Work single Brussels needlelace (see page 56) areas.

G Work bullion knot rose (see pages 114–115) areas.

H Work raised leaf stitch (see pages 116–117) areas.

I Work rosette stitch (see pages 118–119) areas.

J Work French knots over the padding (see page 42).

K Work the raised chain (see page 49) areas.

L Add the wrapped beads (see page 120).

M Add any surface embellishments.

N Construction.

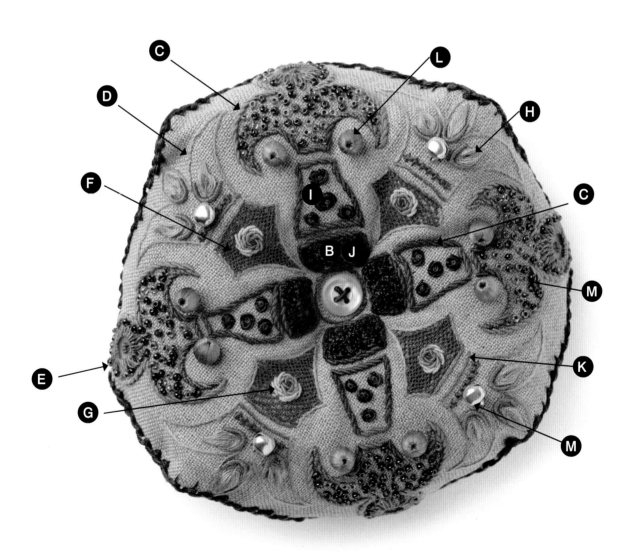

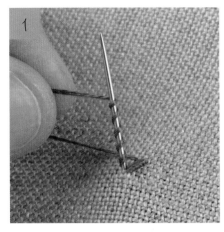 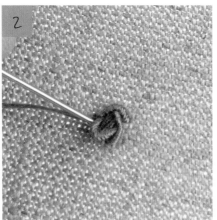 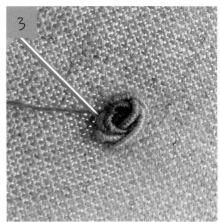

BULLION KNOT ROSE

This can look so impressive, and once you have perfected your curved bullion knot, you'll be churning these out by the dozen. Pick a colourway with subtle shade changes to get the most realistic effect. Two strands of embroidery cotton are the easiest to work with, but you can use more or fewer.

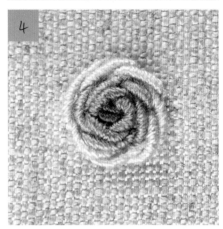

1 Using the darkest shade of the colourway, work two standard-sized bullion knots (see page 43) side by side in the centre of the rose.

2 Make the first roundel of curved bullion knots by working three curved bullion knots which slightly overlap each other at the ends and surround the two bullions made in step 1.

3 Change to a slightly lighter shade of cotton to make a second roundel of overlapping, curved bullions around the first. You will need to make four or five knots at this stage.

4 Repeat the process for any subsequent roundels, increasing the number of curved bullions by at least one or two as required, until the bullion knot rose is the size your design requires.

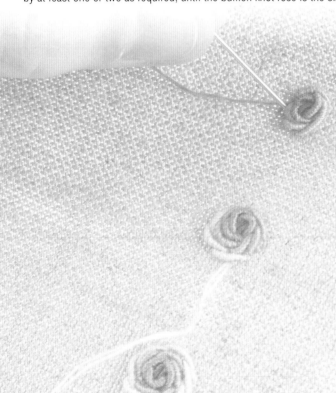

Tip

You can alter the way a bullion knot rose faces by changing how the second and subsequent roundels of knots surround the central knots and first roundel.

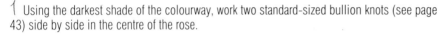

Green rose

These bullion knot roses are worked in three shades of green over a shaped panel of double Brussels needlelace.

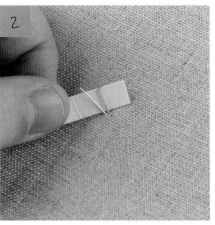

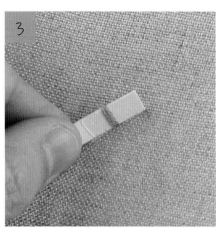

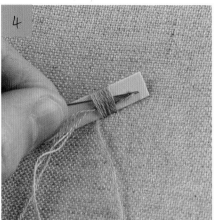

RAISED LEAF STITCH

This is very effective when worked in a variegated thread (I used Gutermann Sulky 12 gauge). You will need a piece of stiff paper or card 0.5cm (¼in) wide and long enough to hold.

1 Bring your needle up at the tip of the leaf shape, over the card and back down into the same hole, then pull taut (see inset).

2 Bring your needle up very close to the first stitch.

3 Take it over the card, and down slightly away from the initial hole. Pull taut.

4 Repeat several more times, then gently slide the eye of the needle back under these stitches on one side of the card strip and the pull the working thread through completely.

5 Carefully remove the card strip.

6 Tighten the thread to secure it, then take it over the stitch to flatten the thread wraps into a leaf shape.

7 Take the working thread down through the fabric at the base of the leaf.

8 Draw through and gently stroke the loops of thread on the surface to neaten the result.

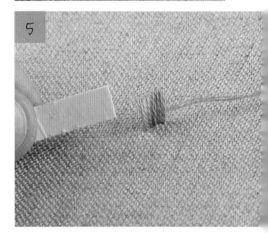

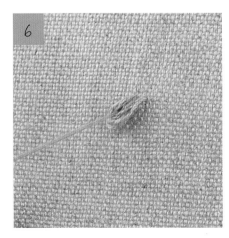

Raised leaf motifs

Here, raised leaf stitch has been worked in
a single strand of variegated cotton thread,
before a curved bullion knot was worked at the
base. Creating new combinations of stitches
and colours means your motifs need never be
the same – enjoy exploring your skills.

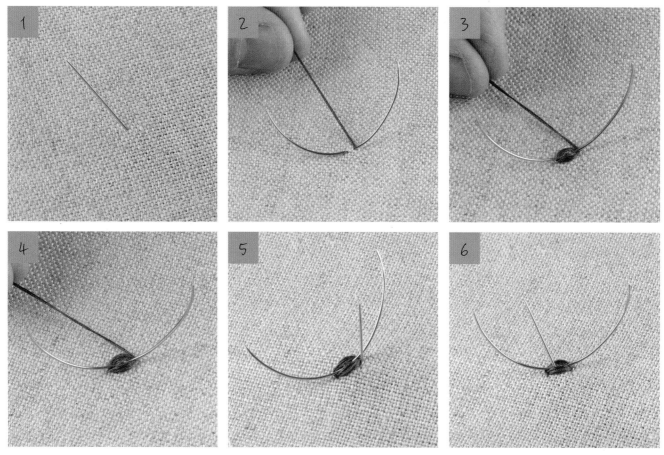

ROSETTE STITCH

This stitch is usually worked on slack fabric with a pin, but a curved needle can be used if your project is stretched tight on a hoop. This technique works well with a variegated thread, embroidery cotton, or a fine twisted silk. I use the latter in this example.

1 Bring your needle up in the centre of the rosette stitch you are about to work (you will need to judge this by eye).

2 Draw the thread through, then use a curved needle to scoop up two or three threads of your base fabric, next to your working thread.

3 Keeping your working thread on the surface of the fabric, wind it around the pin.

4 Continue winding until the resulting roundel is the size you wish.

5 Take your thread down through the fabric at the outer edge of the roundel where it passes near the curved needle and bring it back up directly opposite on the other outer edge of the roundel.

6 Take your needle down on the corresponding inner edge of the roundel, then bring it up directly opposite, also on the inner edge of the roundel.

7 Finish off by taking the working thread down on the far edge of the roundel (the same hole you used to take the winding thread down in step 5).

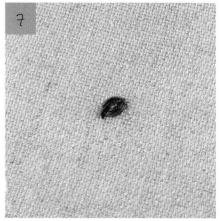

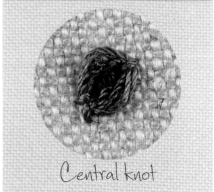

Central knot

You can add a French knot to the centre of this stitch for an attractive result.

Scattered rosettes

Here, four rosette stitches have been arranged in an enclosed area to create an interesting design element that is repeated elsewhere on the biscornu. Each stitch was worked in two colours of silk thread and finished with a single French knot in the centre.

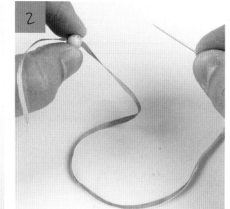

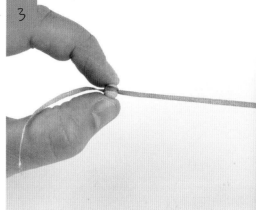

WRAPPED BEAD

This technique can be done with thread or with silk ribbon, as shown here.

1 Thread a chenille needle with ribbon.

2 Take the needle through a bead, leaving a tail of roughly 5cm (2in).

3 Take the needle round and back through the bead. Draw it through and pull tight, being careful to avoid the tail.

4 Take the needle back round and through the bead again, then pull tight as before. Do not let the ribbon twist as it is laid down.

5 Continue working until the bead is covered, then take the working ribbon back through the hole, catching the ribbon inside the bead to secure it. Draw the ribbon through, leaving two tails. These can be used to secure the bead to the biscornu.

Silk wrapped beads

Delicately shaded narrow silk ribbon was
worked around small wooden beads and
attached with the tails of the ribbon. This sort
of addition is not particularly hard-wearing, but
it is perfect for collectibles.

CONSTRUCTION

The distinguishing feature of a biscornu is its distinctive shape. The design may be square, but the way it is attached to the corresponding piece of fabric needs to be deliberately askew. The back piece of fabric is set at forty-five degrees to the decorated front piece and then carefully joined together.

1 Remove the embroidered fabric from the hoop and trim it back to the outline square (marked in blue on the template). Cut a second piece of fabric to the same size and draw a border 1.5cm (¾in) in from the edge.

2 Lay the embroidery piece face-down, then place the backing piece on top as shown (i.e. right sides together).

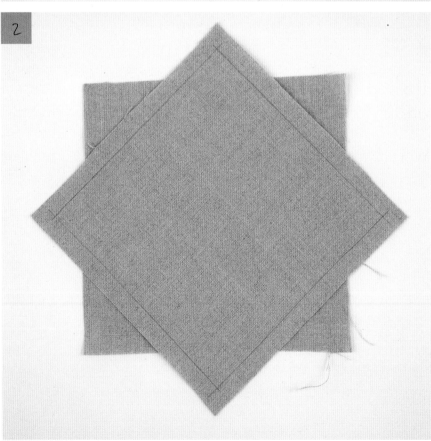

3 Thread a needle with strong sewing thread. Take it through the corner point of the border on the backing, then through the midpoint of the border line on the embroidered piece.

4 Working anti-clockwise, sew back stitch along the lines. Note that you need to make sure that you are keeping the lines aligned on both the embroidered piece and the backing piece. As you reach the midpoint on the backing edge, you will be at the corner of the border on the embroidered side.

5 As you complete one side of the border, you will be able to see the shape emerging.

6 Work all the way round, leaving a 5cm (2in) gap as you near the end.

Turning

To help turn accurately at the corners, bring the needle through from the back at the corner, then hold the needle firmly and swivel the fabric around it.

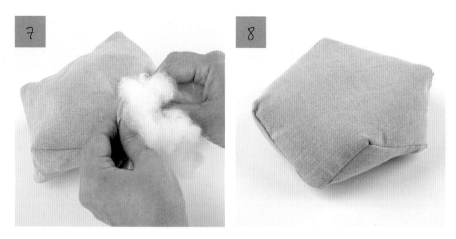

7 Use the gap to turn the piece the right way out, then stuff with polyester toy filling until it is firm.

8 Sew up the gap.

9 Add buttons by making a dimple in the centre. Secure your thread in the centre of the fabric underneath the cushion. Bring the needle out in the centre of the top of the cushion. Take your needle up through one of the button's holes, then back down through the other hole, then back through the cushion of the underside. Do not pull it tight yet. Repeat with the underside button, then take it back through and repeat on the top button again. Once your needle has emerged from the underside of the cushion, gently pull up the slack to draw the buttons together and form a dimple on both sides of the biscornu.

10 Work raised chain stitch (see page 49) round the outside stem.

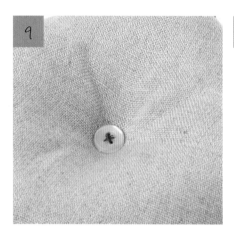

The finished biscornu.

OTHER COLLECTIBLES

Raised work for the sheer fun of it! The examples of raised work on the following pages give you a glimpse into the myriad forms your collectible embroidery can take – from hanging ornaments to framed pictures to sparkling sculpture. Here, beauty becomes its own function.

Flower

Angela Bishop

This stunning piece, which celebrates the beauty of the natural world, is made up of silk petals embellished with couched beetle's wingcase, vermicelli stitch worked in metal thread, beading and free-standing metal wires. It is displayed on a vintage wooden thread spool.

Angela is a recent graduate of the Royal School of Needlework's Future Tutor Programme, which is the contemporary version of the previous Apprenticeship. This piece was her response to the 'Creative Metal' project brief.

Even the underside of the piece is exquisitely and delicately worked. Wired copper petals wrapped in blue silk threads support the silk petals from below.

This detail shows the intricate wandering vermicelli stitch, which has been worked in fine metal threads and embellished with glass beads.

Looping metal bullions are clustered at the centre of the flower to create an eye-catching focal point.

Tiny Dancer
Kate Barlow

This playful piece combines the best of traditional and modern raised embroidery. The delicate 10cm (4in) high artwork is a traditional stumpwork figure worked in fine cottons and satin with bead and lace embellishment.

Detached buttonhole scalloping is used on the knickers, while single and double Brussels needlelace is used on the stockings.

This top-down view shows the decoration on the skirt top and the surface embellishment on the needlelace bodice.

A lovely (and cheeky!) interpretation of the traditional figures seen on seventeenth-century stumpwork boxes and frames. The hands are made with separately wired fingers while the face is made up of several layers and sculpting stitches.

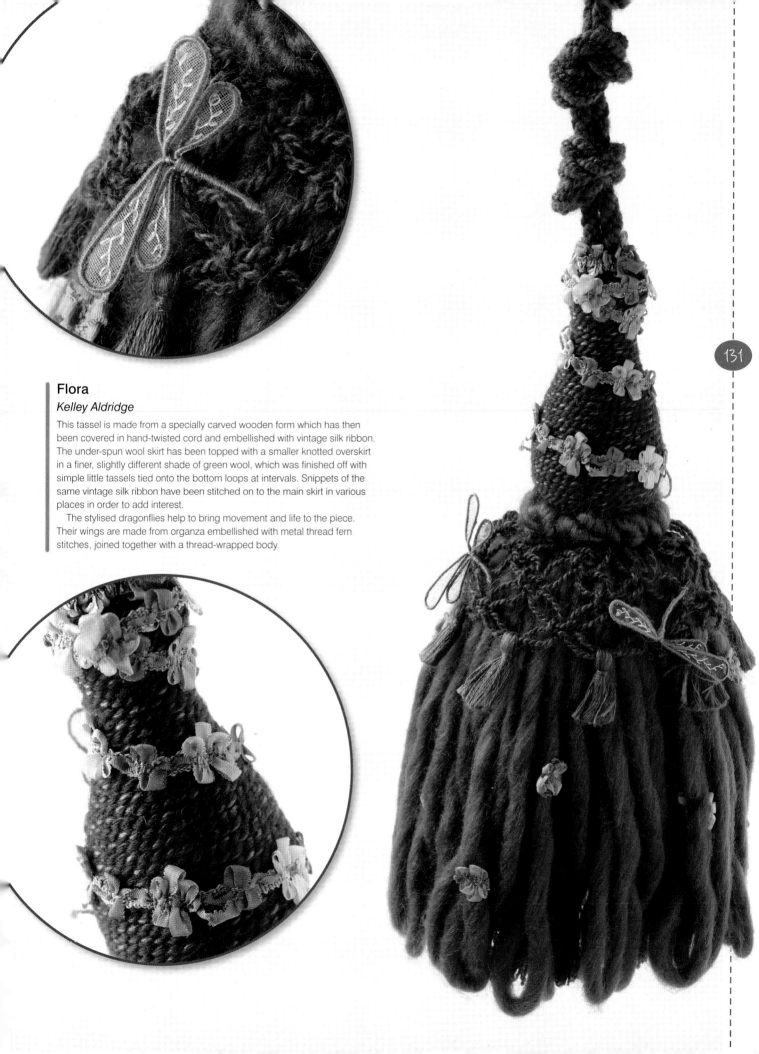

Flora
Kelley Aldridge

This tassel is made from a specially carved wooden form which has then been covered in hand-twisted cord and embellished with vintage silk ribbon. The under-spun wool skirt has been topped with a smaller knotted overskirt in a finer, slightly different shade of green wool, which was finished off with simple little tassels tied onto the bottom loops at intervals. Snippets of the same vintage silk ribbon have been stitched on to the main skirt in various places in order to add interest.

The stylised dragonflies help to bring movement and life to the piece. Their wings are made from organza embellished with metal thread fern stitches, joined together with a thread-wrapped body.

FURTHER INSPIRATION

I am incredibly lucky to know so many talented artists through the Royal School of Needlework's apprenticeship, certificate & diploma, Future Tutor and degree programmes; I hope the following pages showcasing their work provides as much inspiration to you as it does to me.

Opposite:
Botanical
Holly Coleman

This lovely piece has been framed in a deep box frame, so they really do look like specimen plants! The flower stems were worked directly on the backing fabric with a technique known as trailing, and they both have wired leaves filled with long and short shading attached at the side. The left-hand flower has wired fabric petals gathered together into a central fabric bud and attached to a short length of thread-wrapped wire which blends into the background stem. The right-hand flower features Turkey work finished off with a fabric centre and wired beads. The central plant showcases free-standing wired needlelace embellished with spangles, and metal threads couched with different colours in a tube over padding. It has been finished off with beads at the base.

Alexander Beetle
Victoria Laine

This beautiful beast comes with his own embroidered box. His wings are wired organza, while his wing cases are made from layers of fabric with cutaway beaded inserts, shisha mirrors, spangles and gold threads. His legs are thread-covered wires, and his three-dimensional body has thread-wrapped eyes, wire antennae, and a thorax embellished with many lengths of metal smooth purl threads. His boxy home is covered in a variety of counted stitches (repeatedly worked over an evenweave fabric) and features his name printed on a sheer ribbon on the lid.

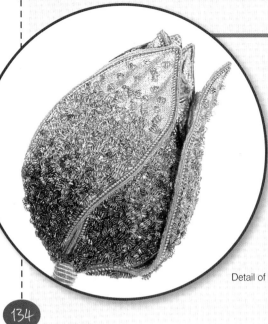

Tulip
Hattie McGill

This sparkling flower has many layered petals, made of wired organza heavily embellished with gold thread, which overlap and spiral around a central bud. The fabric is gilded with 23.5ct gold. All of the wires are joined together at the base of the flower and wrapped around with wire. This creates a sturdy, solid stem to hold the tulip in place in a delightful vintage bottle.

Detail of the raised embroidery work.

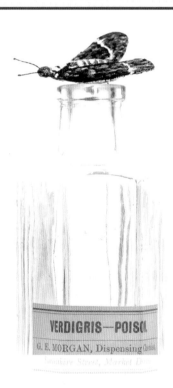

Floral
Hattie McGill

The bottles may once have held poison, but the contents are now beautifully harmless! The left-hand flower is made of very fine, wired pink organza petals, set off by a deep purple velvet padded centre that is surrounded by black wired beads. The right-hand flowers are made of wired petals filled with long and short shading and finished off with beaded centres. As with the tulip (above), the wires of the petals in all the flowers are joined together into central stems which support the blossoms and allow the piece to be displayed. The central bottle provides a perch for a tiny moth which has wired wings filled with long and short shading attached to a central padded body.

Secret Garden

Helen Richman

Wrapped beads, wired long-and-short-shaded petals, raised leaves, fly and stem stitches, French knots, ribbonwork, fabric painting and metal charms are all combined in this beautiful decorative piece, which measures 16cm (6½in) tall.

Aquarium

Helen Richman

Wired fabric shapes and fabric-covered card were used for the basic shapes in this quirky 15cm (6in) collectible. These were beautifully embellished with surface stitching, bead embellishments and appliqué.

Succulent Terrarium
Elena Thornton

The cacti in this charming piece are made of hand-felted wool which has been covered with raised stem stitches and embellished with beads and sequins. The small pink flower on the front cactus plus the large green succulent in the centre are both made of wired and hand-painted silk petals joined at the centre and attached to the body of the cactus. The whole collection is displayed on fine white sand, to complete the playful illusion that these are living cacti.

Stargazer
Laura Baverstock

Part of a larger sampler, this beautiful flower consists of wired petals filled with long and short stitch that emphasises the dark centre of the flower. The tips of the petals have been stitched with a very pale green thread to add a delicate flush of fresh colour. The centre of the petals shows lengths of coloured wires twirling out, and all of the wires (including the petals) have been gathered together into a green thread-wrapped stem which is just visible behind the bloom.

Moth
Laura Baverstock

This bright beast is part of the same sampler as the stargazer lily (above). The moth combines flat stitching on the base fabric with wired organza wings. The body was worked in long and short stitch with couched golden legs and beaded eyes. The wings were made with a combination of straight, running and satin stitches in colours that echo those used in the body.

Opposite:
Jeremy Fisher
Stella Davies

This delightful portrait of the well-known character from Beatrix Potter's book *The Tale of Mr. Jeremy Fisher* was worked by Stella for her Diploma at the Royal School of Needlework. The central figure features thread-wrapped wire fingers, needlelace jacket and trousers, plus a large number of wired petals and appliquéed leaves and wrapped beads in the surrounding plants. The whole piece is embellished with beads, Turkey work, satin stitch, and hand-made cords.

Scarlet Beetle
Kelley Aldridge

The wired calico wings of this beetle were filled with metal thread and couched with yellow and red embroidery threads. The body was padded and covered in kid leather, and the eyes are simply small beads. Note how the legs of the beetle are stitched directly onto the panel with stem stitch.

Flowers

Kelley Aldridge

These little pieces were designed for beginner-level stumpwork classes, and therefore there is a high degree of repetition. Students at the Royal School have a lot of practice working long and short stitch on wired petal shapes. This is excellent training for reliable and high-quality work. Try picking a single theme, like flowers or insects, and work through a number of similar complementary pieces. This can be a meditative and calming project, and you will end up with many small panels that can be combined into a wonderful wall piece.

Each of the three designs include the same stitches and techniques: satin-stitched leaves, split-stitched outlines, bullion-knot bees, and stems worked – very appropriately – in stem stitch. The flowers themselves were worked in long and short stitches, some on the backing fabric, and some over wires, which were added at the last stage.

Daisies
12 x 18cm (4¾ x 7in)

Violets
12 x 18cm (4¾ x 7in)

141

Snowdrops
12 x 18cm (4¾ x 7in)

Apprenticeship sampler

Kelley Aldridge

This was the very first piece of raised embroidery I ever worked, in my first year as an apprentice at the Royal School of Needlework. The inspiration came from a very funny photograph that Jacqui McDonald, one of my fellow students, had taken at a recent wedding, of a grumpy gargoyle wearing a lady's fancy hat. I couldn't resist recreating the gargoyle in a more peaceful – and dignified – setting. My special thanks go to Jenny Adin-Christie, who patiently guided us through our samplers.

ceylon stitch

needle lace rings

wrapped wire

raised leaf stitch

needlewoven picots

textured corded Brussels stitch

Needle-woven picots

I used needle-woven picots for the gargoyle's tongue. Creative thinking will soon get you using all of the stitches in this book in unexpected and interesting ways.

buttonhole-covered woolbead

detached buttonhole
picot — wrapped beads

needle lace scraps
flowers
raised cup stitch

holliepoint
stitch

double brussels
stitch

treble brussels
stitch

½ loop picots

organza
shapes

wrapped
metal
strip

detached
leaves

detached butto
buttonhole
on simple &
wired cordonnets
Single Brussels
Corded Brussels

canvas & calico slips

INDEX

attaching stitches 38

background fabric 27, 29, 92
basic techniques 22
beads 8, 10, 15, 16, 18, 21, 36, 40, 61, 64, 65, 66, 74, 77, 83, 109, 110, 113, 121, 126, 132, 134, 135, 136, 139
biscornu 49, 63, 110, 119, 120, 122, 124
bokhara couching 91, 92
Brazilian embroidery 43, 44, 46, 76
Brussels 56, 57, 80, 113, 115, 128
   corded Brussels 57
   double Brussels 57
bullion knot 12, 43, 44, 45, 46, 69, 76, 77, 82, 91, 100, 106, 113, 114, 115, 117, 140
   bullion knot rose 43, 113, 114, 115
   curved 43
   long 43
   looped 43
   overlapping 77
buttonhole stitch(es) 41, 54, 56, 57, 59, 80

cast-on stitch 12, 44, 45, 46, 69, 76, 77
chain stitch 34, 35, 49, 124
couching 8, 14, 17, 19, 38, 39, 59, 74, 91, 92, 103, 104, 109, 126, 132, 137, 139
couching stitches 14, 17, 39

design 11, 15, 18, 19, 20, 22, 32, 33, 34, 36, 37, 38, 47, 48, 56, 59, 63, 64, 66, 68, 69, 84, 86, 87, 88, 90, 91, 92, 94, 96, 104, 110, 112, 113, 114, 119, 122, 140
   transferring 20, 33
detached buttonhole 54, 56, 78, 80, 128
double cast-on stitch 45

earrings 16, 66, 68
embellishments 8, 13, 16, 17, 38, 69, 113, 128, 135
etui 103, 106

fabrics 13

fly stitch 52, 91, 94, 95, 135
framing up 20, 24, 26
French knots 42, 46, 80, 87, 91, 103, 104, 106, 113, 118, 119, 135

hard string padding 92
history 10, 11, 58, 86, 88, 90
hoop frame 15, 24, 25

inspiration 8, 11, 18, 63, 88, 112, 132, 142

jewellery finding 16, 66, 83

long and short stitch 8, 43, 58, 80, 91, 98, 99, 102, 103, 104, 109, 132, 134, 135, 137, 140

making a wired shape 59
moodboard 21, 68, 90, 112
motifs 19, 90, 91, 117

necklace 19, 64, 65, 66, 68, 78, 81
needle cases 86, 87, 102
needlelace 8, 15, 19, 56, 57, 58, 82, 87, 102, 103, 104, 113, 115, 128, 132, 139
needles 12, 15, 43
   curved needle 12, 24, 60, 78, 118
   embroidery needle 12, 27, 28, 36, 37, 38, 42, 49, 50, 56, 59, 70, 74, 92, 98
   milliner's 12, 43, 44, 45
   tapestry needle 12, 48, 49, 52, 54, 55, 56
needle-woven picots 55, 87, 106, 142

order of work 20, 69, 91, 113

padding 8, 20, 33, 34, 36, 37, 45, 64, 66, 74, 77, 82, 86, 92, 103, 104, 110, 113, 132, 134, 139
felt and stuffing padding 37
soft string padding 36, 74
padding techniques 20, 34
pendant 68

phone sleeve 63, 88, 100, 101
picot 55
prick and pounce 33

raised chain 49
raised leaf 82, 116, 117, 82, 135
raised stem 48, 82, 100, 106, 136
raised stitches 8, 42, 46, 64, 68, 76, 87, 106
raised work 10, 20, 126
ribbon 14, 64, 65, 66, 69, 74, 77, 78, 81, 88, 110, 120, 121, 131, 132
rosette stitch 46, 106, 118, 119

satin stitch 37, 137, 139, 140
securing stitches 22, 60, 72
shaded velvet work *see also* Turkey work 96
shisha 16, 17, 40, 41, 68, 69, 72, 76, 113, 132
slate frame 15, 26
split-stitched 140
stem stitch 48, 69, 70, 71, 91, 109, 113, 125, 136, 139, 140
stumpwork 8, 10, 58, 59, 128, 129, 140

template 68, 70, 78, 88, 90, 100, 112, 122
texture 8, 42, 64, 68, 85, 97, 110, 112
threads 14, 19
Turkey knot 50, 80, 90, 91, 96, 103, 104, 132, 139

velvet work *see also* Turkey knot 46, 50, 90, 96, 97, 99
vermicelli 39, 69, 72, 77, 126

whipped wheel 46, 53, 65
wired shape(s) 58, 59, 60, 80, 140
   securing to your piece 60
wired shape techniques 58
woven wheel 52
wrapped bead 8, 87, 109, 120, 113, 121, 139

144

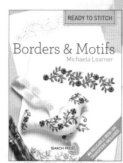

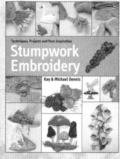
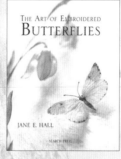

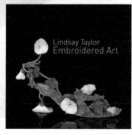

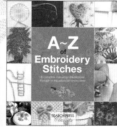
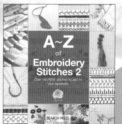

Marc Laurenceau

D-DAY
HOUR BY HOUR

The 24 decisive hours of Operation Overlord
The story of the Normandy Landings on 6th June 1944

OREP
EDITIONS

INTRODUCTION

The conclusion of painstaking preparation and of the commitment of several hundreds of thousands of individuals ready to serve victory, D-Day was an extraordinary military feat during World War II, which marked the dawn of Western Europe's liberation.

Thanks to a description of some 357 specific events that punctuated D-Day, relive – hour by hour and minute – operation Overlord, by land, air and sea. These chronological 'instants' offer us an insight into the stakes, the resources engaged and the consequences of one of the boldest military offensives of World War II. They bring to light the very many D-Day stakeholders who, each at their own level, contributed towards the success of this perilous expedition.

These particular events, some of which only involved a handful of individuals, gradually combine to illustrate this historic event, so that the reader can fully grasp its every angle. Hence, you will come to understand the role and the importance of each of the many pieces that formed the extraordinary puzzle that led to the success of the Allied armies in Normandy.

The presentation of these decentralised events is further highlighted by means of period photographs that enable you to immerse yourself into each and every one of operation Overlord's key events.

The times that are presented throughout this work are local French times in 1944; they are presented so in order to standardise information from military reports that equally referred to British or to French times.

This work is humbly dedicated to all the military staff who strove to offer Europe newfound freedom. It pays particular homage to those who shall remain forever young.

Canadian soldiers from the 9th Canadian Infantry Brigade disembark from their LCI(L), Landing Craft Infantry (Large) transport ships at Bernières-sur-Mer, in the Nan White (Juno Beach) sector, shortly before midday on the 6th of June 1944. IWM (A 23938).

CONTENTS

2   **INTRODUCTION**

4   **PART I: Last minute preparations**

8   **PART II: The longest night**

58   **PART III: The Landings**

124   **PART IV: Consolidating**

148   **PART V: The Key phases of the Battle of Normandy**

159   **ACKNOWLEDGEMENTS**

159   **BIBLIOGRAPHY**

PART I:
Last minute preparations

After two years of painstaking preparation and harvesting of information on all previous military engagements, the preparation of the finer details of Operation Overlord has reached its final phase.

PA 3·27

An LCVP (Landing Craft Vehicle & Personnel) landing barge set to sea from the warship *USS Joseph T. Dickman* has just landed its men during a landing exercise at Slapton Sands. US National Archives.

Wednesday
3rd May *1944*

– General rehearsal of the offensive in Europe with the execution of six military exercises in Great Britain (codename Fabius) over a period of six days.

5th May 1944. During training in amphibious operations, British soldiers land in England from their LCI (Landing Craft Infantry) barges. IWM (H 38213).

Monday
15th May *1944*

– Final decision-making meeting at St Paul's School (London) in the presence of King George VI, the British Prime Minister Winston Churchill, General Eisenhower and the leading Allied military chiefs, to endorse, once and for all, the objectives of Operation Overlord.

The British Prime Minister, Winston Churchill, in the company of the French General de Gaulle. US National Archives.

Landing Craft Assault (LCA) landing barges of British design, with the US Rangers on board, on the 1st of June 1944, off Weymouth. The LCA 1377 is assigned to the transport ship LSI(H) *HMS Prince Baudouin*. US National Archives.

The leading Allied military chiefs involved in operation Overlord, from left to right: Lieutenant General Omar N. Bradley (Commander of the US 1st Army Corps), Admiral Sir Bertram H. Ramsay (Commander of the Allied Expeditionary Naval Force), Air Chief Marshal Sir Arthur W. Tedder (Second-in-Command of the Allied Expeditionary Force), General Dwight D. Eisenhower (Supreme Commander of the Allied Expeditionary Force), General Bernard L. Montgomery (Commander of the 21st Army Group), Air Chief Marshal Trafford Leigh-Mallory (Commander of the Allied Expeditionary Air Force) and Lieutenant General Walter B. Smith (Chief of Staff). IWM (TR 1541).

WHY OPERATION OVERLORD?

The three political leaders of the Allied nations (Roosevelt for the United States, Churchill for Great Britain and Stalin for the Soviet Union) regularly consulted each other and shared their political and military intentions to combat the Third Reich armies. During these exchanges, Churchill made it clear to his counterparts that he was not in favour of a major offensive being launched direct from Britain, for he feared that the war may once more take a heavy toll on his country. The Allies then began to adopt a peripheral strategy to counter the German armies, launching a series of operations in the Mediterranean. On the 13th and 14th of January 1943, Roosevelt and Churchill met in Casablanca to decide on how operations were to be pursued. They endorsed the peripheral strategy and planned continued combat in the Mediterranean, including a landing operation in Sicily. Occupied by the Battle of Stalingrad, Stalin missed this appointment.

After the turn of events in Stalingrad in February 1943, the Red Army recovered lost territories and headed west. However, the conflict remained bitter for the Soviet troops: Stalin renewed his request to the Allied leaders to join forces and to adopt a frontal strategy to finally open a second front in Western Europe. He hoped for this front to be opened by 1943; however, during the Washington Conference from the 11th to the 26th of May, reuniting the US

President and the British Prime Minister, the offensive was finally scheduled for 1944. From the 17th to the 24th of August 1943, Churchill and Roosevelt met once more at the Quebec Conference, baptised 'Quadrant'. They set plans to open the second front, chose its date, its location and its codename: Overlord. It was initially planned to be launched on the 1st of May 1944, a date which was satisfactory to Stalin. The ministers for foreign affairs of the three Allied nations convened in Moscow from the 19th to the 30th of October to confirm and perfect these military choices.

For the first time, from the 28th of November to the 2nd of December 1943, the three Allied leaders met face to face in an aim to make consensual military decisions and to better coordinate their efforts against the Axis Powers, as from the very launch of Overlord and over the months that would follow. The meeting took place in Teheran, the present-day capital of Iran. Committed to a strategy of peripheral attacks, Churchill reiterated his desire to conduct an Allied attack in the Mediterranean and to hit hard into Europe's 'soft belly'; however, his requests were in vain: as a staunch anti-communist, Churchill hoped, above all, to reduce the political influence of the Soviet troops in the Balkans. Relations between the British Prime Minister and Stalin were tense and, between the two leaders, mutual trust was not on the agenda. After long negotiations, the Allies finally opted for Western Europe, the exact landing zone remaining to be defined, even if north-western France appeared the most likely option.

This agreement in principle between the Allied political leaders enabled their military counterparts to initiate preparations in order to choose the best landing site, taking into account information provided by 'combined operations', already engaged against German fortifications in Europe and the Mediterranean. One thing was certain; for logistic reasons, the assault would need to be launched from England.

Several large-scale military operations were imagined by the Allies prior to Overlord. Each action plan was analysed to draw as much useful information as possible for the preparation of a massive landing operation in the West of the European Continent. On the 8th of November 1942, the Allies initiated simultaneous amphibious operations in Morocco and Algeria, at the time administered by France's Vichy government, a German ally. This military action – codenamed operation Torch – involved the Rangers, the United States' special forces, and involved the first massive use of paratroops, who were to take control of airports. However, poor weather conditions and communication hitches prevented them from deploying their planned strategy. Instead of dropping the parachutists, 30 of the 37 transport planes managed an airlanded assault. The operation was also an opportunity for the Allies to conduct coordinated manoeuvres with local resistance, comprised of French forces.

On the 10th of July 1943, the Allied forces launched operation Husky, aimed at capturing Sicily. Husky was the Second World War's most important amphibious operation in terms of landed resources and landing zone surface area. Very soon, after the combat ceased, precious lessons were learned by the Allied airborne forces: transport craft crews needed to be better trained for airborne and airlanded

An American M10 Tank Destroyer, followed by a Sherman tank, landing in Slapton Sands during an amphibious exercise. US National Archives.

action. The pathfinders, who were dropped in advance of the main assault, needed extra time to position their beacons. Parachute drop zones needed to match those of regiments, and not only battalions, in order to simplify future operations. Gliders were not to break their tow-lines by night until they were sure to be flying over solid ground and their landing zones were to be sufficiently large to accommodate all engaged craft. Furthermore, the seamen in charge of anti-aircraft protection in maritime convoys were to receive extra instructions on identification, for several gliders were mistakenly shot down as they flew over the Allied convoys. To facilitate this task, it was decided that three wide white stripes would be painted on the wings of Allied planes. The maritime assault had proven the importance of amphibious vehicles, yet had highlighted poor preparation upstream of the attack: many forces were landed in the wrong place and up to six hours behind schedule.

On the 9th of September 1943, the Allies launched operation Avalanche, aimed at establishing a bridgehead on the Italian peninsula, near Salerno. Given the strategic and tactical location of this sector within the Mediterranean basin, the Allies concentrated on creating an element of surprise, and they decided not to engage prior artillery preparation or to drop paratroops before the amphibious attack. In contrast, ground troops were covered by naval guns as from the very onset of the landing operation. Allied infantrymen were reinforced by special units in the form of British commandos and US Rangers. The fact that no airborne soldiers were dropped behind the enemy lines before the landing phase offered the Germans relative freedom of movement.

All the information gleaned from the various amphibious and airborne operations was gathered together and analysed in order to learn as many lessons as possible, for it was essential for the efficient preparation of operation Overlord.

1Uth July 1943 - Soldiers from the 51st Highland Division unloading material from an LCT landing barge on the first day of operation Husky and the liberation of Sicily. IWM (A 17916).

Wednesday
17th May 1944

– The US General Dwight D. Eisenhower, commander-in-chief of the Allied Expeditionary Force in Europe, confirms the scheduled date for the landings: the 5th of June 1944.

– Exercise Cantab: for forty-eight hours, Allied warships belonging to the Eastern Task Force gather for one last large-scale defensive exercise.

Fascine tank belonging to the 163rd Brigade - 54th Division, under experimentation on the 14th of April 1943 at the military training ground in Dunwich. Its role was to fill up the antitank ditches using wooden stakes, to enable them to be crossed by vehicles and the infantry. IWM (H 29043).

Saturday
20th May 1944

– BBC (British Broadcasting Corporation) and ABSE (American Broadcasting Station in Europe) radio stations begin to broadcast seven recordings entitled *Voices of SHAEF*, targeting the populations in occupied territories throughout Europe. The aim is to encourage inhabitants to provide the Allies with information on the German forces, whilst limiting any aspirations towards popular uprising.

Churchill C Mk II Avre Bobbin tank (also referred to as the Carpet Layer), unrolling a canvas to the front of its chassis, upon which the infantrymen and vehicles could move much faster, in particular on sand or pebbles.

Friday
26th May 1944

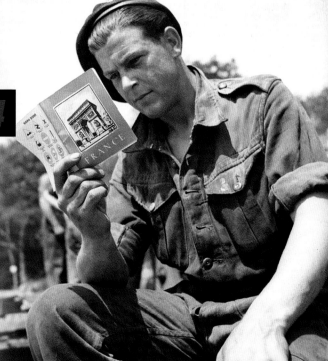

– The Anglo-Canadian troops stationed in Great Britain are despatched to assembly zones to wait for their turn to board their transport ships.

A British soldier from the 101st Light Anti-Aircraft Regiment (12th King's Regiment Liverpool), 3rd Infantry Division consulting the guide on France and the French issued to all soldiers at camp A2 in Emsworth near Portsmouth - 29th May 1944. IWM (H 38831).

GREAT BRITAIN BECOMES A HUGE MILITARY BASE

The Allied generals agreed on the necessity to concentrate troops in Great Britain to prepare for the opening of a second front in Europe. This operation was codenamed Round-up. First and foremost, the Allied armies needed to equip themselves and engage in military training and exercises, so that they could successfully accomplish the great variety of missions they would be entrusted with. The American and Canadian troops had already made use of military facilities in their homelands, but the time had come to tranship both men and material to England, the launch base for the attack on Normandy.

Late 1942, the first transport ships left the North-American continent to head for the British coast. Then, in the Atlantic, began the intense battle between the Allied convoys and the German submarines, which hindered the progression of troops and supplies. Once they had landed in Britain, the Allied soldiers set up quarters in various sites throughout the country, whereas material (tanks, transport vehicles, guns, etc.) was stored in bases that were strictly kept secret. Within the context of the preparations for D-Day, the economic land-lease programme reached its peak and the Americans delivered hundreds of vehicles, warships and individual weapons to the British Army, in exchange for the use of land that, to date, had been occupied by Commonwealth troops. The British military fleet grew fast, whilst the weaponry industry worked at full steam in the United States. To form their armada, the Allies reunited some 5,300 vessels of all sorts and 4,000 relay vessels.

Meanwhile, the objectives of D-Day became clearer. Allied reconnaissance planes contributed considerably: aerial photographs offered precious information for the Anglo-American strategists, who organised their military training and assault plans accordingly. Plane and glider pilots were mass trained, targets were reproduced in England (such as the Merville battery, a copy of which was built on Walbury Hill), parachute drops were made come rain or come shine and a number of amphibious exercises were organised, in order to coordinate naval and land forces. The phase involving the transport of airborne, airlanded and amphibious units was codenamed: operation Neptune.

29th May 1944 - British troops from the 6th or 7th Battalion, Green Howards, 69th Brigade, 50th Infantry (Northumbrian) Division boarding the transport ship SS Empire Lance in Southampton. IWM (B 5237).

Members of No. 4 Commando, 1st Special Service Brigade heading for their assembly point in the Southampton sector before preparing to board their ships. IWM (BU 1178).

Tuesday
30th May 1944

– The American troops based in Britain are sent to assembly zones prior to boarding.

30th May 1944 - Military vehicles belonging to the 51st Highland Division being hoisted aboard transport ships on the East India Docks in London. IWM (B 5215).

Gosport, 1st June 1944 - A Sherman tank belonging to the 13th/18th Hussars, 27th Armoured Brigade boarding an LST (Landing Ship Tank). IWM (H 38977).

Wednesday
31st May 1944

– The first Allied units board their transport ships in British ports.

Thursday
1st June 1944

– General Eisenhower gives orders that, as from the 1st of June, no major change may be made to operation Overlord's general plan (up to division level), to avoid that any alteration fail to be notified to all subordinate troops. This decision is codenamed Y-Day, but is also referred to as Halcyon. The day the landings are to take place is in turn codenamed D-Day.

1st June 1944 - Amphibious DUKW vehicles belonging to the Beach Group Company, 21st Army Group RASC (Royal Army Service Corps) preparing to board transport ships in a port in the south of England. IWM (B 5150).

THE DEFINITION OF D-DAY

D-Day is a code employed in military contexts to refer to a particular date. The use of a code to replace a real date prevents the adversary from gaining knowledge of such a crucial piece of information as the date on which an attack is to be launched. Coding also enables the operation's date to be changed without having to reiterate the change through all other information pertaining to the chronology of events. The day that precedes the attack is referred to as D-Day-1, the following day D-Day+1, and so on. The same applies to times: the hour of the attack is referred to as H-Hour.

French-speaking armies use the same code: *'Jour-J'* and *'Heure-H'*. But it is the English term that has been more commonly perpetuated even in the French language. Indeed, today, D-Day has become a term that, in history books, is inevitably and permanently associated with the 6th of June 1944.

Friday
2nd June 1944

21:30

– Launch of operation Gambit: Two Royal Navy X-class miniature submarines, each with a crew of five men, set off towards the Normandy coast to mark out the access routes to be taken on D-Day by the Allied armada on Juno Beach and Sword Beach.

Saturday
3rd June 1944

21:30

– Land-based troops finalise operations to load men and their vast array of material aboard transport ships berthed in British ports.

– Meeting presided over by General Eisenhower and reuniting the commanders-in-chief of operation Overlord, in order to confirm the date of the Normandy offensive, based on weather forecasts provided by Group Captain James Stagg's team. The operation needs to be postponed 24 hours due to poor weather. A second meeting is scheduled the following morning at 04:15.

Gear inspection for these parachutists from the 82nd Airborne Division, posted in England prior to boarding. US National Archives.

Group Captain James Stagg, in charge of the team of meteorologists that provided real-time updates on changes in weather conditions to the superior Allied officers. *Rights Reserved..*

THE REQUIRED WEATHER CONDITIONS FOR AN AMPHIBIOUS OPERATION

Based on information from their meteorologists, General Eisenhower and his military staff could set the date for the landings, i.e. D-Day, for Monday 5th of June 1944, all the required conditions for successive operations appearing to be reunited. Here are the necessary conditions for the success of the amphibious and airborne assault:

- a full moon, to offer pilots sufficient light during airborne operations, equally on the night before and the night after the landings;

- a sufficiently high cloud cover, leaving potential for Allied airborne support;

- the two aforementioned conditions needed to coincide with dawn (to enable night-time movements over the hours preceding the landings and to reinforce the element of surprise, since not all defenders would be at their positions at sunrise);

- a sea level at mid rising tide, so that the obstacles installed on the beaches by the Germans would be uncovered and, therefore, visible to the naval forces.

The period from the 5th to the 7th of June perfectly satisfied the first three conditions. Although connected, the moon and tide phenomena rarely coincide. Should the dates from the 5th to the 7th of June need to be cancelled (for example if the clouds were finally too low), the military meteorologists estimated that an identical configuration would occur around the 19th of June. But the Allies could not accept such a delay, which was potentially favourable to the Axis forces, for the secret of such an operation could leak.

Hence, on the 4th of June 1944, part of the invasion fleet was already on its way, as per Eisenhower's orders. However, it was called back following meetings attended by military staff to discuss what had become appalling weather conditions. A storm was raging in the English Channel, with force 6 gales and high waves. But the team of meteorologists, supervised by James Stagg, reported to the Supreme Commander of the Allied Expeditionary Force that the climate promised to be more favourable on the 5th of June, and should remain so for the following 48 hours. The forces engaged in operation Overlord were consequently obliged to wait a further 24 hours and, for those who had already boarded their transport vessels five days previously, it was but a short extra wait.

3rd June 1944 - In the port of Southampton, soldiers from the 7th Battalion, Green Howards, 69th Brigade, 50th Infantry (Northumbrian) Division seeing to their weapons aboard the transport ship *SS Empire Lance*. IWM (B 5238).

4th June 1944

04:15

– A further meeting is organised between the commanders-in-chief of operation Overlord and presided over by General Eisenhower and Group Captain James Stagg. They confirm the 24-hour postponement decided the previous day.

12:00

– Operation Gambit: just 20 nautical miles from their target and 20 miles from each other, the X20 submarine (commanded by Lieutenant Kenneth Hudspeth) and the X23 (commanded by Lieutenant George Honour) temporarily surface to observe the shoreline opposite Sword Beach and Juno Beach

13:30

– Winston Churchill, the British Prime Minister, notifies General de Gaulle, chief of the French Free Forces, of the plans for operation Overlord during a journey aboard his armoured train in the region of Portsmouth. The French general is revolted at not having been informed earlier.

Captain Lasdun, from the 693 Road Construction Company, Royal Engineers briefing troops on operation Overlord aboard the Landing Ship Tank (LST) 406 transport ship on the 4th of June 1944 in a southern English port. IWM (B 5157).

21:30

– Meeting with Eisenhower's military staff and review of the weather by Group Captain James Stagg. He announces that conditions will improve over the early hours of the 6th of June and should continue so for twelve hours. Eisenhower chooses the new date for operation Overlord. Pending the next weather bulletin the following morning, it is scheduled for Tuesday the 6th of June 1944.

– Operation Gambit: the two Royal Navy X-class miniature submarines begin to mark out the Allied armada's access routes towards Juno Beach and Sword Beach on D-Day.

DEPLOYED ALLIED FORCES

On the 6th of December 1943, the SHAEF (Supreme Headquarters Allied Expeditionary Force) was born. The US General Dwight Eisenhower was appointed in charge of the force, with the Scot, Air Chief Marshal Arthur Tedder as his deputy. The Allied air forces were commanded by Air Chief Marshal Sir Trafford Leigh-Mallory, the Allied naval forces by the British Admiral Sir Bertram Ramsay and the Allied ground forces by the British Field Marshal Bernard Law Montgomery.

Late summer 1943, the Allies progressively concentrated their efforts on preparations for operation Overlord in Normandy and, from July 1943 to February 1944, some 700,000 soldiers were sent to Britain. The SHAEF comprised several ground forces that were reunited to form three army groups. They were as follows: the 12th US Army Group (US First Army, Third Army, Ninth Army and Fifteenth Army), 6th US Army Group (*1re Armée Française*, US Seventh Army) and the 21st British Army Group (First Canadian Army, British Second Army).

On the 6th of June 1944, the assault was entrusted to the 21st Army Group (which initially reunited the US First Army and the British Second Army). The SHAEF's airborne forces were comprised of the Eighth US Air Force, Ninth US Air Force, Royal Air Force (RAF) 2nd Tactical Air Force, RAF Bomber Command and RAF Airborne & Transport Forces.

In May 1944, some 1,527,000 Americans were in training in Britain pending D-Day. A total of over two million seamen, soldiers and air crew members from 15 different nations were preparing to open a second front in Western Europe. The Allied troops trained relentlessly and their morale was high. The warships and transport ships increased in numbers in the British ports and air raids were intensified along the north-west coast of France. By late spring 1944, the Allies were ready to deploy their 11,590 fighter and transport planes, their 6,939 ships of varying tonnage and their hundreds of thousands of vehicles against the German fortifications that comprised the Atlantic Wall, presented by the Third Reich as impregnable.

4th June 1944, south of England - Training exercise on putting DUKW amphibious vehicles to the water and recovering them. IWM (B 5154).

4th June 1944 - Lance Corporal Smithson, from the 2809 Squadron, RAF Regiment, preparing hand grenades at the rear of a truck. IWM (B 5155).

Team 2 of the 505th PIR (82nd Airborne Division) pathfinders.
US National Archives.

Monday
5th June 1944

01:00

– Operation Gambit: the two submarines in waiting off the Normandy coast are notified of the 24-hour postponement of the Allied attack thanks to a coded radio message broadcast by the BBC. They poise on the seabed the entire night.

04:15

– New meeting with General Eisenhower's military staff to confirm the date of D-Day as the 6th of June 1944, in accordance with the latest information provided by James Stagg.

07:00

– Four years to the day since the German invasion in Normandy in which he took part on the 5th of June 1940, Field Marshal Rommel leaves his headquarters in La Roche-Guyon to head for Germany by car to belatedly celebrate his wife Lucie's 50th birthday (6th of May). He also hopes to convince Hitler to agree to moving armoured divisions within his zone of authority closer to the coast.

09:00

– Group Captain James Stagg calls Major General Harold R. Bull, chief of operations (G-3) for General' Eisenhower's military staff, to confirm the weather forecast he presented the same day at 04:15.

Part II:
The longest night

As the Allied armada headed towards the French coast, bombardment targets and airborne troop operations were designed to disorganise the German forces by destroying communication links and by taking control of strategic locations on the terrain.

Evening of the 5th of June 1944 - Convoy U1 (group 30, flotilla 11, series 9) in the English Channel on its way to Utah Beach. US National Archives.

Opposite: Explosion of a shell fired on the Îles Saint-Marcouf on the 6th of June 1944. US National Archives.

19

Monday

5th June 1944

10:30

– The Allied generals have messages of encouragement distributed and read to all their subordinates.

13:00

– The Allied minesweepers set off and open routes across the English Channel for the Allied armada.

American parachutists from the Fox Company, 506th PIR, 101st Airborne Division (holding the Bazooka: Robert Noody). US National Archives.

THE MESSAGE FROM EISENHOWER PRIOR TO OPERATION OVERLORD

General headquarters of the Allied Expeditionary Force

Soldiers, Sailors and Airmen of the Allied Expeditionary Force,

You are about to embark upon the Great Crusade, toward which we have striven these many months. The eyes of the world are upon you. The hopes and prayers of liberty-loving people everywhere march with you. In company with our brave Allies and brothers-in-arms on other Fronts you will bring about the destruction of the German war machine, the elimination of Nazi tyranny over oppressed peoples of Europe, and security for ourselves in a free world.

Your task will not be an easy one. Your enemy is well trained, well equipped, and battle-hardened. He will fight savagely.

But this is the year 1944. Much has happened since the Nazi triumphs of 1940-41. The United Nations

have inflicted upon the Germans great defeats, in open battle, man-to-man. Our air offensive has seriously reduced their strength in the air and their capacity to wage war on the ground. Our Home Fronts have given us an overwhelming superiority in weapons and munitions of war, and placed at our disposal great reserves of trained fighting men. The tide has turned! The free men of the world are marching together to victory!

I have full confidence in your courage, devotion to duty, and skill in battle. We will accept nothing less than full victory!

Good luck! And let us all beseech the blessing of Almighty God upon this great and noble undertaking.

Signed: General Dwight D. Eisenhower

Official military letter drafted 6th June 1944

THE ALLIED ARMADA

The fleet comprised a total of five leading forces – one for each landing beach. Each force in turn comprised eight to sixteen distinct convoys. Reunited, they represented over 5,300 vessels of all sorts, along with 2,000 relay vessels that would shuttle to and from the shore and the ships out at sea. The fleet was based essentially in five English ports. Admiral Kirk was in command of the American sector (Western Task Force): Task Force U (for Utah) was positioned in Plymouth and Task Force O (for Omaha) in Portland. Admiral Vian was in command of the Anglo-Franco-Canadian sector (Eastern Task Force): Task Force S (for Sword), positioned in Portsmouth, Task Force G (for Gold) in Southampton and Task Force J (for Juno), positioned on the Isle of Wight.

Further support forces (forces B and L) were based near Falmouth and Nore, and twelve minesweepers were to open channels towards the French coast, in advance of the armada. Bombardment forces were designated to offer fire support to cover each landing beach: Task Force A for Utah, Task Force C for Omaha, Task Force D for Sword, Task Force K for Gold and Task Force E for Juno.

The Allied ships that were berthed in different ports were to travel predetermined distances to reach the Normandy beaches. This is why the various maritime convoys set off at different times, depending on the distance to cover. This is also why they gathered at a large assembly zone, 'Y', commonly referred to as Piccadilly Circus (after the famous road junction in London, often prone to traffic jams), off the southern English coast and more precisely 20 miles south-east of the Isle of Wight. They were finally to head for their respective beaches via 5 channels previously cleared by minesweepers.

In order to prepare the terrain for ground troops via a massive bombardment campaign, whilst defending the landing barges from German attacks, the Allied armada comprised a total of 325 warships. Naval support was provided by 6 battleships, 3 monitors, 22 cruisers, 101 destroyers and 93 torpedo-boat destroyers.

Although this Allied fleet was essentially made up of British, and to a lesser degree American, ships, it did also include French, Polish, Norwegian, Greek, Danish and Dutch vessels.

The LCI(L) 84 and 497 landing barges, together with LCH 87 on the Weymouth docks with the US Rangers on board. US National Archives.

5th June 1944 - At the RAF Greenham Common airfield, General Eisenhower encouraging parachutists from the 2nd Battalion, 505th PIR, 82nd Airborne Division before they board their Dakota C-47s to jump over Normandy. US National Archives.

18:00

– The first elements that comprised the Allied armada reach the assembly zone codenamed 'Z' off the Isle of Wight, then head for the French coast.

20:30

– General Eisenhower pays a visit to the American paratroops from the 502nd Parachute Infantry Regiment, 101st Airborne, at the RAF airfield in Greenham Common. He is perfectly aware that estimations of airborne troop losses are high.

21:15

– On the Radio London station, the BBC broadcasts 210 codes for the French Resistance, in particular 'Blessent mon coeur d'une langueur monotone', announcing the landings within 24 hours.

22:15

– The German General von Salmuth, commander of the 15th Army, is informed by Lieutenant-Colonel Helmut Meyer (chief of the 15th Army's 2nd bureau) of the broadcast of the code 'Blessent mon coeur d'une langueur monotone', the meaning of which is known to all. However, the poor weather conditions do not prompt the Germans to alert all units.

22:40

– The *Luftwaffe* radar station located in Guernsey detects echoes corresponding to the presence of planes above the Channel.

PATHFINDERS

The very first parachutists to be dropped over Normandy were pathfinders. Grouped together in teams, each one comprised of a lieutenant squad leader, four radio operators and four parachutists in charge of overall safety during operations. They were dropped into enemy territory without initial marking, simply based on terrain observations and navigation calculations aboard the C-47 Dakota transport planes. The pathfinders were then entrusted with marking out drop zones (DZ) and landing zones (LZ), prior to the arrival of airborne fighting companies, whilst implementing the 'Eureka' transceivers they had been provided with. The latter sent out pulses that were intercepted by the 'Rebecca' transceivers installed in the fuselage of the C-47 planes, in order to help pilots find their way. These devices could also be used to send short messages in Morse code, to communicate equally with pilots or pathfinders.

Pathfinders were also equipped with markings for use by day or by night, for airborne and airlanded reinforcements were also scheduled to arrive on the 6th of June, at 21:00.

For daylight operations, marking consisted in using yellow-coloured panels that were lined up to form the letter 'T', along with smoke. Green smoke was used to indicate a 'clear' DZ or LZ, i.e. no enemy presence, whereas red smoke indicated the presence of adversaries within contact. By night, the pathfinders were equipped with holophane lamps.

Photograph of team E (stick 2) of the 377th Field Artillery pathfinders (101st Airborne Division) and the Air Force crew in charge of their transport. They were dropped at 00:27 on the 6th of June to the north of Hiesville in Cotentin in order to mark out Drop Zone C. US National Archives.

Last brief for the crews of Royal Air Force No. 137 Wing at the Hartford Bridge airfield, before taking off in their Douglas Boston planes to spread the smoke that was to form a screen to conceal the Allied armada as it crossed the Channel. IWM (CL 4).

British parachutists from the 22nd Independent Parachute Company, 6th - GB) Airborne Division listening to the very last tactical instructions and identifying key locations on the terrain, before boarding for France. IWM (H 39089).

22:56

– Launch of the airborne operation Tonga, as Halifax bombers take off from the RAF Tarrant Rushton airfield, taking with them the six Horsa gliders whose mission is to capture the bridges over the River Orne and the Caen Canal.

23:20

– Take-off from the RAF Broadwell airfield of C-47 planes transporting men from the 9 parachute battalions entrusted with taking the German artillery battery in Merville.

British parachutists from the 6th Airborne Division aboard a Dakota C-47, before jumping over Normandy. IWM (TR 1662).

General Walter Fischer von Weikersthal, Commander of the *LXVII. Armeekorps* (wearing glasses), *Generalfeldmarschall* Erwin Rommel, chief of *Heergruppe B* (centre front), and *Generalleutnant* Felix Schwalbe, commander of the *344. Infanterie-Division* (right). Bundesarchiv Bild 101I 298 1758 19.

GERMAN UNITS IN NORMANDY

Once they had invaded France in 1940 and faltered during the Battle of Britain, the German forces concentrated their efforts against the Soviets on the Eastern Front as from 1941. They had the Atlantic Wall built, to form a permanent line of defence against the Allies. However, the installation was limited: alone, it was incapable of driving back an amphibious attack and the Third Reich authorities were perfectly aware of this. Consequently, German submarines patrolled the Atlantic, hence adding a more heterogeneous line of defence.

The German army had stationed several hundreds of thousands of men in the West and took great care to establish and maintain the strictest discipline in occupied territories: this occupation force needed to avoid any disruption or inconsistent behaviour, in order to provide no grist to benefit the French Resistance. Far from Berlin and the Mediterranean or Russian combat zones, the German generals were offered very few opportunities to shine in the eyes of the Führer or to distinguish themselves in combat. Some of them, however, were happy to be positioned far from the front lines, taking advantage of calmer circumstances in their magnificent requisitioned properties, where the war gradually became of lesser interest to them.

These units could equally belong to the *Heer,* the *SS,* the *Kriegsmarine* or the *Luftwaffe.* By 1944, the German troops had been in combat for five years and their morale was on the decline since early 1942. The various armies readily criticised each other, all the more so since the resources at their disposal were unequal: *SS* division forces were, on average, two-fold compared to those of the *Heer.* The *Kriegsmarine* had very few warships and, in the aftermath of the Battle of Britain and due to its efforts to counter the incessant Anglo-American bombardments, the *Luftwaffe* was totally depleted. The multiplicity of military authorities (for example, certain coastal artillery batteries were armed by the *Kriegsmarine,* whereas the infantry units belonging to the *Luftwaffe* rubbed shoulders with those of the *SS*) and the counter-productive competition between all these units (particularly apparent between the *Wehrmacht* and the *SS*) was extremely detrimental to the Third Reich, for decisions were not necessarily taken in Germany's best interest, but sometimes in that of one unit in its competition with another.

What's more, the German high command's decision-making power was limited: Hitler's approval was required before any decision could be made. And this detail was to prove particularly important over the events to come. In all evidence, this structural fragility amidst the German forces was equally problematic in units positioned in the West and those in combat in the East and the Mediterranean.

Tuesday

6th June 1944

Douglas C-47s flying in formation and painted with the white D-Day Stripes to identify them as Allied planes. Each of the parachute infantry regiments was boarded onto three to four serials (plane formations). These serials comprised 36, 45 or 54 C-47 planes, depending on needs, and were sent to the drop zone at intervals of six minutes. Aboard each C-47, the parachutists formed sticks of 15 to 18 men, based on the equipment they were transporting. US National Archives.

00:07

– German sentries spot planes flying at low altitude to the north of Carentan in the Cotentin peninsula.

00:10

– The first American pathfinders from the 101st Airborne Division jump over the Cotentin peninsula, in order to mark out parachute landing zones for the C-47 pilots who are due to arrive a few minutes later.

00:11

– The German parachutists from the *Fallschirmjäger-Regiment 6* - 13th company, report the presence of enemy paratroops in the Carentan sector, in Cotentin.

THE ATLANTIC WALL IN NORMANDY

To prevent any landing operation, the Germans called upon the Organisation Todt, a company specialising in military constructions, such as casemates, roads for armoured vehicles, etc. As from the spring of 1942, work began against the English shores, after Hitler's plans to invade had been cancelled. Reinforced concrete fortifications were built from Norway to the Southern Basque Country and the Mediterranean. They were accompanied by minefields, thousands of miles of barbed wire networks, machine gun nests and flamethrower emplacements, beach defences, antitank ditches, etc.

This fortification, which was rapidly baptised the 'Atlantic Wall', was reinforced in sensitive areas opposite the English coast, such as the Pas-de-Calais, which the German generals were convinced was the most likely zone for a landing operation. Coastal batteries armed with high calibre guns were built at strategic locations along the coast, in order to protect ports and estuaries.

In Normandy and elsewhere, the Germans built powerfully armed coastal artillery batteries that were further protected by strongpoints. From Barfleur to Le Havre, they installed no less than thirty batteries, some worthy examples of which can be found in Merville, Longues-sur-Mer, Cricqueville-en-Bessin (Pointe du Hoc), Azeville and Crisbecq. Six of them boasted a firing range of up to 20 miles and were quite a concern to the Allies during preparations for their amphibious manoeuvres.

00:16

– The first of the 3 Horsa gliders (number 91) lands just 50 yards from the bridge at Bénouville, later to be named Pegasus Bridge.
– The German artillery battery in Merville is attacked by 5 Avro Lancaster bombers from the Royal Air Force's 7th Squadron.

00:17

– The second of the 3 Horsa gliders (number 92) lands near Pegasus bridge.

00:18

– The last of the 3 Horsa gliders (number 93) lands near Pegasus bridge. Stunned by the shock upon landing, Lance Corporal Fred Greenhalgh is ejected from the craft and drowns in a nearby marsh.

00:20

– Six Albemarle's drop 60 pathfinders from the 22nd Independent Parachute Company in Drop zones N, V and K to the east of the River Orne.

The Horsa glider number 2 (serial 92) flown by Staff Sergeants Boland and Hobbs, near the bridge at Bénouville, later to be named Pegasus Bridge. The glider, transporting section number 25 -d Company, 2nd Battalion, Ox & Bucks) commanded by Lieutenant Wood landed at 00:17 on D-Day. IWM (B 7035).

Horsa glider number 2 (foreground), in front of Horsa glider number 1 near Pegasus Bridge at Bénouville on D-Day. IWM (B 5233).

PEGASUS BRIDGE – EUSTON I

The aim if this mission was to secure the invasion's left flank, for there was only one passageway across the River Orne and the Caen Canal, and it was located between the localities of Ranville and Bénouville: these two communes were naturally among the British 6th Airborne Division's prime targets.

Operation Deadstick, which was part of operation Tonga, began on the 5th of June 1944 with the departure of Halifax bombers towing six Horsa gliders as from 22:56. Under Major John Howard's command, the gliders flew by night and cut their tow-lines above Cabourg, at an altitude of 6,000 feet. In the very early hours of the 6th of June 1944, from 00:16 precisely, they arrived within their target zone.

The three gliders in charge of the bridge at Bénouville, later rebaptised 'Pegasus Bridge' after the 6th Division's nickname, managed to land less than 50 yards from the bridge: a performance that largely outshone previous training exercises! A few minutes after landing and once the assailants had engaged as discreetly as possible in their initial action, flares were launched by the Germans who, by now, were totally panic-stricken. They fired in all directions, as the British troops crossed the bridge, covered with smoke and launching phosphorus grenades inside the machine gun nests, which almost immediately exploded.

Bénouville bridge was taken in 10 minutes, but Lieutenant Brotheridge, the chief of the 1st section, was killed and Commander Howard feared a German counter-attack. The coded message 'Ham and Jam', signifying victory ('ham' meant that the British troops had taken control of the site and 'jam' that the bridges were intact) was sent to the Allied armada via carrier pigeon immediately after the attack. John Howard blew his whistle at length, in order to inform all the Allied soldiers in the sector of his men's successful mission. In the drop zone codenamed 'N', to the north of Ranville, the sound of the whistle put a smile on the face of General Nigel Poett, in command of the 5th Para Brigade.

For Major Howard and his men, a very long night had just begun.

MAP OF OPERATIONS EUSTON I AND II

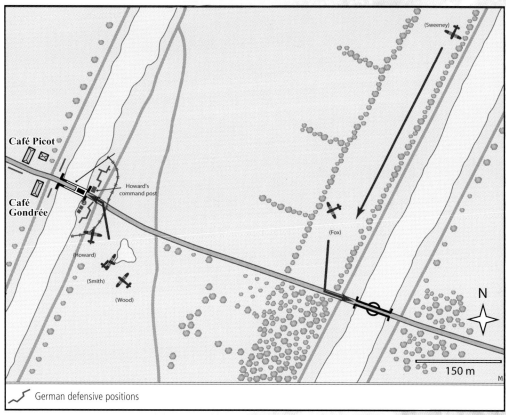

Café Picot

Café Gondrée

Howard's command post

(Sweeney)

(Fox)

(Howard)

(Smith)

(Wood)

N

150 m

M

⌇ German defensive positions

© Y. Magdelaine.

00:21

– Howard and his men have successfully taken control of Pegasus Bridge and German resistance has ceased.

00:21

– During the assault on the bridge at Bénouville (Pegasus), Lieutenant Herbert Denham Brotheridge is mortally wounded in the head. He is the first Allied soldier engaged in operation Overlord to be killed under enemy fire in Normandy.

00:30

– *Oberleutnant Brandenburger*, commander of the *5. Kompanie, Panzer-Grenadier-Regiment 125.* reports to his regimental command post that he has spotted parachute drops to the east of the Orne.

– One hundred and ten bombers belonging to the Bomber Command No.1 Group and No.100 Group attack the anti-aircraft batteries in the region of Caen-Carpiquet.

– Thirty-six French parachutists, reunited within 4 teams, jump over Brittany, in the Duault forest near Plumelec.

– All German troops under the 84th German corps are placed on the alert, from the Orne to the Couesnon.

An Avro Lancaster bomber above its target. Armed with eight Browning 7.7mm machine guns and transporting 6,350kg of bombs. Throughout World War II, the Lancaster conducted a total of around 156,000 missions. US National Archives.

AERIAL BOMBARDMENTS

Within the context of operation Neptune, in the very early hours of the 6th of June 1944, in the dark of night, the Bomber Command, comprised of aircraft piloted by British and Allied crews (French in particular) was entrusted with the mission of reducing to silence all major targets identified over the months prior to D-Day by reconnaissance planes. Hence, 360 heavy bombers, with support from 269 light bombers, flew over the convoys of warships and transport ships that were on their way to Normandy. This massive aerial attack was the conclusion of months of bombing that had already targeted France's entire north-western zone, intensifying as from the spring of 1944.

Despite very cloudy skies, which hindered the identification of targets, the planes attacked the fortifications that formed the Atlantic Wall. A total of 92 radar stations were bombarded, from the Barfleur headland to Le Havre, so that the Allied armada could approach without being intercepted by the *Kriegsmarine* radio operators. Seventy-four stations were destroyed by the Allied aviation, a figure considered as successful. Yet the bombardments on certain coastal targets (artillery batteries, support batteries, fortifications), proved to be a relatively difficult operation. Indeed, the heavy cloud cover was a genuine obstacle to the bomber crews. Of the total bomber fleet, 67 planes cancelled their missions due to poor weather conditions, whilst the others did their best to accomplish theirs.

The stretch of coast from Ouistreham to the east and Asnelles-sur-Mer to the west, i.e. all the landing beaches designated for the Anglo-Canadian troops (Sword to the east, Juno in the centre and Gold to the west), was bombed by Allied planes, and several targets were damaged or destroyed. The American sector on Utah Beach was also massively bombed, the Azeville and Crisbecq coastal batteries in Cotentin in particular.

However, between Longues-sur-Mer to the east and Grandcamp-Maisy to the west, targets had either not been hit or only partly so by the bombardments. One of the landing beaches was located within this sector - Omaha Beach, where elements from the US 1st and 29th Infantry Divisions were to land at dawn. According to reports from different aerial groups deployed to bombard the sector, the presence of clouds had complicated their mission and it only took a second or two's delay for the bombs to land several miles off target. Consequently, the coastal artillery batteries located near the localities of Longues-sur-Mer and Maisy were virtually intact, despite the bombing campaign. The same applied to the eight strongpoints located along the beach codenamed Omaha. The Allies were as yet unaware, but the Germans suffered no major destruction in this sector: the Atlantic Wall installations at Omaha Beach had either been spared or had suffered only minor damage.

OPERATION EUSTON II

Concurrent to the capture of the bridge at Bénouville (Pegasus), three Horsa gliders headed for Ranville, on a mission which had been codenamed Euston II. They were to land within a landing zone codenamed 'Y', located on the strip of land between the River Orne and Caen Canal. Only one Horsa glider, number 6 (Chalk No. 96), managed to land near the Euston II sector, where Lieutenant Dennis Fox's No. 7 Platoon was in position. As soon as they set foot on solid ground, the airlanded troops attacked the bridge, in the wake of previous combat on Bénouville bridge. Alerted by the sound of automatic rifles, the German sentries were ready and waiting to defend their position, which was equipped with just one machine gun.

As Lieutenant Fox's section prepared to launch the assault, light mortar units were set up to cover them. As the British airlanded troops thrust forwards towards the Ranville bridge, the Germans fired several salvoes in their direction, but in vain. The mortars were launched without delay, forcing the defenders to flee. The Allied assailants grasped the machine gun and began to fire against the last remaining Germans, who in turn took to their heels. Combat ceased immediately.

The Horsa glider number 5 (Chalk No. 95), aboard which Lieutenant 'Tod' Sweeneys' No. 23 Platoon was travelling, landed just a mile to the north of the Ranville bridge. The section rapidly made its way to its target and Sweeney's men also prepared to attack, unawares as to whether the bridge had been successfully taken by the airlanded company. The assault was launched, to be just as rapidly brought to a halt when the troops recognised Lieutenant Fox, standing before them. A message was sent to Bénouville to report back to Major Howard that the bridge at Bénouville was now under Allied control and had been taken in less than ten minutes.

The Horsa glider number 4 (Chalk No. 94) made an emergency landing near Varaville, around 6 miles to the north-east of the planned landing zone. In the midst of the darkness, the pilot and his co-pilot (respectively Staff Sergeant Lawrence and Staff Sergeant Shroter), had mistaken the Caen Canal and the River Orne with two parallel waterways, the Divette and the Dives: they consequently landed near a bridge over the Divette, which Lieutenant Hooper and his No. 22 Platoon immediately attacked, taking it for their target. Realising their mistake, they began to head for Ranville, but came across several German patrols on their way. They did their best to avoid them, in order not to lose precious time, however, the airlanded troops were stopped several times in their tracks.

It was during one of these unwanted encounters that Lieutenant Hooper was taken prisoner, until an armed intervention by Captain Priday - who had also travelled aboard glider number 4 - which led to his release. They could then continue their night-time advance, in quest of their company...

5th June 1944, early evening - An Armstrong Whitworth Albemarle bomber, towing a Horsa glider with troops from the 6th Airlanding Brigade (6th Airborne Division) on board, taking off for Normandy. IWM (H 39183).

00:35

– Two Horsa gliders land near the bridge at Ranville, renamed Horsa Bridge, as part of operation Euston II. The third glider taking part in the operation is missing.

00:40

– The French *Caporal* Émile Bouétard, a member of the *4ᵉ Bataillon d'Infanterie de l'Air (SAS)*, is shot down at the Plumelec mill in Brittany.

00:45

– German reports, sent by the 919th Grenadier Regiment's 3rd Battalion, under the orders of Lieutenant-Colonel Hoffmann, inform of the presence of enemy parachutists.

A stick of paras from the 101st Airborne Division waiting for the green light to jump over Normandy. US National Archives.

GERMAN RADARS

The Atlantic Wall was not only comprised of blockhouses and minefields. A large number of radar stations were located along the coast from Norway to Spain, together with listening stations. Located between Cherbourg, Vire and Le Havre: an identification radar, two 'Freya' type radars, five long-range coastal surveillance radars, seven coastal surveillance radars and fourteen impressive 'Würzburg' radars. These radars were often associated with anti-aircraft guns, which were generally of a calibre of 88mm.

00:48

– Start of the parachute drops above the Cotentin peninsula, on zones marked out by the pathfinders, by the American 101st Airborne Division, within the framework of operation Albany.

Portrait of *Caporal* Émile Bouétard, member of stick 1 ('Pierre 1'), commanded by Lieutenant Pierre Marienne from the 4th Battalion, Special Air Service, killed by the enemy near Plumelec in Morbihan (Brittany) during operation Dingson. Rights Reserved..

01:11

– The German 716th Infantry Division informs General Marcks from the 84th Army Corps stationed in Saint-Lô of the presence of enemy airborne units in the Cotentin peninsula.

01:21

– Pathfinders from the 82nd Airborne Division jump over Normandy, above the Cotentin peninsula, to try to mark out three landing zones for the rest of the division (Drop Zones N, O and T), as part of operation Boston.

01:30

– General Dollman places the German 7th Army under general alert.

– The sirens at the Pointe du Hoc artillery battery begin to resonate to warn of the presence of Allied bombers.

00:50

– The British 6th Airborne Division's 3rd and 5th Brigades are dropped to the east of the River Orne.

01:00

– The German navy (*Kriegsmarine* in German) reports the presence of an important armada off the Pas-de-Calais shores.

– Sergeant Ludwig Förster spots the Allied armada off shore from his Wn 62 strong point, in the Omaha Beach sector.

General der Artillerie Erich Marcks, commander of the *LXXXIV. Armeekorps*. Born on the 6th of June 1891, he was one of the rare German generals to immediately engage his forces against the Allies, without waiting for orders from Hitler. Bundesarchiv.

OPERATIONS DINGSON AND SAMWEST

In order to coordinate action by the Breton Resistance, whilst disorganising the arrival of future German reinforcements in Normandy after the Landings, French parachute commandos were dropped over Brittany. Two operations, codenamed Dingson and Samwest, were aimed at deploying a solid secret army in Brittany in order to establish parachute dropping and plane landing zones, in association with local Resistance networks.

In the very early hours of the 6th of June 1944, as the American and British pathfinders jumped over Normandy, 36 commandos belonging to the French *4e Bataillon Special Air Service (SAS)*, later to become the *2e Régiment de Chasseurs Parachutistes* were dropped over Brittany. They were divided into four teams of nine paratroops: two teams were dropped at around 00:30 near Plumelec in the *département* of Morbihan (operation Dingson, commanded by Lieutenants Marienne and Déplante) and two others jumped at the same time above the Duault forest in the Côtes-d'Armor (operation Samwest, commanded by Lieutenants Deschamps and Botella).

As soon as they set foot on solid ground, Lieutenants Marienne and Déplante's sticks, dropped near Plumelec in Morbihan, immediately came face to face with Georgians and Ukrainians from the Russian Liberation Army, who were serving in the German army as proxy forces. *Caporal* Émile Bouétard was killed in the skirmish. Initially wounded, one of the proxy troops finished him off (as per Hitler's orders with regard to all Allied paratroops taken prisoner).

By the 9th of June 1944, some 166 French SAS paratroops were dropped on the Samwest secret base. Those who survived the Samwest cell, came to reinforce the Dingson cell, in order to improve coordination of future action. On the 18th of June 1944, a German attack dislocated the Resistance fighters who suffered severe losses (around 30 were killed in one day). Captain Leblond was then entrusted with the mission of gathering together the survivors and of training new recruits within the context of operation Grog, which began on the 19th of June 1944.

01:45

– General Marcks from the 84th Army Corps, receives new information from *Oberst* Hans-Heinz Hamann (*Artillerie-Kommandeur 118* and interim commander of the *709. Infanterie-Division*) on the presence of enemy paratroops spotted between Sainte-Marie-du-Mont and Sainte-Mère-Église.

01:50

– Start of dropping operations for the paratroops from the 82nd Airborne Division above Cotentin, as part of operation Boston, on zones that have been haphazardly marked out by the pathfinders.

– From his Parisian headquarters near the Bois de Boulogne, Admiral Hoffman, the Western Naval Group's chief of operations, informs his various military chiefs of an increasing number of alarming reports. He sends the following message to Germany, 'Signal to the Führer's headquarters the invasion is on.'

MAP OF THE GERMAN INSTALLATIONS FORMING THE ATLANTIC WALL

The German structures that comprised the Atlantic Wall included a range of installations of varying design and chains of command.

Division batteries, which were exclusively manned by the *Heer* (German land-based army), could be protected by concrete constructions or placed in temporary positions with no particular protection (field batteries).

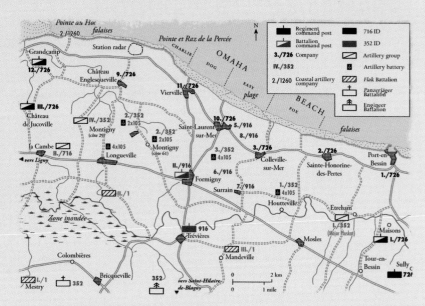

Organisation of the German forces in the Omaha Beach sector on 6th June 1944. © Omaha Beach Memorial Museum

Coastal batteries were equally manned by the *Heer* (*HKA: Heeres Künsten Artillerie*) and by the *Kriegsmarine* (*MKA: Marine Künsten Artillerie*). Artillery pieces were placed in concrete gun emplacements until the Allied bombardments spurred the Organisation Todt (O.T.) to build protective casemates.

The batteries located on railway lines, also referred to as *Eisenbahn Batterie*, were equipped with large calibre guns and were designed to protect strategic locations such as estuaries and ports. The *Eisenbahn-Artillerie-Batterie 688*, located in the Calais/Coquelles (Pas-de-Calais) sector and equipped with two 28cm K5 (E) guns was a case in point. These batteries could be rapidly moved, hence escaping Allied aerial raids.

Finally, the *Flak (Flak Abteilung)* batteries offered various military sites protection against enemy aerial attacks.

THE ATLANTIC WALL AT OMAHA BEACH

Omaha Beach, originally referred to as the *Côte d'Or* (Golden Coast), stretches over a distance of 3.7 miles and comprises the localities of Vierville-sur-Mer to the west, Saint-Laurent-sur-Mer in the centre and the villages of Colleville-sur-Mer and Le-Grand-Hameau to the east. Above the beach stands a plateau and four hanging valleys offer access inland. Eight heavily armed strongpoints defended the access to these valleys: codenamed Wn (for the German *Wiederstandsnest* meaning resistance nest), these defensive positions were comprised of casemates housing antitank guns, machine gun and mortar emplacements, trenches and antitank walls, together with automatic flamethrowers.

The soldiers stationed there belonged to the *Grenadier-Regiment 726 (716. Infanterie-Division)* and the *Grenadier-Regiment 916 (352. Infanterie-Division)*.

PARACHUTE DROPS IN COTENTIN

With the elaboration of the general plan of operation Overlord, the finer details of which began to emerge during the Trident conference in Washington in May 1943, it transpired that the invasion sector flanks were of particular importance, for their control would be decisive in the evolution of future combat operations. This is why the Allied high command entrusted three airborne divisions with securing these zones: the British 6th Airborne Division was to secure the left flank to the east of the Orne, whilst the US 82nd and 101st Airborne Divisions were to look after the right flank in the Cotentin peninsula.

The 82nd (commanded by General Ridgway) and the 101st (commanded by General Taylor) were formed as airborne divisions in 1942. Prior to operation Overlord, the 101st had been engaged in no operational missions, in contrast with the 82nd, deployed in Sicily on the 9th of July 1943: they trained successively in the United States then in England, to ensure that absolutely nothing was left to random.

The Allied generals determined three major targets for the American airborne units: to take control of the communication links between the beach and the inland sector, to maintain control of junctions and nearby localities and, finally, to control the only two bridges over the River Merderet. The finer details of these objectives were as follows:

1. To take control of the communication links between the beach and inland sectors. The terrain, which had been transformed by the German occupier, had been rendered totally unsuitable for establishing a bridgehead. Indeed, the Germans had flooded a vast share of the land from the south of Valognes to Carentan and Isigny-sur-Mer. Utah Beach, the chosen landing zone for the American troops from the 4th Infantry Division, was isolated by a marshy rampart and could only be reached via four narrow roads. The key mission for the US paratroops was to capture the four beach exists, referred to as Causeways, in the early hours of the 6th of June 1944, in order to enable landed troops to rapidly advance westwards and to extend the bridgehead.

2. To take control of key locations out in the field, to maintain control of road junctions and nearby localities. The operation zone was crossed from north to south by the RN13 trunk road, linking - in particular - Caen and Cherbourg. A major road link for the region, it also ran through the market towns of Saint-Côme-du-Mont and Sainte-Mère-Église. Other localities were located along the causeways and their control depended on the possibility for the Allies to circulate freely throughout the region. The paratroops therefore received orders to take control of them and to maintain such control, in particular at road junctions.

3. To control the bridges over the Merderet and the Douve. The land located inland from Utah Beach was blocked to the east by the River Merderet and to the south by the River Douve, with a further obstacle in the form of a vast marshland of a depth of up to 2 miles in certain areas. The two bridges across the Merderet were situated in La Fière and Chef-du-Pont, whereas to the north of Carentan, a total of four bridges enabled the Douve and the Carentan canal to be crossed. These structures naturally became priority targets for the paratroops, for they provided an exit for the Utah Beach bridgehead in the Cotentin peninsula. Whereas the Merderet bridges were to be captured intact, the Allies decided to destroy those over the Douve.

CODED MESSAGES FOR THE FRENCH RESISTANCE

The French Resistance communicated with the Allies via Radio Londres (Radio London) in the form of a series of coded 'messages personnels' (personal messages), each of which had its own particular meaning. Over the days that preceded D-Day, the Allied instructions intended for interpretation by the Resistance took on an increasingly offensive slant and, on the 1st of June 1944, some long-awaited messages were finally broadcast for the attention of specific networks. One of them included verses of the song *Chanson d'Automne* by Charles Trenet, inspired by the poem of the same name by Verlaine, '*Les sanglots longs des violons de l'automne*' intended for Philippe de Vomécourt's 'Ventriloquist' network, established in Sologne, alerted the Resistance fighters that they were to prepare to conduct sabotage missions on communication links in their sector, following specific orders to come over the forthcoming 7 days. Around 160 other 'personal messages' were communicated on the 1st, then rebroadcast on the 2nd and 3rd of June 1944, in order to prepare the Resistance for various acts of destruction. Under no circumstances did they clearly announce the landings: at this point in time, this was but pure supposition.

The day before D-Day, on the 5th of June, increasing numbers of coded messages were broadcast. The three following verses by Trenet ('*bercent mon coeur d'une langueur monotone*'), once more targeting the Ventriloquist resistance network, meant that the sabotage acts in Sologne were to be conducted within 48 hours. Several codes were deployed with specific action in mind, such as '*Il fait chaud à Suez*' (It's hot in Suez), which meant that guerrilla operations were to be launched in all directions against the occupier.

Resistance fighters immediately set to accomplishing their missions, destroying telephone lines, scattering mines across the roads, installing explosive devices on railway tracks. All of this action was intended to hinder communication and to limit coordination between German units during the initial phase of the Normandy assault.

01:55

– Bombers from the 8th US Air Force take off from England. A total of 1,198 planes are deployed.

02:05

– The *1. Panzerjaeger Kompanie* from the 716th Infantry Regiment leaves Biéville to patrol along the banks of the Caen canal, as it heads towards the Bénouville and Ranville bridges.

02:00

– The German Field Marshal von Rundstedt is informed of the alerts initiated following the discovery of paratroops, in particular those spotted by the 352nd Division.

– Captain Wagemann (duty officer) places the 21st Infantry Division on level 2 alert (capacity to engage in manoeuvres in less than an hour and a half).

Generalfeldmarschall Gerd von Rundsted (left), commander of the armies in the West (*Oberbefehlshaber West*), in conversation with *Generalfeldmarschall* Erwin Rommel, chief of Army Group B (*Heeresgruppe B*). Bundesarchiv Bild 101I-718-0149-17a.

American troops being transferred to their landing barges off Utah Beach. US National Archives.

German soldiers from the *21. Panzer-Division* in the bocage. The *Panzer-Grenadier-Regiment 125.*, commanded by Major Hans-Ulrich von Luck, was directly affected by the Anglo-Canadian airborne assault on Caen on D-Day. Bundesarchiv Bild 101I-722-0405-04.

The Allied forces' maritime convoy by the Isle of Wight on its way to Normandy. IWM A 23720 A.

02:15

− The German 352nd Infantry Division informs all its units of the end of the alert.

02:29

− U Force ships approach the coastline and anchor 15 miles off Utah Beach.

02:30

− In Ranville, British troops from the 6th Airborne Division engage in fierce combat with German soldiers from the 716th Infantry Division and the *21. Panzer-Division*.

− A tank from the *1. Panzerjaeger-Kompanie* of the German 716th Infantry Division is destroyed at the crossroads on the road from Caen to Ouistreham near Bénouville by a PIAT (Projector Infantry Anti Tank) belonging to the 6th Infantry Division's 7th Battalion.

− Fixed 'Bagpipe' and 'Chatter' transceivers in England enter into action and jam communication between *Kriegsmarine* and *Luftwaffe* (respectively the German Navy and Air Force) units.

These American (LCI - Landing Craft Infantry) troop transport barges belong to group 30, flotilla 11, serial 9, convoy U1. They are heading for Utah Beach. US National Archives.

A coast guard launch towing a GMC DUKW amphibious vehicle. US National Archives.

02:35

– Two planes towing gliders are spotted by the 352nd Infantry Division's *Feldpostamt*.

02:40

– Field Marshal von Rundstedt notifies the German 7th Army by radio that he does not believe in a large-scale landing operation.

02:45

– The 914th Grenadier Regiment (352nd Infantry Division) alerts on the landing of 50 to 60 parachutists to the south of the Carentan canal.

02:51

– O Force ships arrive off Omaha Beach and anchor 14 miles from the shore.

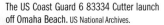

The US Coast Guard 1 Cutter launch off Omaha Beach. US National Archives.

The US Coast Guard 6 83334 Cutter launch off Omaha Beach. US National Archives.

US Coast Guard 53 launch, LCVPs, an LCI and a Liberty Ship off the Normandy shores. National Archives.

OPERATION FORTITUDE

In order to protect both the preparations for and the unfolding of operation Overlord, the Allies devised a vast deception strategy aimed at misleading the Germans as to the date and the precise location of the future offensive. Indeed, the Allied military chiefs were perfectly aware that the success of their assault partly depended on the element of surprise and on their capacity to deceive the enemy on a long-term basis, even after the landing operation was launched. As early as December 1943, they put together a series of active and passive measures to delude the German intelligence department, creating, in particular, fictional combat units and fake messages simulating preparations for an attack in the Pas-de-Calais region or in Norway.

The Allies built inflatable decoys which, when seen from a reconnaissance plane, looked like genuine machines. Rural zones in south-east England were scattered with vast quantities of imitation tanks, transport vehicles and artillery pieces, all painted with the colours of the feared and famed US General Patton's 3rd Army. In ports in and around Dover, warships and transport ships made of wood or of rubber were also 'berthed'.

Operation Fortitude entered a new phase immediately prior to the launch of operation Overlord. Indeed, in order to establish a solid bridgehead in Normandy, the London Controlling Section ordered, just a few hours before D-Day, for a series of manoeuvres to be engaged, indicating that a large-scale amphibious attack was underway opposite the Pas-de-Calais shores. Should the Germans effectively take the bait, they were sure to maintain a substantial military force in the area, which meant that they would not be deployed to other operational sectors such as Normandy.

The aerial bombardments clearly increased in intensity in northern France, particularly off the shores of Dover, as from the early months of 1944. On the night of the 5th to the 6th of June 1944, several thousand tonnes of bombs were dropped in the Pas-de-Calais region by Allied bombers. The German troops from the 15th Army were placed on the alert, their generals fearing an Allied landing in the zone.

To add to the confusion, a naval squadron comprised of small vessels emitting fake radio messages left their ports in south-east England on the evening of the 5th of June and headed for northern France. The German radio surveillance operators noted large echoes on their radars and raised the alarm: according to Germany, the Landings would indeed happen, and they would happen in Pas-de-Calais.

The subterfuge of the London Controlling Section's operation Fortitude proved remarkably effective. On D-Day, confused by a number of contradictory reports from Pas-de-Calais and from Normandy on the night over the 5th to the 6th of June 1944, the Germans considered the Landings on the Lower Normandy beaches as a diversion, convinced that the bulk of the operation was heading for the Pas-de-Calais shores. Even more surprising, they continued to believe in this 'diversion' up to July 1944, maintaining several tens of thousands of soldiers positioned in northern France.

03:00

– – *S-Boote*, the German *Kriegsmarine* speed boats, receive orders to patrol in the English Channel, following the landing of Allied paratroops. However, early reports bring no further information on the possibility of enemy naval forces in the sector.

– The American troops from O Force, waiting off Omaha, begin to embark onto their landing barges.

– The American troops from U Force off Utah Beach begin to embark onto their landing barges.

– Sergeant Ludwig Förster fires three white rockets from the Wn 62 resistance nest near Colleville-sur-Mer (Omaha Beach) requesting that the ships off shore identify themselves. The other resistance nests in the sector do likewise. The ships fail to respond.

– The Royal Air Force bombards targets in Caen.

– The 914th Grenadier Regiment (352nd ID) inform of 'new groups of parachutists spotted to the south of Brévands'. Other parachute units are now positioned near Cardonville, in Cotentin.

– Lieutenant Braatz from the *21. Panzer-Division* heads for Bénouville and Pegasus Bridge to counter-attack.

03:10

– A report is sent from the Pointe du Hoc sector to the military staff of the German 352nd Infantry Division, 'Enemy parachutists have landed on either banks of the Vire estuary.'

– The *8./(Schwere)Pz.Gren.-Kompanie 192* is sent to reinforce the Bénouville sector.

PLAN OF THE LANDINGS ON UTAH

Two beach sectors were created on Utah: 'Uncle Red' and 'Tare Green', located between the village of Saint-Martin-de-Varreville to the north and the locality named La Madeleine to the south. These beaches were controlled by the German 709th Infantry Division, which benefited from seven strongpoints in the sector. Two coastal artillery batteries, located in Azeville and Crisbecq, were a genuine threat, not only along the coast but also out at sea for the guns in both positions had a firing range in the region of 20 miles. Two further mobile artillery positions were also positioned in this sector, one in the vicinity of the Brécourt manor, the other in Holdy, in the village of Hiesville.

Major General J. Lawton Collins' 7th Army was entrusted with the mission of attacking Utah Beach on D-Day. This army was comprised of the US 4th Infantry Division's 8th, 22nd and 12th Infantry Regiments, commanded by General Raymond O. Barton. These units were in charge of taking control of the beach, where they were to establish a solid bridgehead, then to join forces with the paratroops from the 82nd and 101st Airborne Divisions.

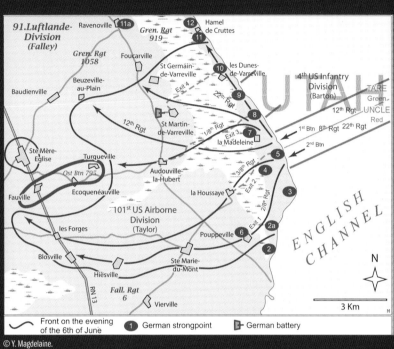

© Y. Magdelaine.

03:13

— The military staff from the German 84th Army Corps is informed that all sectors are calm, with the exception of the south of Brévands, where the equivalent of a battalion has been parachuted, and near Cardonville, where isolated units have been identified.

03:14

— The German commander of coastal troops is informed that naval units have been spotted around 7 miles off Grandcamp.

03:25

— Lieutenant-Colonel Terence Otway, who has only succeeded in reuniting 170 British parachutists, of the planned 635, launches the attack on the Merville battery.

The German *Schnellboot Typ S-38* fast torpedo launch, with three Daimler-Benz MB 501 engines, could reach a speed of 39 knots, i.e. around 45 mph.
Bundesarchiv Bild.

PLAN OF THE LANDINGS ON OMAHA

The US 1st Infantry Division's 16th Regiment and the 29th Infantry Division's 116th Regiment were assigned to attack this beach, which was divided into four large landing zones. From west to east, the zones were codenamed: 'Charlie', 'Dog', 'Easy' and 'Fox'. Depending on the outcome of the simultaneously planned attack on Pointe du Hoc, these units expected reinforcements from the 2nd and 5th Ranger Battalions.

These military formations were commanded by Division General Leonard T. Gerow, commander of the US 5th Army Corps and by General Omar N. Bradley, commander of the First Army.

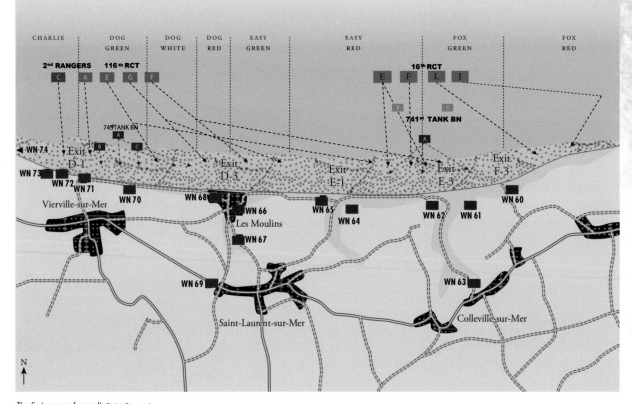

The first waves of assault.

DISPERSAL OF THE ALLIED PARACHUTISTS

Over 75% of the American parachutists were dropped off target, outside their initially planned zones. This terrible reality led to total chaos among the airborne forces, who could only intervene in foreign locations and with teams of men who had been haphazardly reunited depending on other units' similar fate. They, nevertheless, heroically strove to accomplish their respective missions. Pilot errors were such that certain sticks were dropped above the sea, others between Pointe du Hoc and Omaha Beach, over 25 miles from the planned landing zones. In Cotentin, the men from the US 82nd and the 101st Airborne Divisions were mixed together in the field and commanding them became a matter of grade and charisma. The 101st Airborne Division was dropped across a total landing zone of around 25 miles by 10.

To the east of the River Orne, the situation was equally alarming for the British 6th Airborne Division. Of the 9th Battalion's total of 600 parachutists, entrusted with taking the Merville battery, only 150 managed to reach their assembly point at the scheduled hour. Such general confusion led to a series of unexpected encounters throughout Normandy: stunned by the number of ongoing skirmishes, the Germans limited their interventions and were equally disorganised, their units being held down in areas by enemy forces, the firing power and numbers of which were as yet unknown to them. Small groups of Allied parachutists finally managed to organise themselves and headed towards their targets, gathering other isolated soldiers, who had lost contact with their own sections, on their way.

Aerial photograph of the British Drop Zone N, between Ranville and Amfreville, used for dropping parachutists (whose parachutes can still be seen) and for landing Horsa gliders from the 6th Airborne Division on the 6th of June 1944. IWM (CL 59).

IWM (MH 2076).

THE MERVILLE ARTILLERY BATTERY

In the locality of Merville, near Franceville in Calvados, the Germans had built an artillery battery comprised of four casemates housing artillery pieces. The site was manned by the 1st battery of the *1716. Artillerie-Regiment. According* to aerial photographs taken during preparations for operation Overlord, the Allies estimated that this type of casemate must have housed 150mm guns. Such a calibre would enable the occupying defenders to literally pulverise Sword Beach. For the Allies, this seafront military site, which was reinforced by a range of observation and support bunkers located to the west of Franceville, was imperatively to be brought under Allied control before the British and French troops began to land on D-Day.

Lieutenant-Colonel Terence Otway was placed in command of this 600-man commando, belonging to the 6th Airborne Division's 9th Parachute Battalion. Shortly before 01:00 on the morning of the 6th of June 1944, pathfinders commanded by George Smith jumped into the midst of the night above Normandy, reaching their assembly points without ado, as Lancaster bombers launched an intensive raid on the battery. As from 01:00, the 600 British parachutists were dropped above Normandy, on Drop Zone V, located between the battery and Varaville. Otway was dropped 400 yards from his planned landing point, to find himself within a farmstead requisitioned by the Germans for use as a command post. After a rapid skirmish, he managed to reach his assembly point at 01:30, to discover that losses in both men and material were far superior to the most pessimistic of estimations: at 02:50, only 150 of his original 600 men remained. The others had either drowned in the marshes, were wounded or were totally lost across the Normandy countryside. It took some of them over four hours to advance one single mile, without for as much coming across their fellow soldiers. At his disposal, Lieutenant-Colonel Otway had no jeep, just one Vickers heavy machine gun and a few Bangalore torpedoes. He had no news of around 450 of his men, who had been dropped across the four corners of Calvados.

Faced with this rather precarious situation, Otway quickly devised an action plan and divided his remaining troops into four groups. Three were to lead the bulk of the attack from east to west, whereas the last group was to operate a diversion attack from the north. The commander had the assault launched immediately - the Bangalore torpedoes were set off (they were intended to enlarge the breaches through the barbed wire networks and the minefields) and the Vickers machine gun, installed to the south-east of the battery, began to fire. Parachutists then engaged in a brief yet violent confrontation with around a hundred Germans, who staunchly defended their position. The enemy heavy machine guns annihilated the first wave of British parachutists as they advanced across the minefield that had been cleared by the Bangalore torpedoes. Following the aerial bombardments, the reinforced doors of the casemates had

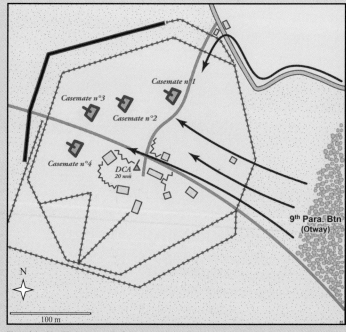

Plan of the Merville battery and of the assault by parachutists from the 9th Parachute Battalion.
© Y. Magdelaine.

A parachutist jumping from a British Dakota.

been left open by the Germans in order to air the firing positions. The parachutists took advantage of these providential openings to launch their phosphorus hand grenades. They also sent several grenades through the ventilation ducts. Only four paras managed to reach the fourth casemate which they captured, the others were either blocked or busy reducing the rest of the complex to silence.

Twenty minutes later, the British troops were in control of the battery, but at a cost of heavy losses (a total of 70 British officers and soldiers had been killed or wounded). The Germans suffered 22 deaths and as many prisoners, the rest of the garrison having managed to escape. Their chief, Lieutenant Steiner, was stationed at the seafront command post in Franceville. He tried to launch several counter-attacks towards Merville (in one particular attack, he deployed a half track armed with a powerful anti-aircraft gun used to fire against his adversaries), but his men were constantly driven back by the British parachutists. Incapable of regaining control of his battery, he directed fire from the 1716th Artillery Regiment's second and first batteries towards Merville.

Back at the battery, the parachutists discovered that the guns were in fact old 100mm Czech models (M.14/19 100mm), far less daunting than the expected 150mm guns. With the means at their disposal, they neutralised the artillery pieces before firing flares, indicating victory, to inform the Allied naval forces, waiting off shore, that the road was now clear. The Merville battery was now (at least temporarily) neutralised.

On D-Day, the Germans regained control of the battery, which had been abandoned by the British troops early in the morning. They managed to bring two of the Czech guns back into working order. With no visual contact over Sword Beach from his command post, Steiner was unable to fire accurately. The 736th Infantry Regiment look-outs posted at La Brèche, nevertheless succeeded in forwarding corrected firing coordinates until their own position was in turn captured by the British.

The Merville battery was the theatre of further combat on the 7th of June, in particular following vain assaults led by commando Number 3. As they disengaged, the British commandos came under enemy fire from guns that were aimed using direct fire sights. A number of confrontations continued on the site throughout the Battle of Normandy and the Merville battery and nearby village only permanently fell into Allied hands on the evening of the 17th of August, thanks to the intervention of the 6th Airborne Division's Ox and Bucks, during operation Paddle.

03:30

– Concerned by Allied aerial activity, *Generalmajor* Wilhelm Falley (commander of the *91. Luftlande Division*) decides finally not to take part in the *Kriegspiel* (tactical exercise using maps) organised in Rennes and takes a u-turn to return by car to his command post. He is killed en route, in front of the Minoterie farm to the north of Picauville, by Lieutenant Malcolm Brannen (HQ Company, 3rd Battalion, 508th Parachute Infantry Regiment, 82nd Airborne Division).

– Troops and vehicles belonging to the *21. Panzer-Division* are ready to engage in action.

03:35

– 48 Horsa gliders boarded by forces from the British 6th Airborne Division land as part of operation Tonga in the vicinity of Ranville, on Landing Zone 'N'.

– Accompanied by his military staff, General Gale, commander of the British 6th Airborne Division, lands his glider in Landing Zone 'N'.

– Situation report sent to the staff of the German 352nd Infantry Division, 'Very heavy bomb attacks at Le Guay, Pointe du Hoc and Grandcamp'.

– Parachutists are reported by the Germans in Amfreville, Hérouvillette and Gonneville.

British Horsa gliders belonging to the 6th Airlanding Brigade, 6th Airborne Division on Landing Zone N, in the Ranville sector on the 6th of June 1944. IWM (B 5202).

SYNTHESIS OF AMERICAN AIRBORNE AND AIRLANDED OPERATIONS IN NORMANDY

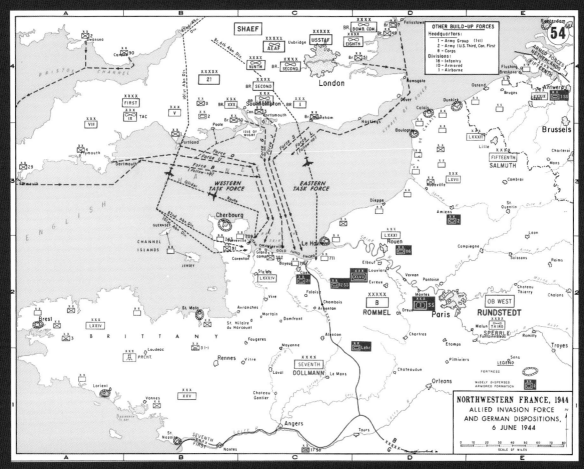

North-western France, 1944. Allied Invasion Force and German dispositions. 6 June 1944.

03:54

– 52 American Waco gliders boarded by forces from the 101st Airborne Division land as part of operation Chicago in Landing Zone 'E', to the north of Hiesville.

03:55

– The 914th Grenadier Regiment (352nd ID) indicates that two camouflaged parachutists have been taken prisoner near Cardonville, and that a further 70 parachutists are reported to have jumped near Isigny.

THE LIBERATION OF SAINTE-MÈRE-ÉGLISE

In the spring of 1944, Sainte-Mère-Église was occupied by German soldiers from the *Grenadier-Regiment 1058*, 3rd Battalion, 14th Company, and by artillerymen from the *Artillerie-Regiment 191*, 4th Battery. The village is located on the RN13 trunk road that crosses the Cotentin peninsula from north to south. Given the many minor roads that converge in the village centre, it is also a mandatory passing place.

During the preparatory phase of the airborne operations that preceded the Normandy Landings, the Americans placed the village of Sainte-Mère-Église at the heart of the 82nd Airborne Division's landing zones. Colonel William E. Ekman's 505th Parachute Infantry Regiment (505th PIR) was in charge of capturing the village in the early hours of D-Day. This specific mission was entrusted to Lieutenant-Colonel Edward C. Krause, commander of the 3rd Battalion. In order to simplify operations to gain control of Sainte-Mère-Église, the Americans defined a drop zone directly north-west of the village, between the River Merderet and the RN13. It was codenamed Drop Zone 'O'.

At around 23:45 on the night of the 5th of June 1944, just a few hours prior to the arrival of the Allied parachutists, a fire broke out in the centre of the village, in a house belonging to Mme Pommier. Transformed into an immense brazier in a few minutes, despite efforts by the local inhabitants to extinguish it, the fire proved to offer a precious landmark for the American pilots. Shortly after 01:50, a stick from the 505th PIR, 2nd Battalion, Company F was mistakenly dropped above the village. The Germans, who had already been alerted twenty minutes earlier of a drop in the church square of two sticks from the 506th PIR and the 101st Airborne Division, began to fire at the US paras. At least one member of the Fox Company, Private Alfred J. Van Holsbeck, landed in the midst of the blazing house. Privates Steele and Russel's parachutes became hooked onto the church (on the side of the present-day Rue du Général Koenig) and

only the latter managed to free himself from this very sticky situation. Wounded in the foot during his jump by a piece of shrapnel fired by the *Flak*, John Steele remained hooked onto the church spire for 45 minutes before being taken prisoner by the Germans. It was Private Rudolf May, who remained inside the belfry throughout the battle, who cut his parachute straps.

The 505th PIR began to drop in Drop Zone 'O' after the arrival of pathfinders at 01:51 on the 6th of June 1944, as per the plans set forth for operation Boston (which consisted in dropping the 82nd Airborne Division). The dropping of the 118 sticks went exceptionally well and the 505th PIR boasted more accurate results than all the other US airborne regiments deployed on the night of the 5th to the 6th of June 1944: 60 sticks (50% of the regiment) landed either within their target zone or less than a mile from the centre of the drop zone, and 20 sticks were within a radius of two miles around the drop zone. A total of 75% of the 505th PIR was in the vicinity of its assembly point. The other elements were scattered across Cotentin. The paras from the 505th were accompanied by the division's military staff, the 307th Engineer and the 456th Parachute Field Artillery Battalion (PFAB), equipped with two howitzers.

The third battalion from the 505th PIR, which set foot on Norman soil as from 02:03, joined forces under Lieutenant-Colonel Krause's orders and headed southwards towards Sainte-Mère-Église. It began to enter the village at 04:00. A few minutes later, the paras were able to hoist the Star-Spangled Banner on the village hall flagpole and Krause reported to his superiors at 05:00 that he was inside the locality, then at 06:00 that it was under his control. Throughout the day, the parachutists set to freeing the bodies of several of their fellow soldiers, either killed or trapped in their parachutes, the straps of which were entangled in the trees that lined the church square.

04:00

— Sainte-Mère-Église is liberated by American soldiers from the 505th Parachute Infantry Regiment's 3rd Battalion. The Star-Spangled Banner is hoisted up onto the flagpole in front of the village hall.

– As part of operation Detroit, 52 American Waco gliders land in Landing Zone 'O', to the north-west of Sainte-Mère-Église.

– Field Marshal von Rundstedt requests permission from the supreme German command in Berlin to deploy two divisions towards the coast.

– Violent airborne attack by the Allies on the Wn 44, 47 and 48 strongpoints to the west of Arromanches-les-Bains.

– Hitler goes to bed late in his home in Berlin after an evening listening to music composed by Wagner.

Two American parachutists from the 505th PIR inspecting the Lemenicier hardware store in Rue de Carentan, Sainte-Mère-Église. US National Archives.

The inhabitants of Sainte-Mère-Église paid a heavy toll during the liberation of Normandy: 43 civilians were killed from May to August 1944 (18 of them on the 6th of June following bombardments in Rue de Carentan, today renamed Rue du Général de Gaulle). On D-Day, they left their houses to avoid the fighting and the bombardments which continued in the village until the 7th of June.

What remains of this CG-4A Waco glider (baptised the Fighting Falcon) bears witness to its violent landing against a hedge to the west of Sainte-Marie-du-Mont. On board, Brigadier General Don F. Pratt (second-in-command of the 101st Airborne Division) and his co-pilot, Lieutenant John M. Butler, were both killed outright during the crash. US National Archives.

American parachutists from the 505th Parachute Infantry Regiment, 82nd Airborne Division patrolling at the foot of the church spire in Sainte-Mère-Église, looking for isolated German snipers. US National Archives.

04:08

– Death of General Pratt, second-in-command of the 101st Airborne Division, after the violent landing of his glider (baptised the 'Fighting Falcon') near Hiesville.

04:10

– The *Panzergruppe West* is placed on level 2 alert (maximum time to engage in manoeuvres - 1 hour 30 minutes).

04:13

– The military staff of the 352nd Infantry Division orders Lieutenant Meyer and his 915th Grenadier Regiment to move towards Montmartin-Deville, via the bridge to the west of Neuilly, in columns and reduced groups.

04:15

– Four American pathfinders from the 2nd and 4th Cavalry Squadrons land on l'Île du Large, one of the Îles Saint-Marcouf.

In Cotentin, this Horsa glider used by the American airlanded troops during operation Chicago has found a new purpose as a parasol for some Normande cows. The chalked figure '401' may indicate that the glider transported men from the 401st Glider Infantry Regiment (which formed the 3rd Battalion of the 327th Glider Infantry Regiment on D-Day). US National Archives.

Explosion of a shell fired on the Îles Saint-Marcouf on the 6th of June 1944. US National Archives.

04:25

– The military staff of the 352nd Infantry Division order for the 914th Grenadier Regiment to attack the opposing airlanded troops to the south of Carentan.

04:30

– 132 American soldiers from the 2nd and 4th Cavalry Squadrons, commanded by Lieutenant-Colonel Dunn, land on the (mined) beaches of the Îles Saint-Marcouf.

British vehicles belonging to the 168 Field Ambulance RAMC, 8th Armoured Brigade aboard an American LST 25 transport ship on its way to Gold Beach on the 6th of June 1944. IWM (A 23890).

– Captain Charles G. Shettle, operations officer for the 3rd Battalion (506th Parachute Infantry Regiment - 101st Airborne Division), takes control of the bridges over the Douve, level with Brévands, and sets up a defensive position near Carentan with fifty parachutists.

– Lieutenant-Colonel Otway launches his 9th Battalion (3rd Brigade – 6th Airborne Division) on the attack of the Merville artillery battery.

– The troops aboard the warships heading towards the Anglo-Canadian beaches who have managed to fall asleep are awakened.

– Field Marshal von Rundstedt orders for the armoured units from the *12. SS Panzer-Division* and the *Panzer-Lehr-Division* to approach the Normandy coastline.

THE LIBERATION OF THE ÎLES SAINT-MARCOUF

During preparations for the Normandy Landings, two islets of a surface area of a few hundred square yards, located a few miles off Utah Beach, posed a serious threat to the Allies. Indeed, they were convinced that the Germans had used this former bastion built under Napoleon III to install an advanced observation post or a submarine control post for the subs positioned in the Bay of Seine (German soldiers had been spotted by the Allied aviation on the largest island in May 1944). Consequently, both islands would absolutely need to be under Allied control prior to any landing operation.

On the 6th of June 1944, shortly before 04:30, four American soldiers, armed only with knives, landed on the island shores to mark out the beaches. Sergeant Harvey S. Olson and Private Thomas C. Killeran from Troop A (4th Squadron), together with Sergeant John W. Zanders and Corporal Melvin F. Kenzie from Troop B (24th Squadron). They were the first Americans to land on the Normandy shores on the 6th of June 1944. The two islands were abandoned but mined.

Hence, at 04:30, i.e. precisely two hours before H-Hour, a combined detachment from the 4th and 24th Cavalry Squadrons, commanded by Lieutenant-Colonel Edward C. Dunn, landed on the Îles Saint-Marcouf. Within an hour, at 05:30, the detachment's 132 men had landed on and now occupied the islands. Type S mines had proven fatal to 2 men and had wounded a further 17 in the US ranks. Apart from mining the shores, the Germans had established no other defensive installations on the islands.

04:35

– The German 916th Grenadier Regiment captures an American officer who confirms the existence of fake mannequin parachutists laden with explosives.

– Allied aerial bombardments over Le Guay, Pointe du Hoc, Grandcamp and Maisy.

– *Korvettenkapitän* Heinrich Hoffmann, commander of the 5th speed boat flotilla based in Le Havre, receives orders from the *Marinegruppen-Kommando West* to patrol in the Bay of Seine.

A Short Stirling heavy bomber dropping dummy parachutists during operation Titanic. US National Archives.

Rupert' dummy used as a decoy during operation Titanic. Some models were equipped with devices capable of emitting noises similar to those of automatic weapons. US National Archives.

OPERATION TITANIC

In an aim to mislead the German military forces, both on their intentions and on their modus operandi and their overall capacity on D-Day, the Allies devised a plan to drop fake units over Normandy simultaneously to genuine paratroops. Aimed at covering their tracks, this diversion involved the use of canvas mannequins attached to real parachutes. The Allies chose specific landing zones in order to draw maximum benefit from this incredible diversion tactic: the areas around Saint-Lô, Yvetot, the south of Caen and the east of the River Orne.

In the midst of the shadows on the very early hours of the 6th of June 1944, the dummies were dropped on their respective zones: 200 over Saint-Lô, 200 over Yvetot, 50 south of Caen and 50 to the east of the Orne. They all measured fifty centimetres in length and were made of hessian. Some models were equipped with devices capable of emitting noises similar to those of automatic weapons.

To increase the realism of the sound effects, six SAS (Special Air Service) commandos, divided into two teams, were dropped at the same time as the 200 dummies over Yvetot. They were carrying equipment that would emit the sound of shootings as soon as they landed. And to make sure that the Germans would not discover this decoy too soon, the mannequins were also equipped with auto-destruction devices that were activated shortly after landing, so that the Germans would only find parachutes without their owners when they came to inspect the landing zone.

Nicknamed 'Rupert', the dummies were dropped from Short Stirling light bombers. During flights over the landing zones on D-Day, two aircraft were shot down by the German anti-aircraft defences.

04:45

– The X20 and X30 midget submarines already positioned off Normandy as part of operation Gambit, respectively mark out the access routes to be taken by the Allied armada towards Juno Beach and Sword Beach, without alerting the Germans.

– Lieutenant-Colonel Terence Otway has a yellow flare launched to inform the cruiser Arethusa that it is in control of the German artillery battery in Merville. Seventy British officers, non-commissioned officers and soldiers are killed during the assault.

X23 midget submarine, commanded by Lieutenant George Honour, off Sword Beach, photographed from the cargo ship *HMS Largs*. Here, it has just accomplished its mission in the framework of operation Gambit. IWM.

THE KRIEGSMARINE *IN NORMANDY*

The term *Kriegsmarine* (German naval forces) equally applies to surface and submarine units belonging to the Third Reich, and to coastal artillery batteries. In Normandy in the spring of 1944, the *Kriegsmarine* was under orders from two military commanders: to the west, Admiral Walter Hennecke (based in Cherbourg) whose sector stretched from the Mont Saint-Michel bay to the mouth of the Orne and to the east, Konteradmiral Hans-Udo von Tresckow (based in Le Havre), whose sector stretched from the mouth of the Orne to the Somme region. The German naval forces positioned along the Channel coast were placed under the command of Admiral Friedrich Rieve, whose command post was based in Rouen.

The principal ports used by the Germans in Normandy were located in Cherbourg, Le Havre, Ouistreham, Port-en-Bessin, Grandcamp-Maisy and in the Channel Islands.

Already severely weakened by years of war, the German navy only disposed of 163 minesweepers (*Raumboote*), 57 patrol boats (*Vorpostenboote*), 42 artillery barges (*Artillerie-Träger*), 34 fast torpedo-launch craft (*S-Boote*) and 5 torpedo boats (*Torpedoboote*).

The historic storm that had been raging in the English Channel since the start of the month of June prevented the *Kriegsmarine* from taking boats out on the days that preceded operation Overlord. When the Allied armada finally headed for the Normandy coast, the German warships were at dock and their crews in their quarters.

In the early hours of the 6th of June 1944, Admiral Krancke, commander in chief of the Naval Group West (*Marinegruppe West*) was concerned by several messages sent to his command post and indicating the presence of parachutists in Normandy and of a mobile Allied fleet off the Pas-de-Calais coast (a diversion devised by the Allies as part of operation Fortitude). He consequently had the fleet positioned on the Channel coast placed on the alert as from 03:00; however, by this time, the Allied armada was already poised off the Normandy shores, waiting for dawn to come, to open fire.

From the coast, the *Kriegsmarine* artillerymen had spotted by night the dark outlines of ships on the distant horizon - ships which had failed to respond to flares requesting they identify themselves. In Port-en-Bessin, the radar listening station had recorded echoes coming from the high seas and indicating the presence of anchored ships: the 6th Artillery Flotilla (*6. Artillerieträger-Flottille*) was deployed but reduced to silence by gunfire from the Allied armada. Further patrols were deployed from Le Havre and Cherbourg. Among them, the 4th and 5th torpedo boat flotillas, and the 15th patrol boat flotilla. As they made their way through the smoke screen created by the first vessels that comprised the Allied armada, they gradually perceived the enemy warships and, as soon as they had fired their torpedoes, they u-turned back to the coast. Two of them managed to approach the Norwegian destroyer *Svenner*: a huge explosion ensued and the warship was literally split in two, before rapidly sinking to the sea bed. Thirty-three crew members (including an English seaman) were killed and fifteen wounded. The others were recovered by escort and support ships.

SYNTHESIS OF BRITISH AIRBORNE AND AIRLANDED OPERATIONS IN NORMANDY

The vast majority of initially identified targets had been reached by elements from the 6th Airborne Division. The 5th Brigade was in control of the Bas de Ranville sector (13th Battalion), Ranville (12th Battalion) and Drop Zone 'N' (7th Battalion); the 3rd Brigade was dispersed over a front in excess of three miles between the south of the Bavent Woods (8th Battalion) to Le Plein to the north (9th Battalion), via Le Mesnil in the centre (Canadian 1st Battalion); the 1st Special Service Brigade was in control of Le Plein, Le Hauger and Amfreville. Lieutenant-Colonel Bradbrooke, commander of the British and Canadian parachutists (himself under General Gale's command) could be proud of his men who, despite encountering difficulties (drop errors, substantial enemy defences, etc.) had successfully accomplished their missions.

The left flank of the Allied invasion was protected by Anglo-Canadian parachutists, who prepared themselves for possible German counter-attacks by consolidating their defensive positions against the *21. Panzer-Division* until operation Paddle was launched on the 17th of August 1944.

04:53

– The German 352nd Infantry Division reports to the 84th Army Corps that it is no longer able to locate enemy ships.

05:00

– Colonel Howard R. Johnson, commander of the 501st Parachute Infantry Regiment (101st Airborne Division), takes the initiative to take control of the Barquette lock on the canal to the north of Carentan, with a total of 150 parachutists.

05:01

– Several four-engine aircraft, towing gliders above Houlgate and Cabourg, are spotted by the Germans, as are parachute jumps over Morsalines, Saint Côme and Sainte-Mère-Église. Three parachutists with maps of the mouth of the River Vire are captured.

05:07

– The German 716th Infantry Division reports that the number of gliders in the Orne sector is constantly increasing.

The American battleship *USS Nevada*, a veteran of the Japanese attack on Pearl Harbor, opens fire on the German positions in Cotentin, in the Utah Beach sector, with its ten 356mm and ten 127mm guns. US National Archives.

PART III:
The Landings

The Allied warships and bombers bombarded the coastal defences
and the long-awaited landings could finally begin.

THE LONGUES-SUR-MER ARTILLERY BATTERY

The Longues-sur-Mer artillery battery is located on the seafront around 5 miles to the north of Bayeux. It stands at the summit of a 200-feet high cliff overlooking the sea. Its construction began in September 1943. From Arromanches to the east to Port-en-Bessin to the west, the Germans built four *Regelbau M272* type casemates and a *Regelbau M262A* command post, equipped with an electrical communication and firing command system that was highly sophisticated at the time. To do so, they employed Third Reich craftsmen and local manpower. The battery was codenamed Wn 48 and was armed with four Skoda 150 mm TK C/36 navy guns with a firing range of around 12 miles. These pieces were installed on a central pivot bearing Torpedolafette (TP) C/36.

In addition to these casemates, the Germans built shelters for servers and ammunition holds, installed a searchlight and three 20mm anti-aircraft guns, whilst protecting the entire site against possible attacks from inland sectors by means of machine gun positions, minefields and an extensive network of barbed wire. The site was further reinforced by a 122mm K390 Soviet gun.

The German garrison at the Longues battery comprised 184 men, commanded by the *Kriegsmarine* – the German naval forces. French Resistance fighters infiltrated the local craftsmen employed to build the site. They informed the Allies of the battery's layout and capacity, whilst sabotaging the concrete used to build one of the M272 casemates, rendering it more vulnerable to shocks.

The MKB (*Mareküstenbatterie*) in Longues is located in the centre of the Allied landing beaches, between the Omaha and Gold sectors. Favourable to the Germans, the position was a concern to the military chiefs, who decided to launch several powerful aerial raids as from May 1944. Over the two weeks prior to D-Day, from the 28th of May to the 3rd of June, no less than 1,500 bombs were dropped on the battery. However, they caused limited destruction, with the exception of the M272 casemates, whose concrete had been sabotaged by the Resistance and whose electric cables linking with the firing command post had been severed by bombs, obliging the Germans to use less rapid and less effective means of communication.

The destroyer *HMS Cottesmore* (L78) opens fire on the German positions in the King sector on Gold Beach on 6th June 1644. IWM (A 23892).

Present-day view of an M272 casemate at the Longues-sur-Mer artillery battery, still equipped with a TK C/36 150mm gun.

Over the night of the 5th to the 6th of June 1944, 404 tonnes of bombs were dropped on the site by 99 four-engine planes. But the 80-inch wide casemate walls made of reinforced concrete withstood several direct hits. At precisely 05:30, the British light cruiser HMS Ajax, positioned in the English Channel within naval force G, received orders to open fire with its 102mm and 152mm guns after flight squadrons had flown over the battery.

The German artillerymen retaliated, opening fire on Omaha Beach shortly before 06:00, but without causing serious harm. As from 06:20, the Longues battery engaged the Force G Flagship (Gold Beach) *HMS Bulolo*, with the staff of the British 30th Corps on board. The ship was obliged to leave its anchorage and to withdraw outside the battery's firing range. The cruisers Ajax and *Argonaut* in turn received orders to approach the coast in order to fire as accurately as possible. The British warships fired a total of 179 times, reducing the German battery to absolute silence as from 08:45, hence leading the naval forces to believe they had successfully destroyed the position.

Later in the morning, after fast and makeshift repairs by the German gunners, the 150mm guns opened fire once more on Omaha Beach. The French cruisers *Georges Leygues* and *Montcalm* were fast to react, as was the American ship *USS Arkansas*. They retaliated in turn, successfully destroying one gun thanks to a bulls-eye hit and damaging two others.

The battery remained silent until the afternoon of the 6th of June, when its fourth casemate, which had escaped the previous artillery duels, opened fire – reinforced by a 122mm Soviet gun – towards Gold and Omaha Beach. However, it was never a genuine concern to the Allies. On D-Day, the Longues battery fired a total of 115 shells against the Allied forces.

On the morning of the 7th of June, the Allies launched a further aerial raid, preceding the assault by British troops from the 2nd Devonshire Regiment's C Company, landed on Gold Beach. By midday, they had taken control of the battery and taken the 120 surviving German gunners and infantrymen prisoner, with no particular resistance from the latter.

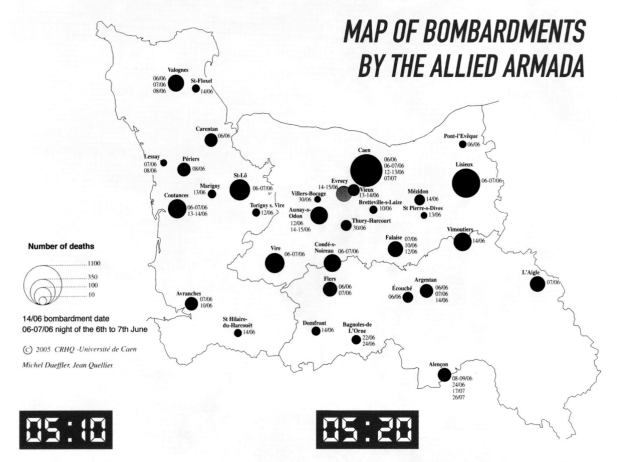

MAP OF BOMBARDMENTS BY THE ALLIED ARMADA

Valognes 06/06 07/06 08/06
St-Floxel 14/06
Carentan 06/06
Lessay 07/06 08/06
Périers 08/06
St-Lô 06-07/06
Marigny 13/06
Coutances 06-07/06 13-14/06
Torigny s. Vire 12/06
Evrecy 14-15/06
Villers-Bocage 30/06
Vieux 13-14/06
Bretteville-s-Laize 10/06
Caen 06/06 06-07/06 12-13/06 07/07
Mézidon 14/06
St Pierre-s-Dives 13/06
Pont-l'Evêque 06/06
Lisieux 06-07/06
Aunay-s-Odon 12/06 14-15/06
Thury-Harcourt 30/06
Vimoutiers 14/06
Vire 06-07/06
Condé-s-Noireau 06-07/06
Falaise 07/06 10/06 12/06
L'Aigle 07/06
Avranches 07/06 10/06
Flers 06/06 07/06
Écouché 06/06
Argentan 06/06 07/06 14/06
St Hilaire-du-Harcouët 14/06
Domfront 14/06
Bagnoles-de L'Orne 22/06 24/06
Alençon 08-09/06 24/06 17/07 26/07

Number of deaths

1100
350
100
10

14/06 bombardment date
06-07/06 night of the 6th to 7th June

© 2005 CRHQ -Université de Caen

Michel Daeffler, Jean Quellier

05:10

– First naval artillery fire in direction of the German positions by the cruiser *Orion*, anchored off Gold Beach, 40 minutes ahead of schedule, followed by the cruisers *HMS Ajax*, *HMS Argonaut* and *HMS Emerald*, together with the Dutch gunboat *HNLMS Flores* and thirteen destroyers.

– Attack on the German artillery battery at Mont Canisy by 18 Royal Air Force Marauder bombers.

– The French warships *Georges Leygues* and *Montcalm* bombard the German artillery battery in Longues-sur-Mer, which in turn opens fire on the American ship *USS Arkansas*.

05:20

– Report sent by the German 352nd Artillery Regiment to the staff of the 352nd Infantry Division, 'Advanced lookouts from artillery groups 2 and 4 signal perceived noises, probably naval units in movement towards the Vire estuary. Other observations towards Le Guay-Pointe du Hoc - 29 ships, 4 of which are relatively large vessels (destroyer or cruiser class) at a distance of 4 to 6 miles. 3 or 4 planes crashed in Formigny, 1 (Polish) pilot captured. The number of barges off Port-en-Bessin is in the vicinity of 50.'

– General Feuchtinger, commander of the *21. Panzer-Division* arrives at his command post established in Saint-Pierre-sur-Dives.

– Operation Gambit: the two X20 and X30 submarines have finished marking out the access channels towards Juno and Sword using signal ramps and radio transmitters.

- Three German gunboats fleeing Ouistreham via the Caen Canal are intercepted by Major Howard's men level with Pegasus Bridge: one is destroyed, another grounds nearby and the third seeks refuge further north, near Maresquier.

— The Norwegian destroyer *Svenner* sinks off Sword Beach, after being hit by a German torpedo, killing 30 seamen and soldiers. Eighteen torpedoes have been fired by three speed boats from the 5th Flotilla (T28, Möwe and Jaguar), based in Le Havre.

– Troops from the first Force S (Sword Beach) wave of assault board their landing barges.

– For the first time of the day, an Allied fighter plane dives to attack a target near Falaise.

PLAN OF THE LANDINGS ON SWORD BEACH

Landings on Sword Beach included British troops from the 8th Brigade (3rd Infantry Division) and commandos (numbers 4, 6, 8, 10, 41 and 45) from the 1st Special Service Brigade (including commando number 4 with the 177 men from the French *1er Bataillon de Fusiliers Marins Commandos*, under *Commandant Kieffer*). These Allied forces were all fighting under the 1st Army Corps, commanded by the British Lieutenant-General John Crocker.

The beach was divided into four large sectors codenamed - from west to east – Oboe, Peter, Queen and Roger. The sectors were defended by men from the German 716th Infantry Division, which was comprised of 29 companies and armed with 500 machine guns, 50 mortars and 90 other guns of varying calibres.

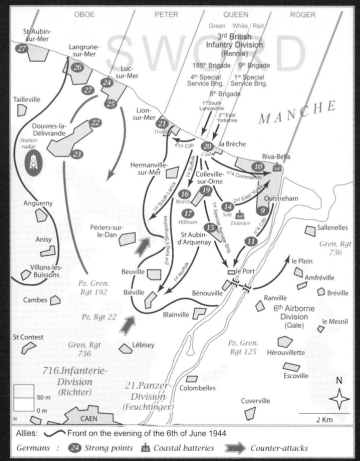

© Y. Magdelaine.

MAJOR NAVAL LOSSES FOR THE ALLIED ARMADA ON D-DAY

TYPE	NOM	PAYS	CAUSE
Destroyer	*USS Corry* (DD 463)	United States	Mine /Shell
Coastal cargo ship	*S/S Dunvegan Head*	Great Britain	Shell
Destroyer	*HNOMS Svenner* (G 03)	Norway	Torpedo
Submarine chaser	*PC 1261*	United States	Shell
Destroyer	*HMS Wrestler* (D35)	Great Britain	Mine

05:31

– The majority of the warships belonging to the *Eastern Naval Task Force*, under Rear-Admiral Philip Vian, open fire for the first time on the British and Canadian sectors on Gold, Juno and Sword.

05:32

– LSI (Landing Ship Infantry) vessels transporting troops towards Juno Beach anchor and prepare for transhipment towards the landing barges.

05:34

– The staff of the 352nd Division receive information that no ship is within sight off Carentan.

05:35

– Twenty-nine American amphibious tanks from the 714st Tank Battalion are launched 11 miles off Omaha Beach. Twenty-seven of them will sink.

05:37

– The guns at the German artillery battery in Longues-sur-Mer open fire on the destroyer *USS Emmons* and the battleship *USS Arkansas*.

The British battleship *HMS Rodney* opens fire on the Benerville Battery and on several German positions around Caen. The day after D-day, *HMS Rodney* collides with LCT (Landing Craft Tank) 427, causing the death of 13 British seamen. It nevertheless continues its mission, offering support to the Allied land-based forces throughout the Battle of Normandy, in particular in the sectors of Carpiquet and Caen, causing major destruction, including the spire of the Church of St Peter in Caen. This photograph was taken from aboard *HMS Holmes*. IWM (A 23961).

PLAN OF THE LANDINGS ON JUNO BEACH

Juno Beach comprised 3 large sectors, codenamed – from west to east – Love, Mike and Nan. The first soldiers to land on this beach, on the dawn of the 6th of June 1944, belonged to the 7th Brigade (comprised of regiments from the Royal Winnipeg Rifles and the Royal Regina Rifles) and the 8th Brigade (comprised of regiments from the Queen's Own Rifles of Canada and North Shore). These men were under the orders of the Canadian 3rd Infantry Division, in turn answerable to the British 1st Army Corps, commanded by Lieutenant-General John Crocker. These units were reinforced by British troops from N°48 (Royal Marine) Commando, landed in the Oboe sector to the west of Sword Beach, opposite Saint-Aubin-sur-Mer.

Juno Beach was defended by men from the German 736th Regiment, 716th Infantry Division, which was comprised of 29 companies and armed with 500 machine guns, 50 mortars and 90 other guns of varying calibres. The 736th Regiment's 5th company defended Bernières, the 6th was positioned in Courseulles, the 7th in the Mike sector, and the 9th in Saint-Aubin-sur-Mer, opposite the Nan sector. Just over a mile to the south, four further companies from the *716. Panzerjäger Abteilung* 1st antitank squadron formed a second line of defence.

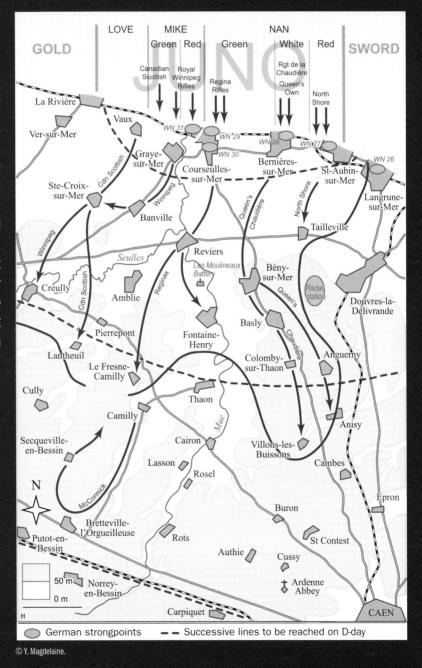

© Y. Magdelaine.

SPECIAL TANKS – 'FUNNIES'

From feedback on the various engagements in combat by the British Army, it transpired that the British armoured vehicles were ill-adapted to the terrain, finding themselves rapidly blocked by the many obstacles of all sorts in their way (the failed Allied landing operation in Dieppe in August 1942 was a case in point). The Americans were confronted with the same problems and the Allies needed to find a solution, and fast. They were quick to realise that armoured reinforcements in Dieppe had been neutralised essentially due to the incapacity of Churchill tanks to overcome the pebbles and the natural and manmade obstacles on the beaches. During preparations for operation Overlord, it became clear that new methods capable of improving both the mobility and the firing power of the Allies' armoured fleet needed to be developed.

The English General Percy Hobart, a man with a genuine passion for combat tanks and in charge – as from April 1943 – of rendering the 79th Armoured Division operational, put forward a plan to test a range of structural modifications or additions to his tanks. His inventions not only enabled fire support missions to be successfully accomplished, they also served for mobility and countermobility support, in particular during amphibious assaults. His armoured vehicles were fittingly nicknamed 'Funnies.' Several tanks were produced for the Normandy Landings, based on the standard British Churchill or American Sherman chassis. The following tanks were developed:

- The Avre tank equipped with a 290mm mortar on a Churchill chassis. Its aim was to provide heavy support fire to land-based troops. Its structure provided the basis for all other 'Funnies.'

- The Ark tank was designed to be used to fill antitank ditches with its chassis and with ramps to enable other vehicles to then cross.

- The Bobbin tank, also referred to as the Carpet-Layer, was a tank equipped with a canvas carpet which it could place on loose soil surfaces to facilitate progression by the infantry and other vehicles.

- The Bullshorn Plough tank was equipped with a plough used to extract mines without them exploding.

- The Crab tank was equipped with chains that hit the ground, setting off any mines before the tank hit them.

- The Crocodile was equipped with a particularly efficient flamethrower against any enemy troops entrenched inside casemates.

- The Duplex Drive was an amphibious tank with an inflatable and watertight skirt, together with propellers.

- The Fascine tank was used to fill ditches and trenches with wooden planks or branches, on which the infantry troops could advance.

From the very beginning, the Americans decided not to develop the 'Funnies' any further. They decided only to keep the Duplex Drive amphibious tank and the Crab and Bullshorn Plough mine clearing tanks for operation Overlord. In contrast, the Anglo-Canadian forces divided the various tank types belonging to the 79th Armoured Division among the units that were to lead the assault.

M4 Sherman tank with a collapsible watertight skirt around the vehicle, which is also equipped with propellers. Referred to as the Duplex Drive, its capacity to float and its initials lead the British and American troops to rapidly give it the nickname of Donald Duck. IWM MH 3660.

A Consolidated B-24 55 CO Liberator (serial 42-99949) bomber belonging to the 93rd Bomber Group, 328th Bomber Squadron, 9th Air Force. US National Archives.

05:45

– Bombardment by the Allied naval artillery of the batteries in Houlgate, Mont Canisy and Villerville.

05:50

– *USS Texas* fires for the first time (on the American sector on Omaha).

05:52

– *USS Arkansas* opens fire once more.

HMCS Prince Henry LSI(M) (Landing Ship Infantry (Medium)), used for troop transport. On D-Day, it transported the staff of Force J1, together with 550 infantrymen, six LCA (Landing Craft Assault) barges and two LCM (Landing Craft Mechanised) barges. National Archives Canada.

05:55

– Four hundred and forty-six American B-24 Liberator bombers from the 8th United States Strategic Army Air Force attack the German coastal installations on Omaha Beach.

– *P.C. 1261*, an American ship charged with the task of guiding the landing barges towards Utah Beach, enters a zone riddled with mines and hits one of them. Other ships sink a few minutes after *P.C. 1261* for the same reason.

05:58

– Sunrise. The weather is grey, the sea heavy with swell and between the clouds, only short sunny spells appear. Wind is force 3 to 4.

THE BRIDGES DESTROYED TO THE EAST OF THE ORNE

Five bridges located to the east of the River Orne were to be destroyed in order to disorganise the German forces and to prevent any major counter-attack from the area, whilst maintaining control of the terrain in order to prepare local Allied counter-offensives. This mission was entrusted to the Canadian 1st Parachute Battalion and to the British 8th and 9th Battalions from the 3rd Brigade.

The soldiers from the 6th Airborne in charge of destroying these bridges advanced towards their targets as soon as they had successfully and sufficiently reunited their units. Robehomme, the first bridge to attack, was destroyed at 06:00 by the parachutists from the 1st Canadian Battalion, commanded by Lieutenant Jack Inman. It was followed by the road bridge in Bures-sur-Dives, destroyed by the 2nd section of the 3rd Parachute Squadron RE. The Varaville bridge was destroyed at 08:30 by Sergeant Davies' men from the 1st Canadian Parachute Battalion's C Company, with support from sappers from the 3rd Parachute Squadron RE. The rail bridge in Bures-sur-Dives was hit at 09:15, by Lieutenant Shave's men from the 3rd section of the 3rd Parachute Squadron RE.

The fifth bridge, in Troarn, was destroyed at 15:00 by Captain Jukes' sappers after having been damaged over the night after a daring feat by Major Tim Roseveare. Commander of the 3rd Parachute Squadron RE, he was informed, at around 04:00 on the 6th of June, that the village of Troarn was occupied by heavily armed elements from the *21. Panzer-Division*. He devised a plan for an audacious raid using a Jeep and a trailer, upon which he loaded 2,000 lbs of explosives, 45 detonators, a lieutenant and seven sappers. They drove through the main street in Troarn, under heavy enemy gunfire, which could have set off the detonators at any time. As soon they reached the bridge, they set to work. Five minutes later, they set off the explosive charges causing a huge hole in the middle of the bridge, but failing to totally destroy it. As they hastily began to withdraw, a sapper by the name of Peachey fell from the trailer and was taken prisoner by the Germans.

Off Utah Beach, US Infantrymen observe landing operations from their LCVP (Landing Craft Vehicle & Personnel) vessel, before, in turn, being thrust into the fray on the beaches. US National Archives.

THE WEATHER ON D-DAY

On the 6th of June 1944, the sun rose at 05:58 and set at 22:07. The moon was full. Out at sea, winds reached force 5 (around 22 mph) and heavy clouds stretched across the Cotentin peninsula over the very first hours of the 6th of June, when the American parachutists were dropped above Normandy. Weather specialists had estimated that the cloud level, although still far too low, could only improve as dawn approached. At the same time, further east in Calvados, the sky was clear. When the sun finally rose, the sky was grey. By late morning, sunny spells finally appeared and the temperature reached 15°C. By the day end, the wind settled to force 4 (around 16 mph).

06:00

– Two hundred and seventy American Marauder bombers drop 4,404 bombs, each weighing in at 240 lbs.

– Major von der Heydte, commander of the German 6th Parachute Regiment begins to interrogate the American parachutists captured in Carentan.

– Sappers from the 10th Section of the 3rd Parachute Squadron, Royal Engineers, commanded by Lieutenant Jack. D. Inman, and parachutists from the 1st Canadian Parachute Battalion, explode the Robehomme bridge over the Dives.

1st Canadian Parachute Battalion shoulder badge.
National Archives Canada.

Royal Engineers Parachute shoulder badge.
National Archives Canada.

06:02

– The 352nd Infantry Division informs of a first group of ships accompanied by four smaller convoys in movement out at sea, and of the presence of groups of small vessels off Grandcamp.

The frigate *La Surprise* (K 292) belonging to the Free French Naval Forces (formerly the Royal Navy's *HMS Torridge*) together with LST (Landing Ship Tank) transport ships off Gold Beach on 6th of June 1944. IWM (A 23902).

06:06

– Violent aerial bombardments are reported on strongpoints located in Arromanches, Sainte-Honorine and Colleville.

– The 726th Grenadier Regiment informs its HQ that the crew of a shot down bomber has been located to the north of Sully.

06:15

— The landing barges positioned at around 4 miles off the Anglo-Canadian beaches begin their progression towards the beaches.

– The German 709th Infantry Division informs that Sainte-Mère-Église is now occupied by Allied parachutists.

06:20

– The 352nd Infantry Division reports that between 4 to 6 miles off Le Guay-Pointe du Hoc, 29 ships (4 heavy tonnages) have been located and that 50 of the same have been seen off Port-en-Bessin.

06:25

– The 726th Grenadier Regiment reports that 30 ships are moving at slow speed 6 miles off Port-en-Bessin. The German battery in Longues is capable of destroying them.

06:27

– Omaha Beach: the bombardments end with a barrage of artillery fire along the coast (with the exception of the ships *Satterlee* and *Talybont*).

06:29

– On Omaha Beach, 32 amphibious tanks belonging to the 743rd Tank Battalion land in the Dog Green and Dog White sectors.

Duplex Drive tank with its floatation skirt raised. IWM.

The crew of an LCF (Landing Craft Flak) vessel, preparing to fire to offer support to landing operations on Juno Beach at Courseulles-sur-Mer on 6th June 1944. IWM (A 23933).

THE TYPOLOGY OF THE ALLIED WARSHIPS

Type of ship	Royal Navy – Royal Canadian Navy	United States Navy	Other nations*
Command ship	3	2	-
Naval trawler	30	-	-
Corvette	17	-	4
Battleship	3	3	-
Monitor	2	-	-
Cruiser	17	3	3
Destroyer	65	30	6
Frigate	11	2	4
Sloop	4	-	2
Minelayer	88	9	-
Patrol ship	-	17	-

*Free France, Greece, Norway, Netherlands, Poland

06:30

– Omaha Beach: aerial attack on Pointe du Hoc by 18 Marauder bombers, then the American warships (including USS Texas) fire on the German battery.

– General Feuchtinger, chief of the 21. Panzer-Division gives orders to attack the bridgehead established by men from the British 6th Airborne Division beyond the River Orne.

– Alfred Jodl, chief of operations for the OKW (*Oberkommando der Wehrmacht*, the German armed forces' supreme command) cancels the order given by Field Marshal von Rundstedt at 04:30, given that Hitler has not personally approved moving German armoured divisions.

A Sherman tank equipped with a snorkel abandoned on Omaha Beach by its crew shortly after landing. US National Archives.

THE LANDING PLAN AT POINTE DU HOC

The assault on this German battery, located at the top of a 100 feet-high cliff, was scheduled for 06:30.

Two hundred and twenty-five Americans belonging to the 2nd Ranger Battalion, commanded by Colonel James E. Rudder, were entrusted with the mission of capturing and destroying the German guns. These Rangers were specially trained in the destruction of fortifications. They were to signal to the Allied warships anchored off the headland as soon as the position was under control, at 07:00 at the latest, i.e. half an hour after the initial assault. Five hundred rangers from the 5th Ranger Battalion were then to be sent in reinforcement.

To capture the position, the rangers were to scale the cliff on either side of Pointe du Hoc - to the west and the east, to seize the bunkers protecting the German artillery pieces which they were then to destroy. Timing was of the essence if the Americans were to obtain the expected support from the 500 reinforcements. They were to hold the battery until the arrival of troops from C Company from the 2nd Ranger Battalion and from the 29th Infantry Division's 116th Regiment, landed between Vierville-sur-Mer and Saint-Laurent-sur-Mer.

If, by 07:00, Colonel Rudder had not reported Pointe du Hoc under his control, the assault would be considered to have failed and the reinforcements would be sent direct to the Charlie sector on Omaha Beach, and would later capture the battery from inland.

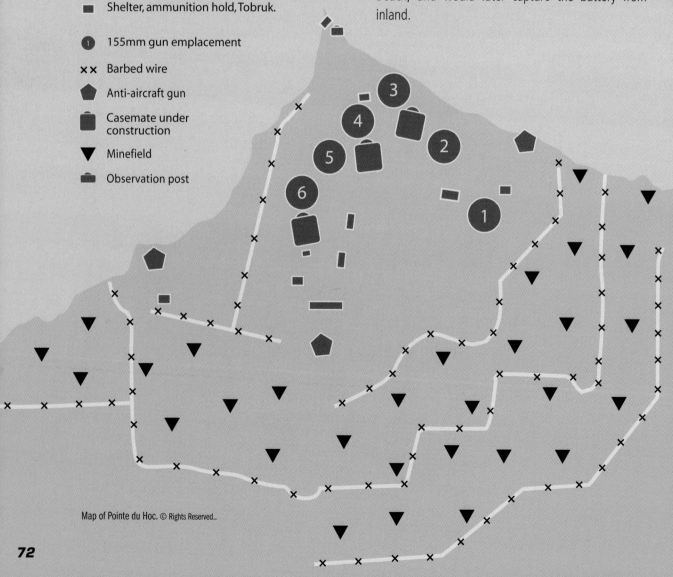

- ■ Shelter, ammunition hold, Tobruk.
- ① 155mm gun emplacement
- ✕✕ Barbed wire
- ⬠ Anti-aircraft gun
- ▣ Casemate under construction
- ▼ Minefield
- ◗ Observation post

Map of Pointe du Hoc. © Rights Reserved..

06:31

– Utah Beach, Uncle Red sector: the 2nd Battalion, 8th Regiment, 4th US Infantry Division lands.

06:33

– Utah Beach: the destroyer *USS Corry* hits an underwater mine. It is simultaneously hit by a shell fired from the Crisbecq battery which leads to an explosion in its ammunition hold. The warship sinks. Twenty-four crew members are killed and 60 wounded.

06:35

– Omaha Beach: landing of the first waves of assault from the 1st Infantry Division's 16th Regiment and the 29th Infantry Division's 116th Regiment.

– Utah Beach: landing of the second wave of assault comprised of infantrymen from the 8th Infantry Regiment and sappers from the 4th Infantry Division.

06:36

– Omaha Beach: landing of the second wave of assault from the 1st Infantry Division's 16th Regiment and the 29th Infantry Division's 116th Regiment.

Landings on Utah Beach in Cotentin. These men from the 4th (US) Infantry Division are gathering together before heading inland.
US National Archives.

THE LANDINGS ON UTAH BEACH

The US troops from the 1st and 2nd Battalions (8th Infantry Regiment, 4th Infantry Division) who had boarded the landed barges could but observe the bombardments as they pounded the French landscape and filled the skies with immense clouds of smoke. Even if many of them suffered from terrible sea sickness, they were relieved to finally see the coast they would attack a few minutes later under the same showers of steel. Two Duplex Drive amphibious tank squadrons were launched two miles off the shoreline, with the mission to head for the beach sectors by their own means thanks to their two propellers and inflatable rubber skirt. They advanced over two waves of assault: the first was comprised of twelve and the second of sixteen Duplex Drive tanks. However, the amphibious vehicles advanced too slowly and were quickly overtaken by 2nd Battalion landing barges, who consequently led the offensive in the Uncle Red sector, to the south-east of Saint-Martin-de-Varreville.

The 1st Battalion landed fifteen minutes later in the Tare Green sector to the east of Saint-Martin-de-Varreville, at the same time as the amphibious tanks from the 70th Tank Battalion's squadrons A and B. The latter reached the beach and immediately engaged in combat with enemy positions. Over the first minutes of landing operations on Utah Beach for the 4th Infantry Division, German gunfire was heavy but inaccurate. The machine guns progressively ceased fire, to be relayed by haphazard but deadly explosions caused by shells fired from field guns belonging to the German 709th Infantry Division. These guns were positioned in locations a few miles to the west of the landing beach (near the Brécourt manor in particular) and were camouflaged to prevent the Allied planes that were patrolling the Normandy skies from locating them.

Very quickly, the beach was under control. The tide was low and the beach defences were visible over a distance of around 300 yards between the dunes and the sea. The fifth wave of assault landed half an hour after H-Hour. By 07:30, engineers had opened breaches through the beach obstacles, enabling the landing barges to approach without mishap.

A German shell exploding on Utah Beach amidst the men from the 4th US Infantry Division, as they take shelter behind the dune. US National Archives.

THE LANDINGS ON OMAHA BEACH

All of the first waves of assault landed on Omaha Beach from 06:31 to 06:35 – 1,450 soldiers in 36 flat-bottomed barges. The sea was at mid-rising tide and the mined stakes installed a few months earlier were visible. However, the assailants needed to cross a 300-yard stretch of uncovered beach before finding any form of shelter. Ready and waiting in their defensive positions, the Germans waited for the last minute before opening fire, to avoid revealing their precise location. As soon as the barge ramps were lowered on the beach and the soldiers set foot on French soil, they met with showers of shellfire and machine gunfire. The first wave of assault was annihilated in no time. Over the first five minutes of the assault alone, around 90% of its men were put out of action. The vast majority of officers and non-commissioned officers had been killed or were wounded, and the survivors organised themselves as best they could in small groups, mainly by affinity or geographical origin, the Texas boys grouping together with fellow Texans, etc.

The 270 sappers who – in the space of 27 minutes – were to hastily open 16 passageways to allow vehicles - tanks in particular - to cross the 300 yards that separated the first German positions from the shoreline, set desperately to their task. They destroyed the beach defences that some landed soldiers were using for shelter, in order to open routes that would only be used far later. Since they had no choice but to remain, without cover, on the beach to accomplish their mission, they became easy targets for the German snipers. By the 27-minute timescale established weeks before D-Day by the Allied officers, only one passageway had been cleared and most of the sappers had been killed or wounded.

As the American waves of assault continued, enemy gunfire was sustained. In the sector, the Germans had established 17 defensive positions, including 8 impassable strongpoints: antitank walls, minefields, machine gun nests, flamethrowers, mortar shelters, guns of varying calibre, etc. Furthermore, the German defenders were not infantry division units as expected in Allied plans. The division had been partly replaced in May 1944 by the formidable 352nd Infantry Division, brought back from the Eastern Front. A message from the French Resistance had been sent to London by carrier pigeon prior to D-Day, but it did not arrive early enough to be taken into account by the military authorities.

The landings on Omaha Beach, a terrifying scene. The troops that are among the first wave of assault are welcomed by intense and deadly enemy gunfire. The smoke from fires and explosions intermingles with the threatening low clouds. US National Archives.

The landed troops sought refuge behind the antitank wall located in front of a projecting edge at the foot of the plateau overlooking the beach. Of varying height, this antitank wall was nevertheless high enough for a crouching man to take shelter without being spotted by the Germans from their casemates. To the extreme west of Omaha Beach, in front of Vierville-sur-Mer in the 'Charlie' sector, the antitank wall was replaced by a natural rampart formed by pebbles. To avoid becoming a target, the American soldiers were obliged to lie down at this spot. But the German mortar shells still proved deadly behind this meagre protection. The beach was strewn with material of all sorts and with human bodies, mutilated by bullets and shrapnel. They were all progressively amassed with the rising tide. Those who were wounded on the beach and incapable of moving were condemned to death by drowning if no-one came to help them. The GIs were all mixed together, and very few had landed in the planned sector. The assault barge pilots had preferred to land the men on spots where enemy gunfire was less intense, rather than strictly abiding by the planned landing zone which would lead to certain death.

Those who had escaped the first waves of assault did their best to survive this hell. German snipers targeted the American officers, or any other soldier who appeared to be trying to organise his fellow troops. Their machine guns spat out their ammunition from bunkers and strongpoints in a deluge of metal, discharged in concert with that of other similar weapons. Guns and mortars hit the only vehicles that had managed to land, provoking explosions here and there. Any movement, any breakthrough, seemed impossible. The situation only took a turn for the better for the Omaha assailants at around 09:30, to the east of the beach, in particular in the Fox sector, where enemy fire was less dense than in the western zone. A group of Americans was heading eastwards towards the village of Port-en-Bessin, in an aim to join forces with British troops established at a distance of around 10 miles.

06:40

– General Dwight Eisenhower wakes after a short nap. He receives an optimistic and reassuring call from Admiral Ramsay.

– Utah Beach: 28 of the 32 amphibious tanks from squadrons A and B of the 70th Tank Battalion reach the beach ten minutes behind schedule.

– Omaha Beach: the first tanks from the 741st and 743rd Tank Battalions reach the shoreline, respectively in Colleville-sur-Mer and Vierville-sur-Mer.

06:42

– The US Rear-Admiral Alan Goodrich Kirk, commander of the Western Naval Task, informs that 'all is going according to plan.'

06:45

– Utah Beach: landing direct on the beach of 16 M4A1 Sherman tanks belonging to squadron C of the 70th Tank Battalion, together with 4 bulldozers, landed across the Uncle Red and Tare Green sectors.

– Utah Beach, Tare Green sector: landing of the 1st Battalion, 8th Regiment, 4th US Infantry Division.

– Omaha Beach, Dog Green sector: landing of Task Force B (C Company, 2nd Ranger Battalion) intended to offer support to Company A of the 116th Infantry Regiment (29th Infantry Division) at the 'D-1' exit towards Vierville-sur-Mer.

– The Royal *Navy destroyer HMS Wrestler* hits a mine in the Eastern Task Force sector.

– The Royal Air Force 8th and 342nd squadrons (the French 'Lorraine' group) finalise the creation of a smoke screen to camouflage the Allied armada.

– General Speidel places the *21. Panzer-Division* under the German 7th Army's command.

06:52

– The 352nd Artillery Regiment reports that between 60 to 80 landing barges are approaching off Colleville-sur-Mer. The regiment is capable of countering all the aforementioned enemy units. The Maisy and Saint-Marcouf artillery batteries are under naval artillery fire.

Barely have they landed on Utah Beach when the amphibious tanks from the 70th Tank Battalion engage in combat against the German strongpoints. US National Archives.

06:56

– The 914th Grenadier Regiment reports that three warships are bombarding the Maisy sector in particular.

The Royal Navy destroyer *HMS Wrestler*. Launched on the 25th of February 1918, this class W warship took part in many convoy escorts in the Atlantic and the Mediterranean, in particular during operations Torch (November 1942) and Husky (July 1943). Too seriously damaged by a mine on the 6th of June 1944, it was scrapped the following month.
Rights Reserved..

EISENHOWER'S MESSAGE IN THE CASE OF DEFEAT

In the event that the Normandy Landings end in failure, General Dwight Eisenhower, commander-in-chief of the Allied Expeditionary Force in Europe, drafted a speech in which he assumed total responsibility for the attack. Immediately after the success of operation Overlord, he crumpled the document and placed it in his waste bin. His military secretary recovered the speech and kept it, so that, today, we can learn of its contents.

'Our landings in the Cherbourg-Le Havre area have failed to gain a satisfactory foothold and I have withdrawn the troops. My decision to attack at this time and place was based upon the best information available. The troops, the air and the navy did all that bravery and devotion to duty could do. If any blame or fault attaches to the attempt it is mine alone. July 5'.

The date of the 5th of July is noteworthy. In 1966, when asked about this date, he replied that it was a minor error on his own part and that he had drafted the note on the 5th of June 1944.

A team of advanced naval artillery observers (Naval Shore Fire Control Party), in position in one of the craters hollowed out by shells, setting up an SCR-284 radio with a GN-45 hand-cranked generator in order to direct gunfire for the Allied armada. The radio operator to the right, using the SCR-536 model, is a Comanche Indian from the 4th Signal Company, 4th (US) Infantry Division, and is using his mother tongue to render messages undecipherable by the enemy. US National Archives.

THE FRENCH FREE AIR FORCE

Three fighter squadrons and two light and heavy bomber squadrons (with previous combat experience in North Africa) belonged to the French Free Air Force (FAFL) or were flown by FAFL pilots. They actively participated in operation Neptune on the night of the 5th to the 6th of June 1944. Other squadrons were engaged in the Battle of Normandy after D-Day.

Squadrons engaged on D-Day with FAFL pilots:

91st Squadron (Supermarine Spitfire XII)

198th Squadron (Hawker Typhoon IB)

329th Squadron 'Cigognes' (Supermarine Spitfire IX)

340th Squadron 'Île-de-France' (Supermarine Spitfire IXB)

341st Squadron 'Alsace' (Supermarine Spitfire)

342nd Squadron 'Lorraine' 1/20 (Douglas Boston III)

345th Squadron 'Berry' (Supermarine Spitfire VB)

602nd Squadron 'City of Glasgow' (Supermarine Spitfire IX)

French pilots and mechanics serving the 'Île-de-France' 340th Squadron, conducting maintenance on the squadron's Spitfire planes. IWM.

THE MAISY ARTILLERY BATTERY

The Maisy battery is located between the villages of Grandcamp and Maisy to the east, and the Vire estuary to the west. In 1944, it was comprised of two strongpoints (Stp 83 'La Perruque' and Stp 84 'La Martinière'), originally built separately, but later connected via the same minefield and a network of barbed wiring. The first fortified bridge at the time was in the locality of La Martinière (Wn 84 or Stp 84), and directed towards the Vire estuary. It was armed by four 100mm Czech FH14/19 (t) guns with a firing range of 6 miles and originally installed on open-air emplacements. Given the increasingly intensive Allied aerial bombardments on the Atlantic Wall, the Germans decided to protect their guns by housing them in firing casemates: thanks to the Organisation Todt, they began the construction of four *Regelbau H612* casemates, but only three were complete and fully operational by D-Day. Stp 84, or 'La Martinière battery' was manned by gunners from the *8./AR1716* and comprised two 75mm anti-aircraft guns, five Vf58c buildings and one R622.

Five hundred yards to the east, stood Stp 83 ('Les Perruques battery'), defended by the 9./AR1716. The Germans installed four open-air gun emplacements to house four 155mm French F414 guns dating from World War I and with a maximum firing range of 7 miles. Two further similar guns reinforced the position; however, insufficient space meant that they were installed in makeshift open-air hollows.

On the night of the 5th to the 6th of June 1944, the Allies launched a massive aerial raid on the Atlantic Wall. It was followed, at dawn, by a naval bombardment executed by *HMS Hawkins*. Despite this deluge of bombs and shells, the site had suffered no major damage when the US troops began to land on Utah and Omaha, the two sectors located the closest to the Maisy battery. The limited range of the battery's 155mm guns nevertheless enabled them to fire on the western border of Omaha Beach, in the Vierville-sur-Mer sector and, according to the G-3 journal drafted by the US 29th Infantry Division on the 6th of June 1944, the 'boys' realised that gunfire was coming from the Maisy battery on the morning of D-Day. The battery was still in action and *HMS Hawkins* resumed fire throughout the day against Stp 83 and Stp 84.

On the 8th of June, General Bradley entrusted Colonel Rudder, commander of the 2nd and 5th Ranger Battalions, who had just captured Pointe du Hoc, with a new mission. This time, they were to take control of the Maisy strongpoint. Already wounded, Rudder knew that his 2nd Battalion was no longer fit for combat. He asked the 5th Battalion, landed on Omaha on the 6th of June 1944, to lead the assault. It began on the morning of the 9th of June. Three 5th Ranger Battalion companies were engaged in the attack, supported by two 2nd Ranger Battalion half-tracks (armed with 75mm guns) and by the 81st Chemical Mortar Battalion's Battery B (armed with 107mm mortars). The rangers also had four 81mm mortars at their disposal. Once the 58th Armored Field Artillery Battalion had neutralised the site, the Americans launched the assault per se, across its 44 hectares. According to veteran testimonies, the fighting was of unprecedented intensity. The barbed wire network was so complex that the Americans lost their bearings several times, adding to the general confusion that reigned throughout the battle and leading to friendly fire incidents. The battery was finally in Allied hands after five hours of fierce combat.

American seamen in charge of transporting the successive waves of assault observe a powerful explosion at the foot of the plateau overlooking Omaha Beach. US National Archives.

07:00

– At his home in Herrlingen in Germany, Field Marshal Rommel is informed by General Speidel of the first details of the Allied offensive in Normandy.

07:04

– The 916th Grenadier Regiment reports that the beach strongpoints are being subjected to a continuous naval artillery barrage.

07:10

– Omaha Beach: the 88mm gun at the Wn 61 resistance nest is unfit for combat, its muzzle brake having been destroyed by a bull's eye hit, either by the naval artillery or by Sergeant Turner Sheppard's Sherman tank.

07:11

– Omaha Beach: the rangers from Task Force A (command company and companies D, E and F from the 2nd Ranger Battalion, reinforced by a coastal control naval detachment), hindered by navigational errors and strong currents, land at Pointe du Hoc 41 minutes behind schedule.

THE LANDINGS AT POINTE DU HOC

The 225 rangers, soaked by the chilly sea swell, suffering from sea sickness and laden with their packs, headed towards the cliffs aboard their LCA landing barges, piloted by British seamen. Their vessels were concealed by the smoke of the explosions, fires and by the smoke screen created to protect the Allied armada. One team was in charge of taking control of Pointe de la Percée, to the east of Pointe du Hoc, a site surmounted with a German radar station. However, due to strong currents, the barges drifted eastwards and, just a few yards before reaching the foreshore, Rudder realised that the cliff they were heading to was not the right one... The landing barges that were to take the troops to Pointe du Hoc changed direction and continued westwards along the shoreline. One of them (LCA 860, transporting soldiers from Company D and their unit commander, Captain Slater) became the target of automatic weapons and mortars and sank. Its crew was rescued by a launch.

The rangers finally arrived within sight of their target at 07:00. At this point in time, the Allies that were still aboard their ships had not yet seen the flare indicating the successful capture of the battery and presumed that the operation had turned into a fiasco. The 500 rangers that were to reinforce Rudder and his men were consequently sent to Omaha Beach, where the landings had already begun...

The Germans in turn had been offered thirty minutes of respite, which had enabled them to gather their spirits after the bombardments, to head for their bunkers, to establish a defensive position, to rearm, etc. And there they were, ready and waiting, with their weapons and grenades, as the Allied troops approached their position. One barge sank amidst the currents and the waves. Only one of its passengers survived, the other rangers dragged down to the depths by their packs. The German machine guns crackled as they spat out their showers of steel over the assault barges. Some of them began to fill with water; one, which was only transporting ammunition supplied for the rangers, exploded in a deafening din, sending shrapnel flying all around. The first LCA reached the pebbled beach to the east of the headland. The rush which resulted from the previous navigational error prevented the rangers from climbing up either side of the Pointe. They all headed for the east side. Then the US Rangers set off, across a five to six-yard stretch of beach, hollowed out by several mortar shells. The first bodies fell to the pebbles, as the escapees used mortars to fire grappling hooks attached to ropes against the cliff, under close-range naval artillery cover. However, the ropes were heavy with water and the hooks fell back onto the beach. Certain rangers then decided to climb the cliff bare-handed, hollowing out holds in the rock with their daggers. The Germans sent showers of grenades along the narrow stretch of beach, along with sustained sprays of MG submachine gunfire.

Some rangers finally managed to reach the summit by means of simple ropes, rope ladders or narrow metallic ladders, whereas others successfully climbed the rock face. A few minutes later, the first American soldiers thrust forwards towards the bunkers to discover a lunar landscape, hollowed out by the bombs. The Germans had disappeared, apart from a few isolated snipers, who opened fire. They used the hollowed craters as shelter, to come as close as possible to the rangers. In just fifteen minutes, Pointe du Hoc was recaptured and secured by the Americans. But the Germans had removed the position's 155mm artillery pieces. Following multiple bombardments, and pending the completion of construction of all the concrete gun shelters, they had been replaced by dummies in the form of wooden stakes, aimed at deluding the Allied reconnaissance planes. Once the element of surprise behind him, Lieutenant-Colonel Rudder organised the defence of the small corner of land that was now under his control.

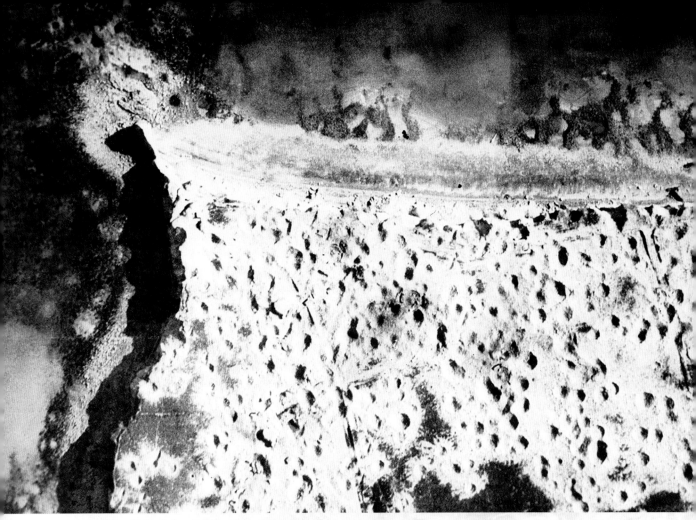

Aerial view of Pointe du Hoc at low tide and the craters caused by the bombardments. The landing barges used to transport the US Rangers can still be seen on the narrow strip of sand, also strewn with craters. IWM (MH 24806).

07:15

– Pointe du Hoc: failing the signal requesting reinforcements at Pointe du Hoc, the rangers from Task Force C head for Dog Green (Omaha Beach).

– Omaha Beach: the 726th Grenadier Regiment reports that Wn 60 has been severely bombed and that 20 landing barges, spotted by Wn 37, are approaching.

– Gold Beach: the landing barges, armed with 127mm rocket launchers, open fire on the coastal defences.

07:20

– Omaha Beach: the 916th Grenadier Regiment reports that amphibious tanks have been identified in the Vierville bay.

– Naval artillery bombardments cease on Gold, Juno and Sword.

– Sword Beach: simultaneous landing of 31 (of a total of 41 engaged) amphibious Sherman tanks belonging to squadrons A and B of the 13th/18th Royal Hussars, along with special tanks belonging to squadron A (reinforced by elements from squadron C) of the 22nd Dragoons, transported by ten LCT (Landing Craft Tank) barges.

THE LANDINGS ON SWORD BEACH

Just like the other invasion beaches, this assault was preceded by aerial then naval bombardments prior to the landing operation which was scheduled for 07:25.

Special assault tanks (a total of 25, familiarly referred to as 'Funnies') and amphibious tanks were the first to land, before the infantry, between Colleville-Plage to the east and the locality of La Brèche to the west. Despite difficult navigation due to very heavy swell, the vessels successfully reached the beach according to schedule. The Germans fired relentlessly, their shells and mortars exploding in the vicinity of their Allied units, wounding or killing the assailants. By the time the infantry began to land, the tanks had already destroyed certain German resistance nests, but the British troops struggled to progress between the shore and the line of houses directly behind the beach, equally because of defensive German gunfire and because of the many beach obstacles that had been installed over such a small area. The rising tide further reduced the beach area which gradually became almost entirely cluttered with an array of material, destroyed vehicles and the bodies of the most unfortunate Allied soldiers.

When Brigadier Simon Fraser, aka Lord Lovat, landed in command of the 1st Special Service Brigade, he was in the company of Bill Millin, a bagpipe player who, prior to the war, had acted as his personal piper. During the ship's journey towards the beach, Lovat said to Millin, who had brought his instrument with him and had played continuously in his military base in England, 'Play *Highland Laddie* for us.' And the piper began to play the requested tune, followed by *The Road to the Isles*. When he set foot on Norman soil, he began this well-known melody, which was even heard by a few Germans, as reported by the veteran Maurice Chauvet from the *1er Bataillon Fusiliers Marins,* 'Suddenly, when Millin began to play, the Germans stopped firing for a few seconds; they couldn't believe their eyes… nor their ears!' »

The assailants sought protection behind the dune or the roadside antitank wall, grouping together, crossing the lines of barbed wiring under fire from the last German resistance nests still in action on the beach, and heading inland, with close-range support from the 'Funnies.' The infantry companies then embarked on the difficult task of cleaning the beaches and of clearing the German defences, some of which still put up staunch resistance.

An LCI (Landing Craft Infantry) landing barge on its way to Sword Beach. The first vehicles from the 27th Armoured Brigade (79th Armoured Division) have just landed.
IWM (B 5102).

Men from the 47th (RM) Commando disembark from their LCA (Landing Craft Assault) barges in the Jig Green sector on Gold Beach, 6th June 1944. IWM (B 5246).

THE LANDINGS ON GOLD BEACH

The British, who had favoured the use of 'Funnies', those tanks of all trades developed by the Allies, were the first to use them to provide close-range support to the infantry and to create access routes in order to evacuate the beach as quickly as possible. Some of them, called 'Crabs', were among the first to land, with the mission of clearing a route through the minefields. As they progressed along the sand between the various beach defences, the landing barges approached the shoreline under fire from the German positions.

The first wave of assault, comprised of men from the Royal Hampshire 1st Battalion - 231st Brigade, began to reach the beach at 07:25. Violent gunfire was exchanged and several soldiers collapsed onto the sand, stopped in their tracks by bullets or shrapnel.

To the east of the Item sector, in front of the village of Le Hamel, which was the departure point for the British troops on their inland advance towards Arromanches, the Germans put up fierce resistance against the adverse units. Indeed, elements from the 352nd Division, who were positioned at the top of

a cliff to the west of Le Hamel, pounded the beach and the landing barges with an 88mm gun. The British infantry then attacked the cliff from behind, supported by special tanks, in particular a 'Petard', which in turn opened fire on its enemy position.

The members of commando N° 47 landed under sustained enemy fire to the east of Arromanches. Then they headed west in order to capture Port-en-Bessin, where they were to join forces with the American troops landed on Omaha Beach. They were welcomed by a wall of projectiles that wreaked death and destruction: of the 14 vessels that were transporting them towards the beach, 4 were destroyed by gun or mortar fire from German positions.

British Sherman tanks landing on Gold Beach from their LCT 1076 (Landing Craft Tank). 6th June 1944. A bulldozer is clearing a pathway across the beach to avoid the tanks becoming stuck in the sand. IWM (B 5259).

British troops from the 50th Infantry Division, landing on Gold Beach with a Sexton self-propelled gun on 6th June 1944. IWM (B 5262).

07:25

– – Gold, Juno and Sword: the special tanks used for beach obstacle and mine clearance land.

– Gold Beach: the British 50th Infantry Division, commanded by Major General Graham, lands.

– Sword Beach: the Avre tanks belonging to the 5th Assault Regiment RE (79th Armoured Division) land.

07:30

– The parachutists from the 3rd Battalion, 502nd PIR (101st Airborne Division) capture exit N° 3 to the west of Utah Beach, near Audouville-la-Hubert.

– Omaha Beach: the surviving rangers from C Company reach the plateau to the east of exit D-1 (Vierville-sur-Mer).

In the Fox Green sector, to the east of Omaha Beach, American soldiers (most of them from the 29th Infantry Division) are stopped in their tracks by German gunfire. Incapable of moving away from the beach, they find short-lived refuge from direct fire at the foot of the cliffs. US National Archives.

The piper Bill Millin (his bagpipes are visible), and Lord Lovat (to the right of the column) landing on Sword Beach on the 6th of June 1944. IWM (B 5103).

Commandos from the 1st Special Service Brigade aboard their LCI (Landing Craft Infantry), prepare to land in the Queen Red sector on Sword Beach on the 6th of June 1944. IWM (MH 33547).

British soldiers from the 3rd Infantry Division in the Queen sector on Sword Beach on the 6th of June 1944. To the left, nurses are tending to the first wounded soldiers, under the protection of an Avre tank from the 5th Assault Regiment, Royal Engineers. IWM (B 5096).

The French commandos from the *1er Bataillon de Fusiliers Marins Commandos* (Commando No. 4) attacking the strongpoint at Ouistreham casino, at a cost of heavy losses. British armoured units support them during their progression. Jose Nicolas / Jacques Witt / Sipa.

– Sword Beach: the French Kieffer commando lands opposite Colleville-sur-Orne.

– Omaha Beach: the 726th Grenadier Regiment reports that 'the first landing barges have grounded by Wn 65 and Wn 69, with amphibious tanks on board.'

Commandos from the staff of the 4th Special Service Brigade landing at Saint-Aubin-sur-Mer in the Nan Red sector on Juno Beach on the 6th of June 1944.
IWM (B 5217).

07:40

– Omaha Beach: the LCI (Landing Craft Infantry) ship number 91 is hit by a mine and by the German artillery, causing the death of 73 soldiers.

07:45

– Pointe du Hoc: the rangers establish temporary headquarters in a crater in front of the L409A anti-aircraft bunker (37mm gun) to the east of the German battery.

– Omaha Beach: the German soldiers at resistance nest Wn 70 announce a breakthrough by six American tanks, three of them now level with Wn 66.

– Omaha Beach: Task Force C, comprised of companies A and B of the 2nd Ranger Battalion, prepare to land between the Dog Green and Dog White sectors. The entire 5th Ranger Battalion heads for Dog Green.

– Juno Beach: the 3rd Canadian Infantry Division, commanded by General Keller, lands.

Landing of Canadian soldiers from the 9th Canadian Infantry Brigade, after leaving their LCI(L) (Landing Craft Infantry (Large)) barges at Bernières-sur-Mer, in the Nan White sector (Juno Beach) shortly before midday on the 6th of June 1944. IWM (A 23938).

THE LANDINGS ON JUNO BEACH

Early in the morning of the 6th of June 1944, the sea was extremely rough in the Juno Beach sector. There are very many underwater rocks off Courseulles-sur-Mer Bernières-sur-Mer and Saint-Aubin-sur-Mer, and the height of the waves increases as it approaches the beach. What's more, on the 6th of June 1944, although it had considerably calmed down since the previous day, the storm that was raging in the English Channel was not yet over. The assault, scheduled for 07:35, was delayed due to heavy swell and poor visibility, both of which prevented the Allied seamen from correctly manoeuvring. Several landing barges hit the mined beach defences that were concealed under the water. The Duplex Drive amphibious tanks were also submerged by the waves, as they gushed over their floating skirts. The landing barges struck the rocks which burst open the hulls, sending them hurtling to the sea bed along with their load.

Immediately, this poor weather was synonymous to delays: the sappers in charge of opening and clearing breaches across the dense fields of beach defences were unable to efficiently accomplish their task with such wild sea conditions. They quickly accumulated a half-hour delay on schedule and, just like on Omaha Beach, they were unable to clear enough openings before the tanks and assault barges arrived. Despite the risks, the ships transporting armoured vehicles (LCT - Landing Craft Transport), came as close as they could to the beach in an attempt to keep losses to a minimum. Indeed, certain amphibious tanks needed to cross a distance of around 600 yards, amidst continuously threatening waves. This is why some of the LCT landing ships unloaded their vehicles direct on the beach. In insufficient numbers and having failed to destroy all the main resistance nests in time, the tank support that was supposed to accompany the infantry was as yet impossible, leaving the latter to face the shock of the attack without direct cover.

This delay enabled the Germans to reorganise themselves, for a time, and to regain their spirits after the preliminary bombings, which although intense had lacked accuracy. They waited for the barges to be sufficiently within range before opening fire with their machine guns, mortars, antitank guns, etc. In this sector, the Canadians found themselves face to face with a formidable and particularly deadly Atlantic Wall.

Of the 306 landing vessels, 90 suffered damage before even reaching French soil. The 3rd Canadian Infantry Division's 7th and 8th Brigades suffered heavy losses and severe delays: 10 minutes for the 7th, 20 for the 8th. The infantry landed before the tanks and entered into action without cover off Bernières-sur-Mer: the men from the Queen's Own Regiment were welcomed by enemy gunfire of extreme intensity, slaying many men as they crossed the 100-yard wide stretch of beach. The assailants were hindered by a 6-feet high protective sea wall that the Germans had taken care to associate within their defensive system, across which the many access routes that linked their various strongpoints were concealed. Without armoured support, the Canadians did their best – in vain – to overcome this obstacle for fifteen minutes. It was only when the amphibious tanks finally arrived (in particular the seven DD tanks belonging to the 6th Armoured Regiment's squadron A, to the west of Courseulles-sur-Mer) that the course of events finally took a turn for the better. They destroyed the German defences one by one, enabling the men from the first waves of assault to attack enemy positions further inland.

08:00

– Utah Beach: four battalions have now landed.

– One of the two Czech 210mm Skoda K52 guns at the Crisbecq battery is put out of action by Allied naval fire.

– Omaha Beach: American soldiers reach the top of the plateau at the Wn 60 resistance nest.

– Omaha Beach: landing of men from the 5th Ranger Battalion, initially planned to land at Pointe du Hoc.

Isolated after an inaccurate drop, this stick of parachutists from cell S2 (intelligence) of the command company, 508th Parachute Infantry Regiment, 82nd Airborne Division, is crossing the village of Saint-Marcouf on D-Day before heading to the positions already held by the regiment. US National Archives.

THE CRISBECQ ARTILLERY BATTERY

The Crisbecq battery is located in the Cotentin peninsula, near the hamlet of the same name, on high ground around two miles from the shoreline. It was the most powerful artillery battery in all the German defences in the Landing Beach zone. It is also known as the Saint-Marcouf battery.

Its construction, which began in 1942, was entrusted to the Organisation Todt, the body in charge of all the Atlantic Wall installations. On this site initially comprised of six 155mm guns, which were later moved to a nearby position in Fontenay-sur-Mer, the Germans planned to build four *Regelbau R683* casemates, each one to house a 210mm gun (Skoda K39/40 guns with a firing range in excess of 20 miles), along with a firing command post.

By the spring of 1944, only two *R683* casemates were complete and operational (even if the mobile gun shields had not yet been added) and only three 210mm guns had been installed: the Allied bombings, which had accelerated since the month of April the same year, prevented work from continuing according to plan. On the 5th of June 1944, a third casemate was still under construction and work on the fourth had not yet begun. The *Regelbau R683* casemate proved to be difficult and costly to build, each casemate requiring around 100 tonnes of steel and over 70,000 cubic feet of concrete. The battery was reinforced by one 105mm gun.

In addition, the site of the Crisbecq battery boasted six 75mm guns of French origin and three 20mm guns, used for anti-aircraft defence. The area around the battery was protected by means of 70 machine guns, which could be equally installed in small Tobruk type bunkers or on simple firing positions. The site was surrounded by a wall of barbed wire fencing and minefields, across which ran a number of trenches, with troop shelters and ammunition holds. The coastal artillery position also housed an observation post for the Azeville battery, located just over a mile away.

In June 1944, the Crisbecq battery was manned by a garrison of 320 soldiers, commanded by *Oberleutnant Zur See* (Naval Sub-Lieutenant) Walter Ohmsen. Similar to the other German batteries located along the Normandy coastline, Crisbecq was heavily bombed by the Allied aviation on the night of the 5th to the 6th of June 1944. A total of 598 tonnes of bombs were dropped, killing dozens of German soldiers and destroying all the anti-aircraft guns and one of the 210mm guns.

In the early hours of D-Day, American parachutists belonging to the 502nd Parachute Infantry Regiment (101st Airborne Division) attacked the Crisbecq battery. These soldiers, who had been dropped in the region of Saint-Martin-de-Varreville, well beyond their planned zone, had done their utmost, but found themselves face to face with steadfast German defences. Twenty of them were taken prisoner. At 05:55, the Crisbecq battery opened fire on the Allied armada off Utah Beach, one of the American sectors. At the same time, an Allied plane in charge of creating a smoke screen to protect the warships positioned around the Îles Saint-Marcouf, off Crisbecq, was shot down by the German anti-aircraft defence. Benefiting from an excellent viewpoint over the destroyer, the Crisbecq gunners opened fire on *USS Corry*. Simultaneous to the first landings on Utah, the American destroyer was hit by shells just under the surface of the water, level with the keel and began to sink.

Both the Crisbecq and the Azeville batteries then concentrated their firing power on the sinking warship. One of the shells hit the ship's 40mm gun carriages setting off the explosion of the nearby ammunition. At 06:40, George Dewey Hoffman, the ship's commander, gave orders to evacuate.

At 08:00, one of the battery's last two 210mm guns was put out of action by gunfire from the American warships *USS Arkansas, USS Nevada and USS Texas*. At 09:00, a direct hit destroyed the only remaining gun. The German artillerymen immediately set to assessing the damage sustained by the guns and embarked, wherever possible, upon repairing them (one of the guns was brought back to working order on the 8th of June, to immediately suffer further damage by the Allied warships).

From the 6th to the 11th of June, the German soldiers barricaded themselves inside the battery and were subjected to a series of attacks by units from the US 4th Infantry Division, landed on Utah Beach on D-Day. Reinforced by artillery observers and men from the *919. Infanterie Regiment*, Walter Ohmsen steadfastly defended his battery, even asking for the 105mm guns in Azeville to fire in its direction when the American assailants managed to penetrate the site. He finally received orders to break off contact and to abandon his position, now encircled by enemy units.

On the night of the 11th to the 12th of June 1944, he left the battery undetected and managed to reach the German lines further north, along with 78 other soldiers. Twenty-one of them were left inside the battery to be cared for by a volunteer nurse. The Americans from the 9th Infantry Division's 39th Regiment could then take control of the battery without further combat. A few days later, Ohmsen was decorated with the Iron Cross for his resistance over almost a week against the American military forces.

Over the weeks that followed the capture of the Crisbecq battery, the American military engineers conducted resistance tests on the German casemates, using large quantities of explosives, the effects of which caused more damage than the previous bombardments.

One of the four *Regelbau R683* casemates at the Crisbecq coastal artillery battery, manned by the *Marine-Artillerie-Abteilung 260*. Each of the casemates housed a 210mm gun (Skoda K39/40) with a firing range of over 20 miles. US National Archives.

08:05

— Juno Beach: the 3rd Canadian Infantry Division informs of the explosion of around sixteen shells per minute in the Mike Green sector.

– Orders are given to the German 200th Tanks Destroyer Regiment to advance towards the region of Martragny, Vendes and Basly.

– Report from the 916th Grenadier Regiment to the staff of the German 352nd Infantry Division, 'Relatively weak enemy units have penetrated Pointe du Hoc. The 1st section of the 726th Infantry Regiment is engaged in an immediate counter-attack. Fifty men have landed before Wn 68 at Vierville. Others in smaller numbers before Wn 62.'

08:06

– Omaha Beach: the 726th Grenadier Regiment reports that Wn 60 is under enemy fire and that 40 soldiers with an amphibious tank have just landed in front of the strongpoint.

08:09

– Omaha Beach: all the amphibious tanks that were supposed to land on the Fox Green sector have sunk between their departure point and the beach.

THE DRAMATIC FATE OF THE AMPHIBIOUS TANKS ON OMAHA

In contrast with the soldiers on the Anglo-Canadian beaches and on Utah, the Americans that landed on Omaha Beach benefited from unequal cover from armoured units. A total of 112 tanks (Sherman amphibious Duplex Drive tanks equipped with snorkels and Sherman bulldozers) belonging to the 741st and the 743rd Tank Battalions were supposed to land at 06:30 on Omaha to offer close-range support to the infantry.

As from 03:00 on the 6th of June, 64 Sherman DD tanks were to be put to the water before reaching the beach by their own steam. The other armoured vehicles were to be unloaded direct on the beach, as per the assault plan.

The amphibious Duplex Drive tanks from the 741st Tank Battalion (TB) were in charge of offering support to the 16th Infantry Regiment (1st Infantry Division) at Colleville-sur-Mer. However, the sea was extremely rough and these vehicles, designed to navigate in mild conditions, failed to withstand the heavy swell. All the tanks belonging to squadron C, i.e. 16 vehicles, sank in the Channel. Thirteen of the 16 DDs belonging the squadron B also sank. After the first of the four DDs aboard the LCT (6)-600 barge had sunk, Ensign Henry Sullivan decided to take the squadron's three other tanks direct to the beach. For the 741st Tank Battalion, 5 amphibious tanks, 6 snorkel tanks and 5 bulldozer tanks managed to reach the shore. Unfortunately, several crews were taken down with their vehicles.

The 743rd Tank Battalion decided to operate differently and to land the tanks directly on the Dog Green and Dog Red beach sectors, at Vierville-sur-Mer, at the risk of losing or damaging the transport ships. But the LCT (Landing Craft Tank) vessels, successfully came within reach of the shoreline and managed to return to higher seas without encountering major difficulty. Thirty-two Sherman DDs, 7 snorkels and 3 Sherman bulldozers from the 743rd Tank Battalion also managed to reach the beach.

A total of 58 tanks had made their way to solid ground on Omaha Beach: but as early as 07:00, 14 of them had already been destroyed or abandoned. The others remained on the beach, blocked by the antitank wall, or struggled to progress along the pebbles and shingle. Lacking sufficient firing power, the infantrymen were incapable of reducing the German defensive positions to silence. The tanks from the 741st Tank Battalion became a prime target for the German gunners and only three of them were still fit for combat at the day end.

Omaha Beach, Easy Red sector, to the west of Le Ruquet: shortly before 11:00, three Sherman tanks from the 741st Tank Battalion manoeuvre as best they can on the pebbles, with their guns targeting the beach exit codenamed Easy-1. The one on the left is a Duplex Drive amphibious tank: it is one of the three (of a total of sixteen) remaining tanks belonging to Squadron B. The two others, equipped with snorkels, belong to Squadron A. US National Archives.

08:15

– Utah Beach: Colonel Cassidy, commander of the US 1st Battalion, 501st Parachute Infantry Regiment announces that the Saint-Martin-de-Varreville battery has been destroyed.

– Pointe du Hoc: 1st Sergeant Leonard G. Lomell and Staff Sergeant Jack E. Kuhn (D Company, 2nd Ranger Battalion), discover five field guns less than a mile to the south of the battery. They are immediately neutralised.

08:19

– Pointe du Hoc: the 916th Grenadier Regiment informs the staff of the German 352nd Infantry Division that, 'Near Pointe du Hoc, the enemy has scaled the cliff (with ladders and ropes fired with hand weapons).

08:20

– Omaha Beach: the 726th Grenadier Regiment reports that the 88mm gun at Wn 61 is unfit for use and that barges are preparing to land in front of Wn 37 and Wn 37a (the latter having been bombarded by naval artillery).

– Gold Beach: the Green Howards 7th Battalion lands.

– Sword Beach: landing of Commando N°4 in its entirety.

LCT (Landing Craft Tank) landing barges crossing the English Channel on their way to Normandy. IWM (B 5108).

THE KIEFFER COMMANDO

Philippe Kieffer, one of the first French citizens to join the Free French Forces, was entrusted with commanding 16 volunteer troops in April 1942. They trained at the Camberley camp in Britain, in the company of Lieutenant Jean Pinelli. Early May 1942, the small troop of 23 men was certified at the Achnacarry camp in Scotland and officially named the *1re Compagnie, Fusiliers Marins Commandos*. When in training at the Eastney depot, the men were reinforced a little later when Lieutenant Charles Trepel was appointed as Kieffer's second-in-command. Their commando training was arduous and involved selective tests. The men were expected to conduct manoeuvres in all weather conditions, amidst all sorts of obstacles, and to do marches, to train with real bullets, to train in close combat, etc.

On the 14th of July 1942, the small company, by now comprised of around thirty men, paraded in the streets of London on the occasion of Bastille Day. On the 10th of August, the 1st Company was attached to the N° 10 (Inter-Allied) Commando, based in Wales and within which troops could be of all origins (not only from Belgium, Holland, Norway, Poland or Czechoslovakia but also Anti-Nazis from Germany and Austria). On the 31st of May, the N° 10 Commando established its headquarters in Eastbourne in Sussex. The 1st Company (aka Troop 1) then comprised a total of 81 men. Fifteen French soldiers took part in the Dieppe raid on the 19th of August 1942. The 1st Company, which had been divided into three groups with the mission to reinforce other commandos and the Canadian troops, had refused to wear helmets, preferring caps and the red pompom sailor caps worn by the French Navy. The men had also kept the 'France' strips that were sewn onto their uniforms. Commander Guy Vourc'h landed opposite the casino in Dieppe, in the centre of the assault zone. The two other commando groups headed for the coastal artillery batteries, in particular in Varengeville, where Privates Rabouhans and Taverne from Lord Lovat's Commando N° 4 did a fabulous job in securing the escape route which proved vital for the rest of the operation. However, by early

Soldiers from Commando No. 4 on their way through Colleville-sur-Orne on D-Day. IWM (B 5067).

afternoon the situation had turned to catastrophe and the French commandos received orders to cut contact and to return to their ships. One of them, S. Montailler, was seriously wounded and died in the field. Initially taken prisoner, M. César managed to escape and to return to England via Spain. After the Dieppe raid, the existence of this French commando was made official.

In March 1944, all of the French commandos were officially named the *1er Bataillion Fusiliers Marins Commandos*. At the end of the month, the battalion headed for Scotland (near Nairn) for a series of large-scale manoeuvres that lasted five days and involved the British 3rd Infantry Division, Royal Navy units and several elements from the Royal Air Force. At the end of the exercise, the battalion was attached to Lord Lovat's Special Service Brigade (Commando N°4). Throughout the month of April, training intensified in Sussex (specifically in Bexhille-on-Sea). During an inspection in May 1944, Admiral Dargenlieu decorated the unit. On the 25th of May, the battalion was isolated at the Titchefield base, where contact with the outside world was strictly forbidden for all men. From the 2nd to the 5th of June, the French commandos, along with Commando n°4, boarded their transport ships.

At 17:00 on the 5th of June 1944, the French commandos boarded two LCI (Landing Craft Infantry): LCI 527 for Troop 1 and LCI 528 for Troop 8. The commando's 177 men were informed of the invasion fleet's destination at 22:00 on the 5th of June: Normandy. Their specific destination was in the vicinity of the village of Hermanville-sur-Mer, opposite the locality called La Brèche (Sword Beach). At 07:32 on Tuesday the 6th of June 1944, the French soldiers set foot on home soil. They set off immediately to attack Ouistreham, along with their British counterparts from the 1st Special Service Brigade, Commando N°4.

6th June 1944. Captain Sir Harold Campbell and Commander A. Kimmins from the Royal Navy observe landing operations by the 50th Infantry Division on Gold Beach, from the passenger ship *HMS (MV) Bulolo*, the flagship of Task Force G. I IWM (A 23882).

Aboard the American transport ship USS LST 25, American 20mm gun servers and British soldiers observe the ongoing assault on Gold Beach. 6th June 1944. IWM (A 23894).

08:24

– Omaha Beach: the landed troops report that they are under enemy fire from the Maisy batteries.

08:25

– Omaha Beach: Wn 62 is infiltrated by isolated American soldiers, whilst Wn 61 is attacked from the front and the rear. German radio contact with Port-en-Bessin is cut.

– Gold Beach: landing of the Royal Marines Commando N°47.

08:30

– Omaha Beach: landings are temporarily interrupted due to insufficient space on the beach. For a few minutes, the Germans believe they have won.

– Omaha Beach: counter-attack by the 915th Grenadier Regiment aimed at recapturing Wn 60.

– Omaha Beach: General Cota, second-in-command of the 29th US Infantry Division has established his command post on the beach.

– Sword Beach: the German pilots Priller and Wodarczyk (*Jagdgeschwader 26*) take off from their base in Bondues to the north of Lille and fly over the beach aboard two Focke Wulf 190 planes. They land without difficulty at the Creil (*Jagdgeschwader 2*) airbase.

– Sergeant Davies' men from the 1st Canadian Parachute Battalion's C Company explode the bridge over the Dives at Varaville with help from sappers from the 3rd Parachute Squadron RE.

LCT (Landing Craft Tank) landing barges off Gold Beach on the 6th of June 1944. IWM (A 23912).

THE INTERMEDIATE SITUATION ON OMAHA

At 10:00, American forces had been making no or little headway on Omaha Beach: a few men from the 1st Infantry Division's 16th Regiment (1st, 2nd and 3rd Battalions) attempted a breakthrough. Miraculously, they managed to group together to form a force of around 200 men. Taking advantage of the thick smoke that was emanating from a fire on the plateau caused by Allied bombing, the soldiers progressed, sometimes using their gas masks for protection.

General Bradley observed the evolution of events on Omaha from the deck of the cruiser *USS Augusta*. Naval reports were catastrophic and losses excessively high. Bradley even considered for an instant permanently putting a stop to the waltz of reinforcements that were being sent to Omaha, to redirect them towards Utah Beach, where reports were far more encouraging. However, he finally persuaded himself that the only way the Allies could hope to take control of the beach was to send more and more reinforcements. The Germans were bound to give in at some point in time under the weight of the immense American war machine.

The Americans nevertheless feared that the Germans might manage to bring in reinforcements over the hours to come. Should their adversaries obtain reinforcements, tanks in particular, breaking through the line of defence appeared increasingly complicated. However, these German reinforcements never arrived - the Third Reich generals were ill-informed of the situation and did not deem necessary the detachment of heavy units towards the beaches, in particular their armoured divisions (the *21. Panzer-Division* was positioned to the south of Caen).

On the beach, the vehicles that had not yet been destroyed by German guns found themselves unable to break through the chaos of dead and wounded soldiers, burning vehicles, helmets, weapons, cartridge belts and clothing... all abandoned and transforming Omaha, to the eyes of those who remained, into the most realistic of hells on earth. Genuine concern grew among the US Army officers as the shadow of defeat began to swathe the contours of Omaha Beach. Major General Clarence Huebner, commander of the 1st Infantry Division, asked for the naval artillery to offer the closest possible cover to the landed infantry units. Certain Allied ships came within 800 yards of the beach to fire almost at point-blank range on the German fortifications, which continued to spew out bullets and shells on the assailants as they swarmed over the beach.

At around 11:00, more and more breakthroughs were made towards the plateau and hundreds of soldiers, dazed by the cold and the noise, thrust forth to attack the ever-active German positions that loomed above the foreshore. Whilst vehicle landings had been temporarily suspended, hundreds of infantrymen continued to set foot on the beach that was already referred to as Bloody Omaha. The 18th Infantry Regiment, freshly landed on the Easy sector, headed for the plateau and advanced towards the village of Colleville-sur-Mer, where the 16th Regiment was already engaged in combat. The German positions that overlooked the shoreline were captured one by one from the rear and, little by little, the deafening din on Omaha died down in the afternoon. The vehicles were once more allowed to land, for the sappers had cleared a further 5 beach exits, giving a total of 6 possibilities from the initially planned 16. By late afternoon, the beach was under control, but only on an intermittent basis. Early in the evening, the coastal road linking Vierville-sur-Mer, Saint-Laurent-sur-Mer and Colleville-sur-Mer was reached by different groups of American troops. The bridgehead, which had previously reached a length of 3.1 miles, i.e. the total length of Omaha Beach itself, grew to cover a 6 mile-long and 2 mile-deep front.

At the extremities of Omaha Beach, near Vierville-sur-Mer and Colleville-sur-Mer, natural pebbled walls offer elementary protection to the American soldiers stuck on the beach. US National Archives.

THE LUFTWAFFE IN NORMANDY

On the 6th of June 1944, only squadrons *I/JG 2*, *I/JG 26*, *III/JG 26* and the Stab were present in the zone.

Richthofen's squadron I/JG 2 had its 19 FW 190 planes take off and head for the Normandy coast, armed with rocket launchers. Lieutenant Fischer from the *III/JG2* claimed to have successfully fired on a Victory class Allied ship.

I/SKG 10 (*Schnellkampfgeschwader* - rapid bomber squadron) was engaged on the night of the 5th to the 6th of June, with four destroyed Allied Lancaster bombers to its credit. *SKG 10* claimed its first Lancaster at 05:01 on the 6th of June, in the vicinity of Isigny-sur-Mer.

IV/ JG 3 had all its planes stationed in Normandy take off. These units were specialised in fighting against Allied bombers.

Three He Heinkel 177 belonging to *KG 30* (*Kampfgeschwader* - bomber squadron) took off from Bordeaux for a bombing mission by night (with the bridgehead as its target), but the three planes were shot down by Allied Mosquitos (fighter planes) before they could begin their operation. For the day of the 6th of June alone, the *SKG 10* and *JG 2* squadrons, which completed their task at around 21:00 claimed to have eliminated 23 Allied craft. Considerable reinforcements arrived over the following days: 200 extra fighter planes over the 36 hours that followed D-Day and 100 more by the 10th of June 1944.

One intervention by two German planes met with particular renown thanks to the book *The Longest Day* by Cornelius Ryan. It was led by *Geschwaderkommodore* Joseph Priller from *JG 26*. Priller and his winger Heinz Wodarczyk were the only pilots from *JG 26* to gun the Allied beaches at Sword and Juno during the landing operations. They were the first Germans in contact with the landed troops. The squadron's other planes, based in the north of France, were on a mission to combat Allied bombardments in Germany. Although the two *Luftwaffe* pilots were convinced they would never come back to base, they returned safe and sound. When they flew over the beaches, no anti-aircraft defence had yet been landed and prepared to fire. Furthermore, they were flying at low altitude and Allied fighter planes, which were at higher altitude, were of no threat to them.

Oberstleutnant Josef Priller preparing to board his Focke-Wulf Fw 190A-8 fighter plane. On D-Day, he commanded *Jagdgeschwader* 26 over the Calvados beaches, along with his compatriot Heinz Wodarczyk. Bundesarchiv.

On 6th of June 1944, these commandos from No. 4 Commando, 1st Special Service Brigade have produced a makeshift stretcher to take one of their wounded men to Sword Beach, as the rest of the unit heads for Ouistreham. IWM (BU 1190).

These men from the Royal Marine Commando are clearly proud to be finally engaged in combat near Colleville-sur-Orne (today Colleville-Montgomery), Sword Beach, 6th June 1944. IWM (B 5075).

08:33

— Omaha Beach: LCT 538 reports that it has been unable to unload its vehicles due to gunfire from an 88mm gun that has wounded 5 American soldiers.

08:35

— Omaha Beach: the Americans take their first four German prisoners among men from the 916th Regiment's 8th Company (352nd Infantry Division).

— Omaha Beach: the 352nd Infantry Division reports to the 84th Army Corps that between 100 and 200 soldiers have penetrated defences at Colleville and that a battalion (Meyer Battalion) has engaged in combat to reinforce German defence.

08:45

— Omaha Beach: the 916th Grenadier Regiment reports that Wn 70 has fallen into enemy hands. Three tanks have crossed the Wn 66 resistance nest and the upper casemate at Wn 62 has been destroyed.

— Sword Beach: landing of the Royal Marines Commando N° 41.

These men from the 3rd Infantry Division are continuing landing operations in the Queen Red sector on Sword Beach. In the foreground, the sappers from the 84th Field Company Royal Engineers, No.5 Beach Group can be easily recognised thanks to the white stripe on their helmets and the anchor on their shoulder badges. IWM (B 5114).

WN 62

Wn 62 was located to the west of a plateau dominating a dell called La Révolution, near Colleville-sur-Mer. It was one of the three defensive positions around the village of Colleville, immediately inland from Omaha Beach. It was comprised of two *H669* casemates and one *H667* casemate and was manned by 23 soldiers from the *3. Kompanie* (*726. Infanterie-Regiment*, *716. Infanterie-Division*).

Composition of Wn 62:

- Two 75mm (FK 235 b) guns housed in an *H669* casemate

- One 50mm mortar (Gr.W 201 f) housed in a Tobruk.

- One 50mm gun (KWK L/42) housed in an *H667* casemate.

- Several flamethrowers and machine gun emplacements.

Configuration of Wn 62 on Omaha Beach

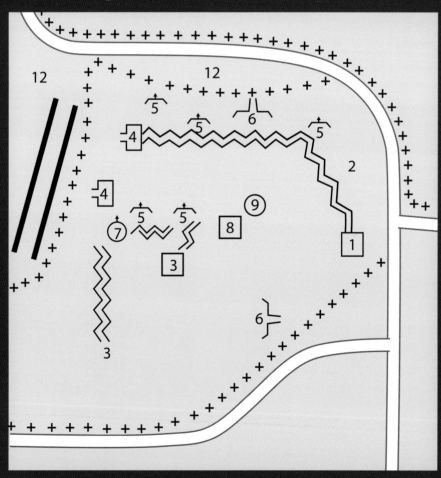

1. Villa used as a kitchen.	6. 50mm antitank guns.	11. Antitank ditch.
2. Ammunition shelter.	7. 50mm mortar housed in a Tobruk.	12. Mined ground.
3. Personnel and ammunition shelter.	8. Observatory.	+ Barbed wire networks and barrages.
4. *Blockhaus* housing a 75mm gun.	9. Platform, temporary gun emplacement.	// Trenches.
5. Machine guns of different calibres and origins.	10. Tobruk housing a projector.	

08:49

– Omaha Beach: the US 116th Infantry Regiment's 1st Battalion signals that it is at a standstill due to heavy machine gunfire and requests support from the naval artillery.

08:55

– Omaha Beach: the 352nd Artillery Regiment struggles to maintain radio contact with Wn 60.

08:57

– Omaha Beach: the 726th Grenadier Regiment reports that 30 enemy tanks have landed between Wn 35 and Wn 36.

09:00

– The second 210mm gun at the Crisbecq battery is put out of action by Allied ships.

– Pointe du Hoc: the rangers drive back a counter-attack by the German 916th Infantry Regiment's 1st Company.

– Omaha Beach: the Wn 60 resistance nest (Red Fox sector) protecting the beach exit F1 is reduced to silence by men from the US 1st Infantry Division.

– Sword Beach: the survivors from the Kieffer Commando's Troop 8 set up support positions at the Riva-Bella strongpoint.

– The high speed craft belonging to the German 5th Squadron have returned to Le Havre.

– Hitler awakes after a late night listening to Wagner.

British soldiers from the 3rd Infantry Division on their way out of the Queen sector on Sword Beach, to head inland. Some of them have bicycles to quickly reach their targets. IWM (B 5078).

THE INTERMEDIATE SITUATION AT POINTE DU HOC

Lieutenant-Colonel Rudder organised the defence of the small spot of land he was in control of. He established communication links with the Allied armada shortly after 08:00, from the command post he had set up behind the anti-aircraft defence bunker to the east of the battery, 'This is Rudder, the Hoc is under control… I need reinforcements and ammunition… Heavy losses!' A little later, he received a reply, 'Good job. No reinforcements available, all rangers have landed on Omaha.'

Losses were indeed extremely high, but Rudder had to make do. The warships off shore launched an artillery barrage around the zones under American control. 1st Sergeant Leonard G. Lomell and Staff Sergeant Jack E. Kuhn from Company D of the 2nd Ranger Battalion discovered five field artillery pieces less than a mile to the south of the battery, camouflaged behind a hedge and in firing position. Dozens of German soldiers were ready to intervene a further 100 yards to the south. The young American sergeant gave orders to his buddy to observe the German positions as he personally launched two thermal grenades on the first two guns. Also referred to as thermites, these grenades produced an aluminothermic chemical reaction that melted any nearby metal. Lomell destroyed the sight systems of the other howitzers with the stock of his Thompson submachine gun which he swathed in his jacket to avoid making too much noise. After this successful operation, the patrol then retraced its steps to recover extra grenades and to finish the job. Ten minutes later, it was all over and the two rangers immediately withdrew.

The eastern sector of the cliff was bombarded around midday and Lieutenant-Colonel Rudder was wounded. A small US flag was hoisted to mark out the zone and to indicate to the warships out at sea that the sector was now held by friendly forces. Throughout the afternoon, the rangers were subjected to successive attacks, one from Grandcamp-les-Bains by the *2. Kompanie, 914. Grenadier-Regiment* (*352. Infanterie-Division*), and from a company belonging to the 3rd Battalion, *726 Grenadier-Regiment* (*716. Infanterie-Division*). Rudder's men were lucky to have the destroyer *USS Satterlee* nearby. The ship provided continuous and life-saving support, exhausting 70% of its total ammunition by 17:00. All the rangers were now to do was to wait for the reinforcements that were supposed to land on Omaha Beach.

6th June 1944 – a DUKW amphibious vehicle put to sea from its transport ship before heading towards the Normandy coast. IWM (B 5014).

At Pointe du Hoc, these US Rangers climb the 100 feet cliff with whatever means are at their disposal: ropes, rope ladders and metallic ladders. Ladders borrowed from the London fire brigade were also used after D-Day. US National Archives.

09:05

– The Canadian soldiers landed on the Mike Red sector report that the situation is now excellent.

09:10

– Omaha Beach: the rangers who landed on the beach report that the tide is rising fast and that the beach obstacles have still not been demolished. By radio, they request demolition teams in reinforcement.

09:15

– The German 352nd Infantry Division records in its log book the loss of resistance nests Wn 65, Wn 68 and Wn 70.

– Lieutenant Shave's men from the 3rd section of the 3rd Parachute Squadron RE explode the Bures bridge over the Dives.

09:16

– Two companies from the *21. Panzer-Division* (*7./192* and 8.(*schw.*)/192) receive orders to set up resistance positions to the north of Périers-sur-le-Dan and Saint-Aubin-d'Arquenay.

09:17

– Issue of Communiqué N°1, 'Under the command of General Eisenhower, Allied naval forces, supported by strong air forces, began landing Allied armies this morning on the northern coast of France.'

09:20

– The ships positioned off Omaha Beach organise a new artillery barrage on the German defences, as per General Huebner's request, despite the risk of hitting American soldiers. The attack lasts 25 minutes.

– The German artillery battery in Longues-sur-Mer temporarily ceases fire towards the sea.

09:21

– The 716th Infantry Division reports that around 30 enemy tanks are moving towards Meuvaines.

09:25

— Omaha Beach: the 352nd Artillery Regiment reports that around 6 amphibious tanks have been destroyed by mortar fire in front of Wn 35.

– Sword Beach: at Ouistreham, the amphibious tank (belonging to the 13th/18th Hussars) requested by *Capitaine de Corvette* Kieffer in reinforcement arrives at the Casino bunker and opens fire, enabling the French commandos from the *1er Bataillon Marins* to reduce the position to silence.

Universal Carrier vehicles belonging to the 1st Dorsetshire Regiment, 231st Brigade, 50th Infantry Division leaving their barges in the Jig sector on Gold Beach on 6th June 1944. The LCT 928, LCT 710, LCT 858 and LCM 244 can be seen in the background. IWM (B 5244).

THE OUISTREHAM CASINO

After capturing the various German fortified positions around the assault zone, landed troops needed to gain control of the neighbouring villages before continuing their advance towards Caen, which was expected to be under Allied control by the evening of the 6th of June. At around 09:30, the British infantrymen from the 1st South Lancs entered Hermanville and found themselves face to face with pockets of German resistance.

It was only around midday that the beach was finally cleared and of its debris and that enough breaches had been opened for the freshly landed reinforcements to rapidly leave the shore. The troops from the first assault accelerated inland towards Ouistreham and its famous 'Casino' defensive position. It was resistance nest Wn 10, a fortification located on the seafront at Riva-Bella in charge of defending access to the Stp 08 strongpoint (comprised in particular of the 1260th Artillery Regiment's firing command post). Wn 10 comprised a 626 type flanking casemate (still under construction at the time of the landings) equipped with a 75mm FK 38 gun. This strongpoint was also armed with an antitank gun housed within the bunker that had replaced the famous casino (inelegantly represented in the film *The Longest Day*) and with an sMG 34 machine gun housed under a cupola on top of an *H644* type construction.

The Kieffer Commando Troop 8 took up a support position to the east and Troop 1 launched a northwards assault. But the Germans resisted. Despite being wounded, *Capitaine de Corvette* Philippe Kieffer, managed to obtain support from British tanks which managed to unsettle the defensive positions. Robert Lion, a medical officer in Kieffer's commando, was killed by a lone German sniper who shot him in the heart during the assault, as he was trying to help *Matelot* Paul Rollin who was seriously wounded. The bunker was under control by late morning, but Stp 08 continued to withstand the Franco-British attacks. The strongpoint was only totally captured three days later.

Amphibious Sherman tanks from Squadron B, 13th/18th Royal Hussars offer support to the French and British commandos from No.4 Commando, 1st Special Service Brigade at Ouistreham on 6th June 1944. IWM (MH 2011).

The beach at Saint-Aubin-sur-Mer (Juno Beach) on 6th of June 1944, the landing site for the British commandos from the 49th (Royal Marine) Commando, 4th Special Service Brigade. They sustained heavy losses there, in particular when two of their landing barges hit beach obstacles and sank. IWM (B 5225).

Canadian soldiers from the North Shore (New Brunswick) Regiment's Company B, protecting themselves from enemy gunfire amidst the obstacles in front of the German strongpoint codenamed Wn 27 at Saint-Aubin-sur-Mer (Juno Beach) on 6th June 1944. IWM (B 5228).

09:30

— Omaha Beach: As the men from the US 1st Infantry Division's 16th Regiment are on their way to Port-en-Bessin, General Omar Bradley receives an estimation of losses – 3,000 men unfit for combat.

– Gold Beach: the 352nd Artillery Regiment reports that the Wn 35 and 36 resistance nests have been destroyed, whereas the Wn 40 guns have destroyed 4 Allied tanks and 3 landing barges.

– Gold Beach: ten German Focke Wulf 190 fighter planes attack the beach.

– Juno Beach: the village of Bernières is liberated by men from the North Shore Regiment and the Queen's Own Rifles.

– Sword Beach: the village of Hermanville-sur-Mer is liberated by the South Lancashire Regiment, as the 1st Suffolk lands.

09:45

– End of the second artillery barrage on Omaha Beach.

– A Royal Air Force reconnaissance patrol reports the presence of armoured vehicles to the north of Caen.

09:55

– The German 352nd Infantry Regiment signals that all radio contact with the 916th Grenadier Regiment has been cut.

British commandos from the 48th (Royal Marine) Commando, 4th Special Service Brigade, head inland with their equipment, near Langrune-sur-Mer (Juno Beach) on D-Day. IWM (B 5220).

THE INTERMEDIATE SITUATION ON JUNO BEACH

As from 08:35, Companies C and D of the Regina Rifles Regiment landed in the Nan Green sector and, in turn, launched their attack on the village of Courseulles. Landed Duplex Drive amphibious tanks from Squadron B of the 6th Canadian Armoured Regiment (1st Hussars) increased the Canadians' firing power and enabled them to progressively silence Wn 29 thanks to direct fire from the tanks.

The Queen's Own Rifles of Canada landed off Bernières-sur-Mer as from 08:12. Finding itself immediately face to face with Wn 28, Company B sustained heavy losses. Also behind schedule, the Fort Garry Horse amphibious tanks were cruelly lacking on the beach. The infantry finally managed to bypass the German defences and to take them from the rear. By the time the first line of German defence fell into Canadian hands, the Queen's Own Rifles had lost 65 of its men on the beach. Having suffered less than Company B, Company A engaged westwards towards Bernières and began its slow progression under fire from mortars and isolated snipers. The *Régiment de la Chaudière* (8th Brigade), comprised of French-speaking Canadians, landed at Bernières-sur-Mer as from 08:30 to reinforce their exhausted compatriots who had already borne the brunt of the battle. The tanks belonging to the Fort Gary Horse B Squadron finally arrived on the beach to offer support to the *Chaudière*. Bernières-sur-Mer was totally under Canadian control by late morning. Major General Rodney Keller and the staff of the 3rd Infantry Division set up headquarters in the Château de Semilly, in the village's Rue des Ormes as from 12:45.

To the west of Courseulles, the Royal Winnipeg Rifles faced staunch resistance, worsened by gunfire from another German strongpoint in Graye-sur-Mer: Wn 31. In the village, several isolated snipers also considerably hindered Allied progression. Courseulles-sur-Mer was entirely under Canadian control by late afternoon. The landing of Duplex Drive amphibious tanks belonging to the 6th Canadian Armoured Regiment (1st Hussars) increased the firing power of the Canadian forces and toppled the force ratio in their favour. The stunned Germans either withdrew or were killed in their positions. Companies A and C of the Royal Winnipeg Rifles successfully liberated Graye-sur-Mer early afternoon.

On Juno Beach at Bernières-sur-Mer, Victor Deblois, a Canadian soldier from the *Régiment de la Chaudière*, poses for military propaganda purposes as he keeps these German prisoners in check with his Sten submachine gun. National Archives Canada.

– Omaha Beach: 2 American destroyers (*USS Doyle* and *USS Emmons*) approach within less than a mile of the beach to provide close-range support for isolated groups as they try to leave the beaches.

– Omaha Beach: around 200 soldiers from the 1st Battalion, 116th Regiment (US 29th Infantry Division) have reached the plateau and are progressing towards Vierville-sur-Mer.

– Omaha Beach: the Wn 64 resistance nest is reduced to silence by American assailants.

– Sword Beach: the British soldiers from Commando N°4 reach the harbour at Ouistreham where the German defences are concentrated.

– Sword Beach: the 'Cod' position (*Stützpunkt 20* for the Germans), located in the locality of La Brèche falls into the hands of the 1st Battalion South Lancashire Regiment and the 2nd Battalion East Yorkshire Regiment.

– Caen: the Gestapo has French resistance fighters taken from their cells in the prison and shoots them down in groups of 5 or 6.

– General Marcks decides to counter-attack with the *21. Panzer-Division*.

– General Edgar Feuchtinger receives orders to counter-attack with his tanks along the River Orne against the British parachutists from the 6th Airborne Division.

Universal Carrier vehicles from the 2nd Middlesex Regiment (MG Battalion, 3rd Infantry Division) encounter a Churchill Avre tank from the 77th Assault Squadron, 5th Assault Regiment at La Brèche d'Hermanville on D-Day. IWM (B 5040).

THE 21. PANZER-DIVISION *COUNTER-ATTACK*
TO THE EAST OF THE ORNE

Alerted by reports by soldiers from the *716. Infanterie-Division*, who were now incapable of maintaining control of the situation to the east of the Orne, the *P21. Panzer-Division* gave orders to several mechanised patrols, as from 02:30 on the 6th of June, to set off on reconnaissance on the east and west banks of the river. Elite elements from the *Panzergrenadier-Regiment 125*, commanded by Major Hans-Ulrich von Luck, established contact with the 6th Airborne Division at 03:00. The 12th Yorkshire's 17-Pounder antitank guns, brought in by glider and now positioned at Le Bas de Ranville, drove back the enemy patrols. Meanwhile, the 6th Airborne's commander General Gale established his command post in Ranville.

At around 15:00, a counter-attack by the *Kampfgruppe* von Luck (*21. Panzer-Division*) in turn sent the British troops back in their tracks during reconnaissance around the village of Escoville. They retreated to Hérouvillette and set up resistance positions, under constant enemy artillery fire. However, the Germans were still unable to break through the Allied lines. Overlord had taken them totally by surprise and they needed, first and foremost, to reunite both men and material before becoming a genuine threat to the Allies.

These British commandos from the 1st Special Service Brigade are keeping a watchful eye over their German prisoners aboard a jeep in the Ranville sector. The 6th Airlanding Brigade, 5th Airborne Division Horsa gliders can be seen in the background. IWM (B 5203).

10:12

– Omaha Beach: the 726th Grenadier Regiment's command post receives the following message from resistance nest Wn 62, 'Wn 60 is holding out, Wn 62 is still in action with a machine gun, but the situation is critical. Elements from the 1st and 4th companies are counter-attacking.'

– The 914th Grenadier Regiment reports that several enemy vessels are now within the Carentan canal, but have not yet begun landing operations.

10:15

– Omaha Beach: at Wn 62, near Colleville-sur-Mer, the two 76.5mm guns are simultaneously destroyed by naval artillery.

– Omaha Beach: the 916th Grenadier Regiment reports that between 60 and 70 barges are currently unloading soldiers in front of Wn 65 at Saint-Laurent-sur-Mer. The German troops at Pointe du Hoc are no longer responding to radio calls.

10:25

– Gold Beach: three tanks are reported by the 916th Grenadier Regiment to the west of Wn 38.

At around 10:30, these American soldiers from the 2nd Battalion, 18th Infantry Regiment, 1st (US) Infantry Division are preparing to land to the west of the German strongpoint codenamed Wn 65, near Saint-Laurent-sur-Mer (Omaha Beach). US National Archives.

THE INTERMEDIATE SITUATION ON UTAH BEACH

Brigadier General Theodore Roosevelt Jr., the eldest son of the former US President (1901 to 1909), landed with the staff of the 4th Infantry Division. He was the first superior officer to land (with the first wave of assault with the 8th Infantry Regiment's E Company) and he was quick to realise that the assault barges had drifted due to strong currents. Indeed, the US troops landed over a mile to the south of their initially planned invasion zone. Instead of finding themselves north of La Madeleine, they were south of the village, directly in front of the German strongpoint Wn 5. This beach sector only offered one single exit route (baptised 'exit n°2') for the Allies to head inland, where German troops were swarming. The sector was nevertheless less exposed to potential gunfire from the German artillery batteries in Azeville and Crisbecq.

Attempts to break through the enemy lines in a northerly direction were driven back by the German defenders, with artillery support. Despite the risk of creating a jam, Roosevelt decided to advance inland via the only route at his disposal. For some 20,000 American soldiers and 3,500 vehicles needed to be landed on Utah Beach by the day end and this narrow country path, nestling between zones deliberately flooded by the Germans, seemed insufficient for such a dense flow. Congestion on the beach was a genuine threat to the Allies.

Meanwhile, the American tanks waited for the military engineers to destroy the antitank walls before continuing their progression. Two hours later, at 08:30, they crossed the dune and headed inland along exit N°2 towards Sainte-Marie-du-Mont, with the infantry following immediately behind. Although light weapon gunfire on the beach had become rare, deadly mortar explosions and artillery fire continued. This desperate harassment by the Germans only ceased late evening.

At 10:30, landing operations continue to the west of the German strongpoint codenamed Wn 65 in Le Ruquet on Omaha Beach. Sherman tanks offer support to the men from the 16th Infantry Regiment, 1st (US) Infantry Division. When they are not grounded, the landing barges are used to evacuate the wounded. US National Archives.

10:30

– To the west of Utah Beach, the American parachutists from the Dog Company (505th PIR) engage in combat near the locality of Neuville-au-Plain.

– Omaha Beach: the two 75mm guns at Pointe de la Percée are put out of action by artillery fire from the destroyer *USS McCook*.

– Omaha Beach: the Wn 65 fortification, located at the junction between the Easy Green and Easy Red sectors and protecting exit E1 is reduced to silence by the American soldiers.

– At Neuville-au-Plain, Lieutenant Turner B. Turnbull and his 42 parachutists (chief of the 3rd section, B Company, 505th Parachute Infantry Regiment, 82nd Airborne Division), firmly in position to the north of Sainte-Mère-Église engages in combat with a column of 200 Germans. He only retreats in the evening, by which time the Americans have been afforded enough time to establish solid defences in Sainte-Mère-Église. Twenty-six parachutists are killed in the battle.

– General Feuchtinger receives orders to move his *21. Panzer-Division* to the west of the Orne canal and to engage in combat north of the Bayeux-Caen route.

11:00

– The radio station at Pointe de la Percée is attacked with 127mm shells fired by the destroyer *USS Thompson*, positioned off Omaha.

– Pointe du Hoc: the 3rd company, 726th Grenadier Regiment reports to the staff of the 352nd Infantry Division that, 'the enemy has penetrated the Pointe du Hoc strongpoint with 2 companies. From ships off shore, it is firing special shells equipped with ladders onto the cliff, enabling the men to climb the obstacle.' These shells are in fact grappling hooks, which are fired by mortars installed on the LCA landing barges.

– Gold Beach: 6 beach exits have been cleared.

Captain Kenneth Johnson from HQ Company, 508th PIR, 82nd Airborne Division with Norman civilians at Ravenoville. US National Archives.

Under the shelter of the dunes on Utah Beach, Major General Raymond O. Barton (in the centre), commander of the 4th (US) Infantry Division, reviews his unit's situation after the landings with his second, Brigadier General Theodore Roosevelt Jr. (left). US National Archives.

Omaha Beach, Fox Green sector. This nurse is giving blood to a wounded American soldier whose head is protected by means of an inflatable belt, ordinarily used as a life belt. Worry and disarray are clearly visible on the faces of these men. US National Archives.

Aerial photograph of Gold Beach and of the junction between the King Red and the King Green sectors, where the men from the British 50th Infantry Division have landed. The Mont Fleury battery (codenamed Wn 35a) and an antitank ditch can be seen in front of the village of Ver-sur-Mer, 6th of June 1944. IWM (CL 3947).

11:20

– Omaha Beach: elements from the 5th Ranger Battalion reach the locality of Surrain (south of Colleville-sur-Mer).

11:27

– Omaha Beach: the 916th Grenadier Regiment reports that the Allied assailants are now in control of the heights above the beach at Saint-Laurent-sur-Mer. The commander of the 352nd Infantry Division once more gives orders to 'counter-attack to throw the enemy back into the sea.'

11:45

– Omaha Beach: the 1st Battalion from the 18th Infantry Regiment (US 1st Infantry Division) lands.

11:58

– The 726th Grenadier Regiment reports that three landing barges have been sunk in the harbour at Port-en-Bessin.

12:00

— Utah Beach: the 4 exit causeways are in the hands of parachutists from the 101st Airborne Division.

– Utah Beach: the 2nd Battalion (8th Regimental Combat Team) enters Poupeville.

– Utah Beach: The 501st Parachute Infantry Regiment's Dog Company reaches the village of Angoville.

– Pointe du Hoc: the last six defenders at the strongpoint's observation post surrender to the US Rangers.

– Pointe du Hoc. Colonel Rudder forwards a message in Morse code, 'Located Pointe du Hoc. Mission accomplished. Need ammunition and reinforcement. Many casualties.'

– Omaha Beach: due to lacking ammunition, the Houtteville battery (located around 3 miles from the beach near Colleville-sur-Mer) refuses an order to fire salvoes against the approaching landing barges. Instead, its 105mm guns fire shell by shell.

– Churchill makes his speech before the House of Commons, informing the British MPs of Rome's liberation and the beginning of landing operations.

THE US PARACHUTISTS IN COMBAT IN THE COTENTIN PENINSULA

In Cotentin, the south-west flank and control of the bridges over the Douve had become absolute priorities for General Taylor in the hours after the American parachutists set foot on French soil. In order to reinforce its forces, both with extra men and material, the 101st Airborne Division launched the second phase of its assault in Cotentin in the form of operation Chicago, as from 04:00 on the 6th of June 1944. This reinforcement was brought in by 52 Waco gliders which landed on Landing Zone E to the west of Hiesville.

The vast majority of the missions entrusted to the 101st Airborne Division were accomplished at dawn, even if a few others still remained out of the paras' reach. When the 4th Infantry Division began to land on Utah Beach, three of the four exit causeways were controlled by the 101st Airborne parachutists, the fourth exit finally falling into American hands early in the afternoon. Although they had taken the bridges over the Douve and the Barquette lock, on the evening of the 6th of June the paras had still not managed to liberate Saint-Côme-du-Mont.

Within its assigned sector, the 82nd Airborne Division made both the most accurate (DZ 0) and the most chaotic (DZ T) landings. Of the three regiments to be dropped above Normandy, only the 505th PIR had, on the whole, accomplished its mission, whereas the 507th and the 508th PIR had failed to establish a continuous front on the west bank of the Merderet. Although all of the various missions that comprised operation Boston had not been pulled off, the 82nd Airborne Division had nevertheless gained relative control, despite the difficulties encountered during drops. As from 04:00, the division was reinforced with extra men and equipment, brought in by glider within the context of operation Detroit. Over and above fresh airborne troops, reinforcements were also in the form of heavy weapons, special equipment for sappers and nurses and light vehicles. The German reaction came at dawn. The La Fière road became a priority target for both sides and extremely violent confrontations ensued throughout the day. Organisation of the American troops from the 507th and the 508th PIR was irregular to the west of the Merderet and the Germans managed to infiltrate the Allied ranks relatively easily. However, they met with considerable and tenacious resistance and the Americans held their positions. Their bravery enabled the critical position at La Fière to stay in Allied hands and prevented the enemy from using the route to reach the eastern bank of the river.

Human losses were high for the division - on the evening of the 6th of June, some 195 parachutists had lost their lives. Whilst the first confrontations between American and German troops had taken many lives, other paras had drowned in the Merderet marshes, which had been deliberately flooded by the Germans to prevent both airborne operations and the establishment of a bridgehead in Cotentin.

A moment's respite for this stick from HQ Company, 508th PIR, 82nd Airborne Division, dropped far from its drop zone on D-Day. US National Archives.

12:14

– Omaha Beach: the Americans have succeeded in reaching the church in Colleville-sur-Mer.

12:40

– Omaha Beach: the 726th Grenadier Regiment reports that the south exit at Colleville-sur-Mer has been reached by the Americans and that several tanks have been stopped in their tracks by antitank ditches.

12:45

– Juno Beach: Major General Rodney Keller and the staff of the Canadian 3rd Infantry Division set up positions in the freshly liberated village of Courseulles-sur-Mer, near the Château de Semilly, in Rue des Ormes.

13:00

– Pointe du Hoc. Colonel Rudder receives a reply to the message he sent at midday, 'No reinforcements available. All Rangers have landed on Omaha.'

– Omaha Beach: General Bradley learns that a few groups of soldiers have broken through enemy lines at the top of the cliffs.

– Omaha Beach: resistance nest Wn 72 (Vierville-sur-Mer, Dog Green sector) is reduced to silence.

– Sword Beach: the men from the 1st Suffolk Regiment capture the Morris battery located in Colleville-Montgomery (at the time called Colleville-sur-Orne).

– Sword Beach: the Germans counter-attack to regain control of Wn 21 (Trout), defended by the British troops from the 41st RM Commando, under Lieutenant-Colonel Gray.

– Field Marshal Erwin Rommel leaves his home in Herrlingen and heads for Normandy after cancelling his appointment with the Führer.

The routes – some of which have been flooded – that lead through the marshes towards Cotentin are largely exploited by the 4th (US) Infantry Division. Damaged or broken down vehicles are mercilessly pushed to the side to clear the way as quickly as possible. US National Archives.

13:30

– Aerial bombardments over the town of Caen.

– Omaha Beach. General Omar Bradley, aboard the flagship *USS Augusta*, receives the following report, 'Troops formerly pinned down on beaches Easy Red, Easy Green, Fox Red advancing up heights behind beaches.'

Lieutenant-Colonel James E. Rudder (still carrying his gas mask, contrary to most of his subordinates), commander of the Rangers, at Pointe du Hoc. US National Archives.

In front of the fountain in the church square in Sainte-Marie-du-Mont, the villagers welcome the parachutists from the 101st (US) Airborne Division, sharing with them bottles of cider and calvados to celebrate their liberation. US National Archives.

The routes – some of which have been flooded – that lead through the marshes towards Cotentin are largely exploited by the 4th (US) Infantry Division. US National Archives.

As a bulldozer continues to clear the beach, a Sherman tank belonging to the 27th Canadian Armoured Regiment (Sherbrooke Fusiliers), in support of the 9th Canadian Infantry Brigade, lands in the Nan White sector on Juno Beach, in Bernières-sur-Mer on the 6th of June 1944. IWM (MH 3097).

BOMBARDMENTS IN NORMANDY

Aerial bombardments were used for different aims, equally tactical and strategic. Tactically, the aim was to hit identified military targets, such as grouped units, command posts, V1/V2 rocket launching ramps or radar stations. Strategically, bombardments were intended to slow down the adversary's war effort (by attacking – for example – its industrial installations or its resources) and to hinder its freedom of movement, by striking towns and specific structures, in particular communication links such as sorting stations or rural and urban road junctions.

After the Battle of Britain, the Allies had acquired excellent command of the air and almost systematically reverted to bombardments prior to and during their military operations. Whereas the Royal Air Force's Bomber Command was in charge of the majority of raids by night, the American bombers were entrusted with most of the daytime attacks in order to ensure that pressure was constantly exerted on the Third Reich forces.

In June 1943, a year before operation Overlord, the Allies initiated the Combined Bomber Offensive. This programme of planned aerial bombings was developed by the United States and Britain and relied on available military airfields in England. Its aim was to prepare for the ultimate outcome of combined operations on the European continent. In other words, this inter-army aerial offensive was designed to pave the way for the fatal blow that would lead to the surrender of Nazi Germany.

On the 26th of June 1943, Air Marshal Trafford Leigh-Mallory was appointed in charge of aerial operations during operation Overlord. The key aim was to destroy the adversary's means of communication and the secondary aim to attack the railway lines and maintenance centres. Meanwhile, bombardments were multiplied over Germany, forcing the *Luftwaffe* (German air force) to engage a vast share of its bomber planes to defend the Reich, hence moving several squadrons away from occupied territories such as France.

Given that the tactical bombardments in preparation of the Normandy landings targeted some specific sites (radar stations, coastal batteries, military headquarters, etc.), the Allies feared that repeated raids over Normandy may arouse suspicion among the Germans as to the precise location of the dreaded offensive. This is why the aerial raids against tactical - but also strategic - targets were deliberately scattered throughout the entire north-west of France, from Pas-de-Calais to Brittany.

On the 25th of October 1943, Air Chief Marshal Arthur T. Harris, commander-in-chief of the Royal Air Force Bomber Command, wrote to the British government to inform of, 'the destruction of houses, public utilities, transport and lives, the creation of a refugee problem on an unprecedented scale, and the breakdown of morale both at home and at the battle fronts by fear of extended and intensified bombing, are accepted and intended aims of our bombing policy. They are not by-products of attempts to hit factories.'

Although these instructions were clearly intended for integration by the German people, they were applied to all territories occupied by the Reich armies. Normandy was no exception.

The Allies then applied the Transportation Plan. Adopted on the 10th of January 1944, this plan specified targets (a total of 75) and locations (northern French and Belgian coasts) for aerial attacks for the rest of the war. The objective was to strike the majority of railway junctions likely to be used after the landings to transport troops towards Normandy. The idea was to isolate the region by bombarding stations, sorting centres and bridges. Many of these targets were located in or close to French towns and the attacks cost the lives of hundreds of civilian victims. On the night of the 9th to the 10th of April 1944, the Allies bombarded the stations in Villeneuve-Saint-Georges and in Lille, killing 687 civilians and wounding a further 799.

Rouen was also the target of an aerial raid on the night of the 18th to the 19th of April 1944, during which 812 civilians lost their lives. All of the road and rail junctions, bridges (with the exception of Asnières) and other structural works in the Seine valley were destroyed late May 1944.

The Transportation Plan was criticised by Winston Churchill in April 1944. He deemed the bombings to be particularly deadly for the civilian populations. Probably in response to Churchill's reluctance, General Eisenhower stuck to his guns and, on the 2nd of June 1944, drafted a note for the attention of Arthur Harris and Lieutenant General Carl A. Spaatz (commander-in-chief of the US Strategic Air Forces). He provided instructions on what to do during the aerial raids, asking to, 'be careful that nothing is done to betray the trust or to prejudice our good name in the eyes of our friends still dominated by the Nazi tyranny. He added, 'I request that those instructions be brought to the attention of every member of aircrews fighting over Europe.' (Public Record Office WO 219 325).

These attacks were multiplied over the early hours of the 6th of June 1944 and those that followed. Hence, the towns of Caen, Rouen, Évreux, Le Havre, Avranches and Saint-Lô were subjected to massive and lethal destruction aimed at transforming their historic centres into piles of ruins. The movement of German reinforcements towards the Allied bridgehead were consequently rendered far more difficult, if not impossible through these towns.

View of aerial bombardments over the town of Caen, the aim of which was to slow down progression by any German reinforcements on their way to the beaches. US National Archives.

13:32

– Pegasus Bridge: Brigadier Simon Fraser (aka Lord Lovat), commander of the 1st Special Service Brigade, reaches the bridge at Bénouville with his commandos landed on Sword Beach. He apologises for being 2 minutes and 30 seconds behind the initially planned schedule. Major Howard and his men welcome him with relief.

13:41

– Omaha Beach: the 726th Grenadier Regiment reports that the Germans have regained control of Colleville-sur-Mer.

– Omaha Beach: German resistance on the Dog Green, Easy Green, Easy Red and White Red beach sectors has ceased.

14:00

– Pointe du Hoc: German defenders from the 84th Infantry Regiment abandon the west flank of the strongpoint.

– Considering that the Allied offensive in Normandy may just be a diversion, Hitler maintains his 15th Army in northern France, in case of an amphibious operation in Pas-de-Calais. The intoxication of the German intelligence via the Allied operation Fortitude is working to perfection.

Pegasus Bridge in Bénouville, with the three Horsa gliders that took part in the assault visible behind the line of trees. IWM (B 5288).

View of Pegasus Bridge with the gliders in the background. The facade of the Café Gondrée, with its shutters closed, can be seen to the right. The British have baptised the bridge after the 6th Airborne Division's defining symbol, Pegasus, the winged horse in Greek mythology. IWM (B 7032).

After installing the Canadian 3rd Infantry Division's command post in Bernières-sur-Mer, General Rodney Keller prepares to give his first press conference. National Archives Canada.

PART IV:
Consolidating

On Omaha, the last deadlock, the remaining German defenders left their positions, one after another. The Allies' aim was now to establish a solid bridgehead in Normandy.

The church of St Andrew in Vierville-sur-Mer - the target of forty 127mm shells fired by *USS Harding* from a distance of 1.8 miles. US National Archives.

– Omaha Beach: the destroyer *USS Harding* destroys the church spire in Vierville-sur-Mer, believing it to house German artillery observers.

14:25

– The village of Périers-sur-le-Dan, to the south of Sword Beach, is liberated by the Staffordshire Yeomanry tanks after fierce combat.

THE LIBERATION OF PÉRIERS-SUR-LE-DAN

The British 3rd Infantry Division, landed on Sword Beach on the 6th of June 1944, advanced along the Caen-Bayeux road and, late morning, the men from the King's Shropshire Light Infantry, 185th Infantry Brigade came within sight of Périers-sur-le-Dan. However, the Germans temporarily thwarted their progression by confronting the Allied troops on the outskirts of Beuville.

With armoured support from the Staffordshire Yeomanry Regiment and the Royal Norfolk Regiment, which attacked Beuville, the King's Shropshire Light Infantry successfully took control of Périers-sur-le-Dan and the heights around the village, overlooking the surrounding countryside. The Staffordshire Yeomanry made use of this strategic position, setting up firm resistance when the *21. Panzer-Division* decided to launch a counter-attack towards the coast. The offensive met with failure thanks to decisive action by the British antitank guns installed along the Périers-sur-le-Dan crest.

On the evening of the 6th of June, the Staffordshire Yeomanry Regiment's C squadron set up a night-time look-out position facing south and south-east of the village, in order to offer support – the following morning – to the 3rd Infantry Division's 9th Brigade in its assault towards the village of Mathieu.

Périers-sur-le-Dan is located within a short distance of the ALG B-10 airfield to the south of Plumetot, which was installed by British troops as from the 10th of June 1944.

At Pointe du Hoc, a weapon is planted in the ground: it indicates the presence of a soldier out of action. The weapon is a Twin Vickers K machine gun, initially installed on climbing ropes and recovered by the Rangers. National Archives.

A Sherman VC Firefly from Squadron C of the Staffordshire Yeomanry, 27th Armoured Brigade. This tank, designed for antitank combat, is equipped with a 76.2mm QF 17 Pounder gun. IWM (B 7558).

14:30

– A rescue barge is launched by the ship USS Barton to offer assistance to the wounded rangers at Pointe du Hoc (however, a German artillery barrage prevents access to the position).

14:35

– Juno Beach: General Rodney Keller, commander of the Canadian 3rd Infantry Division, gives a press conference in an orchard near Bernières-sur-Mer.

14:58

– Omaha Beach: the 352nd Artillery Regiment reports that the village of Colleville-sur-Mer has, again, fallen into enemy hands.

15:00

– Omaha Beach: the 916th Grenadier Regiment counter-attacks the advanced American units in position between Wn 62a, 62b and 64.

– Around 80 French Resistance fighters are shot down in by the Gestapo in the prison in Caen, because it was impossible to move them (the first execution takes place as from 10:00, the second in the afternoon).

– General Marcks asks Colonel von Oppeln-Bronikowski to counter-attack with the *21. Panzer-Division*, specifying, 'the outcome for Germany and for the conflict depends on the success of your counter-attack.'

15:26

– Omaha Beach: failed counter-attack by the German 916th Grenadier Regiment in Colleville-sur-Mer.

A Resistance fighter preparing cartridges for light infantry weapons in a hideout. IWM

A French Resistance fighter placing an explosive charge on a railway track. IWM.

ACTION BY THE FRENCH RESISTANCE ON D-DAY

Although they only had extremely limited resources at their disposal (heavy weapons were, in particular, cruelly lacking), the Resistance fighters played a crucial role during the preparation and after the launch of operation Overlord. Prior to the Allied offensive, their mission essentially consisted in providing information on German units and installations within occupied territories, and in conducting sabotage operations. Hence, plans of the Atlantic Wall installations were drafted and sent across the Channel by carrier pigeons or via radio messages, as was a multitude of information potentially of interest to the Allies.

Upon request from the Special Operations Executive (SOE), the *Bureau central de renseignements et d'action* (*BCRA*) conducted several colour-coded sabotage plans. For example the Blue plan was intended to cut the electricity supply on the French coast for three days, from the 5th to the 7th of June 1944. The Green plan aimed at hindering the transport of German men and ammunition by sabotaging the railway lines. The operation met with success. In just two days, a total of 98 locomotives were destroyed and the routes likely to be taken by the Germans (the *275. Infanterie Division* in Brittany and the *2. Panzer-Division* around Toulouse) became prime targets. The Violet plan was conducted by volunteer engineers from the French telecommunications board's LSGD department (long distance underground lines) and was aimed at paralysing the German command up to the 7th of June 1944.

The day before D-Day, the Resistance launched a series of sudden and brutal attacks, providing vital support to operation Overlord. On the night of the 5th to the 6th of June, some 950 sabotage operations were conducted from a total of 1,050 targets throughout the north-west of France.

When the first Allied soldiers set foot on Norman soil, the Resistance fighters – along with ordinary inhabitants – came to meet them and to guide them through the quite particular bocage landscape. The quantity of information they provided (occupier positions, enemy resources, military units they belonged to, troop morale or even the location of fuel and ammunition depots) proved particularly beneficial to the Allied combat troops.

15:30

– Omaha Beach: Heinrich Severloh, the last defender at resistance nest Wn 62, abandons his position after firing 12,500 times with his K98 rifle and MG 42 machine gun.

– Sword Beach: the British troops have captured the port of Ouistreham, with support, in particular, from an Avre tank.

15:40

– Sword Beach: the men and tanks from the East Yorkshire Regiment's 2nd Battalion and the 19th/18th Hussars take control of the 'Fort Sole' strongpoint.

15:45

– Von Rundstedt's Chief of Staff, General Günther Blumentritt, informs Field Marshal Rommel's Chief of Staff, General Hans Speidel, that the Führer has approved the engagement of two armoured divisions already posted in Normandy.

In the village of Rots, *SS-Schütze* Günther Streelow from the 3rd section of the *15. Aufklärungskompanie (S.S Pz.Gren.Rgt 25., 12. SS-Panzer-Division Hitlerjugend)*, visibly marked by a night of violent combat and an attack late morning on the 9th of June 1944 in Norrey-en-Bessin, retreats before the Canadian 2nd Armoured Brigade. Bundesarchiv Bild 146-1983-109-14a.

THE MG 42

Created in 1942 (hence its name) by the German firm Johannes Grossfuss AG, this heavy machine gun took over from the MG 34. The MG 42 boasted the fastest rate of fire of all WWII machine guns (up to 1,800 rounds/minute for certain versions).

It was requested by the German military authorities, who were looking to reduce the production time and cost of the MG 34 machine gun. Compared to the previous version, the time to produce the new gun was divided by two to a new total of 45 hours. The MG 42V, an improved version of the MG 42, was first brought into action during the Battle of Normandy as from the 6th of June 1944. Its weight had also been reduced to only 9kg (20 lbs).

The MG 42 is considered by specialists to have been the best heavy machine gun in use during World War II, and even of all time. The German *Bundeswehr* military forces today use the MG 3, a heavy machine gun inspired by the MG 42. It has been adopted by several other armies across the globe. The American M60 machine gun was also largely inspired by the MG 42's operating mode.

Total production:
400,000 guns (during WWII).

Firing action: automatic

Calibre: 7.92mm.

Charger: belts of 50 to 250 cartridges.

Effective firing range: 1,000m.

Rate of fire: 1,200 rounds/min
(up to 1,800 for certain versions).

Weight: 11.5kg.

Length: 1,225mm.

COMBAT AT LA FIÈRE

The hamlet of La Fière, which in the spring of 1944 was within the sector controlled by the *Grenadier-Regiment 1058* (*91. Infanterie Division*), was located within the immediate vicinity of a passageway over the River Merderet and the sector's flooded zones. During the preparatory phase before operation Overlord, this 550 yard-long causeway became a priority target for the Allies. The maintenance of the bridgehead in Cotentin – encircled to the south by the Douve and to the north by the Merderet - depended on its control.

The capture of La Fière and its precious bridge was entrusted to the 1st Battalion of the 505th Parachute Infantry Regiment (82nd Airborne Division) commanded by Major Frederick C. A. Kellam. Although the drops made by the 505th PIR were the most accurate of all those recorded on the night of the 5th to the 6th of June, Kellam was unable to reunite enough men to divide his forces into two groups as planned (one was to head for the La Fière bridge, whilst the other was to advance to Chef-du-Pont). He therefore decided to concentrate his forces on La Fière. Company A, commanded by Lieutenant John J. Dolan, led the attack. On their way, they encountered parachutists from various 82nd Airborne Division regiments, with which they joined forces pending the latter being despatched to their respective units. General Gavin, the division's second-in-command, progressed through the marshes along the River Merderet before, in turn, joining forces with the 505th PIR's 1st Battalion, on its way to La Fière.

Lieutenant Dolan, then Lieutenant John. H. Wisner (a 507th PIR intelligence officer) attacked the bridge shortly before dawn, but they were driven back by enemy gunfire. Later in the morning, around 550 parachutists from a diversity of units were gathered together in the La Fière sector. They were under orders from Colonel Roy E. Lindquist, commanding officer of the 508th PIR. He organised an assault on the hamlet of La Fière, relying on the best manned groups for support: Company A – 505th PIR, Company G – 507th PIR and Company B – 508th PIR. At midday, he ordered for the assault to be launched on the hamlet, where the German soldiers were entrenched. After fierce combat, the Americans gained control of the position and the parachutists from the 507th PIR's Company G, commanded by Captain Schwartzwalder, succeeded the

16:00

– Omaha Beach: the first American Sherman tank reaches the road linking the beach with Colleville via a valley. It is destroyed by an antitank gun.

– The German strongpoint Wn 35a (Mont Fleury) at Le Hamel is under control after violent combat involving the Royal Hampshire's 1st Battalion.

– Bombardment of the German artillery battery at Mont-Canisy by 37 Marauder planes which drop a total of 61 tonnes of bombs on the site.

– The Shropshire Regiment liberates the village of Biéville to the south of Sword Beach, as its armoured support from the Staffordshire reaches Blainville.

– Pegasus Bridge: Commando N°4 (Kieffer Commando) attached to the 1st Special Service Brigade reaches the bridge at Bénouville to progress towards Amfreville, its final target for the day.

feat of crossing the La Fière bridge and the road to Amfreville. They even managed to establish a link with other parachutists from the 507th PIR's 2nd Battalion to the east of Amfreville, before withdrawing in the Cauquigny sector.

A few hours later, the 505th PIR's 1st Battalion set up position around the La Fière bridge and replaced Colonel Lindquist's men who were subsequently posted to the rear, along the railway line. Mid afternoon, little by little, gunfire directed at the American positions became increasingly intense and the 505th PIR parachutists found themselves under continuous fire, particularly from the German artillery. Suddenly, at 16:00, two Renault R35 *Beutepanzer* (captured from the enemy) tanks, now belonging to the *Panzer-Ersatz-Abteilung 100*, appeared on the road, heading towards the bridge. Two teams of tank destroyers armed with bazookas were positioned in combat holes on either side of the road and, when the order came, they destroyed the first tank. The enemy infantry (from the *Grenadier-Regiment 1057*), immediately intervened from behind the tanks and engaged in extremely short-range combat. With support from their fellow troops, the two tank destroyer teams opened fire on the second tank, which was in turn destroyed. However one of the bazookas was out of action and the team retreated. The Americans had exhausted their stock of antitank rockets as a third tank appeared on the road. Observing the scene from the east bank of the Merderet, Major Frederick Kellam and his second, Captain Dale Roysden, gathered together antitank ammunition and crossed the bridge to resupply the contact line. They were both killed. Losses were particularly heavy and the defence on the western bank of the bridge had become extremely vulnerable.

Realising that the antitank team that had withdrawn due to a firing incident had left bazooka rockets behind, a para by the name of Marcus Heim went to recover what he needed and took it back to Gordon Pryne, his supply officer. Together, they managed to destroy the third tank and, in doing so, to stop the violent German charge along the La Fière road. Lieutenant-Colonel Maloney reinforced the sector with around a hundred men despatched from the Chef-du-Pont defences at around 20:00.

Work continues to clear the beach in the Queen sector on Sword Beach on the evening of the 6th of June 1944. IWM (B 5116).

– Broadcast of a radio message to the French people from Marshal Pétain (recorded on the 17th of March 1944 on the Germans' request). He asks them not to hinder action by the German forces and not to assist the Allies.

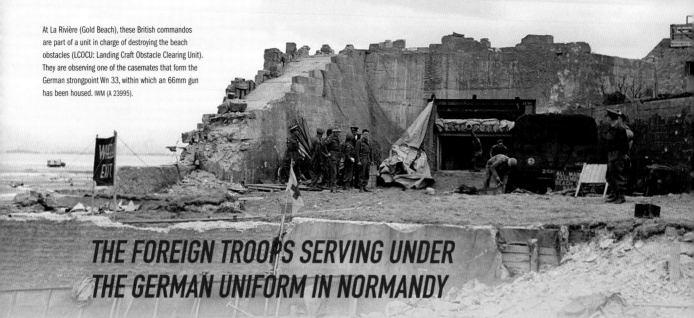

THE FOREIGN TROOPS SERVING UNDER THE GERMAN UNIFORM IN NORMANDY

Throughout the Second World War, Germany reinforced its military forces with units composed of foreign soldiers donning the Third Reich uniform. These 'eastern troops' (Osttruppen in German) were also present during the Battle of Normandy. They were of Slavic origin and most of them were volunteers, who had preferred serving under a different uniform to remaining in catastrophic detention conditions in a Nazi POW camp. In the spring of 1944, around 75,000 of these combatants were positioned in France. They were engaged to watch over ammunition depots or logistics centres, as beach look-outs along the Channel and Atlantic coasts and to fight against Resistance networks in occupied territories... It was within this particular context that many war crimes were committed by the 'eastern troops' who took part in the execution of French resistance fighters along with German soldiers.

Despite their poor quality resources and equipment, their presence nevertheless relieved the German troops, who could consequently be concentrated on the Eastern Front.

On the 6th of June 1944, around 16,000 *Osttruppen* were serving in Normandy, in the form of at least one regiment per German division. Not only Russians, Georgians, Ukrainians and North Caucasians, but also Turkestanians stood against the Allied assault during operation Overlord. To a far lesser extent, Asian soldiers also fought in Normandy in German uniform, such as Yang Kyoung Jong, a Korean who was taken prisoner by the Americans in Cotentin. Also worthy of note, troops referred to as *Malgré-Nous* (literally 'despite ourselves' in reference to their reluctance) from the Alsace and Moselle regions were forced to serve the Reich under threat of reprisals against their families.

Despite Hitler's meagre consideration for the Slavic populations, several German officers testified for their genuine worth in combat, particularly in Normandy on D-Day. Hence, the British parachutists found themselves opposed to fearsome Russian soldiers from the *Ost-Battalion 642*, attached to the *716. Infanterie-Division*, whose command post had been established in Amfreville. On Juno Beach, the Canadians from the 3rd Infantry Division in turn fought against Ukrainians from *Ost-Bataillon 441 (716. Infanterie-Division)* in positions in Graye-sur-Mer and to the south of Courseulles-sur-Mer. The American parachutists also met with fierce resistance between Turqueville and Ecoquenéauville, in Cotentin, by Georgian forces from *Ost-Battalion 795 (709. Infanterie-Division)*.

However, many of the *Osttruppen* and *Malgré-Nous* surrendered to the Allies over the early days of the Battle of Normandy, due to an obvious lack of motivation. The majority of the soldiers from Eastern Europe having fought feared being sent back to their homelands, where they risked forced labour or even summary execution.

A Royal Air Force Halifax bomber during the raids over Normandy. National Archives Canada.

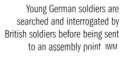

– 25 German tanks from the *21. Panzer-Division* counter-attack in the vicinity of Périers-sur-le-Dan.

16:30

– Aerial bombardment over the town of Caen.

Young German soldiers are searched and interrogated by British soldiers before being sent to an assembly point. IWM

133

GENERAL DE GAULLE'S SPEECH ON D-DAY

'The Supreme battle has begun!

After so much combat, fury and pain, we now face the decisive blow, the blow we have so hoped for. It is, of course, the battle of France and the battle by France!

Immense means of attack, intended for us, in aid, have begun to flood forth from the shores of old England. Before this final bastion of Western Europe, the tide of German oppression was already halted once. Today, it is the departure point of the offensive for freedom. France, submerged for the past four years, but under no circumstances reduced, nor beaten, France is standing proud and taking part.

For the sons of France, wherever they may be, whoever they may be, the simple and sacred duty is to fight by all possible means at their disposal. We must destroy the enemy, the enemy who crushes and sullies our fatherland, the loathed enemy, the dishonoured enemy.

The enemy will do its all to escape its fate. It will stand fast on our soil as long as possible. Yet, for a long time already, it is no more than a retreating wildcat. From Stalingrad to Tarnopol, from the banks of the Nile to Bizerte, from Tunis to Rome, it has become accustomed to defeat.

This battle, France will lead it with fury. She will lead it in good order. It is thus that we have, for over fifteen hundred years, won each of our victories. It is thus that we shall win this one.

In good order! For our armies on land, sea and in the air, this shall be no problem. Never before have they been more ardent, more skilful, more disciplined. Africa, Italy, the ocean and the sky have seen their reborn force and their glory. The Homeland will see them tomorrow!

For this nation that is fighting, bound hand and foot, and to the teeth against the armed oppressor, good order in battle demands several conditions.

The first is that the orders given by the French government and by the French chiefs it has qualified to do so at national level be abided by to the letter.

The ruins of the town of Caen, the target of Allied bombardments aimed, in particular, at hindering any movement by German reinforcements. US National Archives.

The second is that the action undertaken by us behind the enemy lines must be done so in the closest possible collaboration with that of the Allied and French armies. Now, everyone must expect the action undertaken by the armies to be tough and to be long. Hence the importance of continued and amplified action by the Resistance forces, until the German retreat.

The third condition is that all those capable of action, be it by means of weapons, by destruction, by information, or by refusal to do useful work for the enemy, must not allow themselves to be taken prisoner. That all those take prior measures to escape imprisonment or deportation! Whatever the difficulties, anything is better than being made unfit for fighting, without a fight.

The Battle of France has begun. There is only, in the Nation, in the Empire, in the armies, one single will, one single hope. Behind the heavy clouds of our blood and our tears, the sunshine of our grandeur is re-emerging.'

General Charles de Gaulle

17:00

– Omaha Beach: General Clarence Huebner lands in the Easy Red beach sector.

– Omaha Beach: the ruins of the Saint-Laurent-sur-Mer church spire, now a shelter for German snipers, are the target of the US artillery.

– Omaha Beach: Wn 73, the most westerly resistance nest, is reduced to silence by men from the 5th Ranger Battalion and the 116th Regiment (29th Infantry Division).

17:10

– The German 916th Grenadier Regiment reports to the headquarters of the 352nd Infantry Division that the village of Saint-Laurent-sur-Mer has fallen into enemy hands.

17:30

– General de Gaulle's speech is broadcast by the BBC. Fearing that the Allies establish an Allied Military Government of Occupied Territories (AMGOT), he insists on the fact that liberated territories must now come under the authority of the Free French government.

– German armoured units, commanded by Major von Gottberg launch a counter-attack towards Biéville aimed at driving back the Canadian troops.

General de Gaulle's message to the French people is broadcast by the British Broadcasting Company in London. Getty Images.

COMBAT BY THE 6TH AIRBORNE DIVISION ON D-DAY

Generally speaking, the quality of work by Allied pilots during glider parachute drops enabled the 6th Airborne Division to accomplish fast and accurate action, whilst taking the Germans totally by surprise. Each of the targets that were essential for the success of their missions were met within the scheduled timescale, thanks to preparatory work and to the courage of the British soldiers engaged in the battle. The unit sustained heavy losses during the night and over the morning of the 6th of June, temporarily threatening the continuation of its action on the left flank of the Allied invasion. Operation Mallard, launched at 21:00 on D-Day, considerably reinforced the British positions to the east of the Orne, where the situation on the evening of the 6th of June remained particularly precarious given the firing power of the *21. Panzer-Division*.

The overall logics of airborne operations conducted simultaneously within such a large area totally escaped the German high command, which also needed to cope with the temporary absence of ranking officers on the front. This was one of the consequences of the dispersal of Allied units to the east of the Orne. Failing to grasp the intentions of the British assailants, the Germans lost precious time examining the airborne units' plan in an attempt to understand its general outline and comprised missions. The occupiers were too slow to react (at around 10:00 on D-Day) and their action lacked coordination to genuinely threaten the integrity of Allied action on the left flank.

18:00

– The French warship *Georges-Leygues* opens fire on the Longues-sur-Mer artillery battery (which has just attacked the Allied ships) to the west of Gold Beach, plunging the site into silence.

– Juno Beach: in Saint-Aubin-sur-Mer, the last German defenders surrender from their coastal positions in the Nan Red sector.

– Sword Beach: the men from the East Yorkshire Regiment's 2nd Battalion overwhelm the 'Daimler' strongpoint (Wn 12) in Ouistreham.

18:10

– Omaha Beach: the 915th Grenadier Regiment reports that it has bypassed the Americans to the rear of their lines near the Château de Colleville-sur-Mer and that the wounded cannot be evacuated.

18:25

– Pointe du Hoc: General Dietrich Kraiss, commander of the 352nd Infantry Division, informs the officer in charge of the 916th Grenadier Regiment that, 'the 914th Grenadier Regiment's 1st Company must counter-attack at Pointe du Hoc to resolve the situation. Detachments from the Le Guay strongpoint must also attack from the east.'

18:30

– Omaha Beach: the 26th Infantry Regiment (US 1st Infantry Division) begins to land.

18:54

– The destroyer *USS Harding* resumes bombing on the ruins of the Vierville-sur-Mer church spire. Firing ends at 18:57.

19:00

— Omaha Beach: violent combat continues between the landed American troops and German defenders in Colleville-sur-Mer.

19:25

– Pointe du Hoc: the Germans launch a counter-offensive to the east with support elements from Le Guay.

German prisoners being escorted on Gold Beach, 6th June 1944. IWM (B 5257).

19:35

– Once more, the destroyer *USS Harding* bombs the church spire in Vierville-sur-Mer and the surrounding area, for two minutes. Shells fall on the Château de Vierville-sur-Mer.

19:40

– Pointe du Hoc: General Kraiss is informed of the German progression and that, 'the 726th Grenadier Regiment's 9th Company has encircled the enemy from the east and the south.'

– Omaha Beach: German artillery barrage on the beach in the Colleville-sur-Mer sector, where landing operations are continuing. The American troops sustain minor losses.

19:45

– Pointe du Hoc: the 916th Grenadier Regiment informs of, 'parachutist landings near the Le Guay strongpoint.'

A patrol of German soldiers inspecting the wreck of a Waco glider, stopped in its tracks before one of the many wooden stakes installed to counter airlanded assaults. Bundesarchiv Bild 146-2004-0176.

SUMMARY OF THE COUNTER-ATTACK BY THE 21. PANZER-DIVISION

At around 16:20, elements from the *Panzergrenadier-Regiment 192* (*Pz.Gr.Rgt. 192*) attached to the *21. Panzer-Division* and forming the *Kampfgruppe Rauch*, commanded by *Oberst* (Colonel) Josef Rauch, advanced towards the coast. Their forces comprised the 1st Battalion of the *Pz.Gr.Rgt. 192*, the *2. Kompanie* of the *Panzer-Pionier-Bataillon 220*, and the 2nd Battalion of the *Panzer-Artillerie-Regiment 155* commanded by *Hauptmann* Hans Thannenberger. By chance, this tactical group was advancing between the Gold and Juno Beach sectors, which the Allies had not yet succeeded in reuniting, and Rauch's men completed their reconnaissance as far as the western limit of the village of Lion-sur-Mer.

The Germans sought information on Allied missions until 21:00, taking advantage of their position to analyse the terrain and to prepare a counter-offensive directed at the enemy positions. However, at this point in time, the 6th Airborne Division reinforced its positions thanks to operation Mallard. Captain Wilhelm von Gottberg, commander of the *I./Panzer-Regiment 22*, also in position in Lion-sur-Mer with six tanks, observed the airborne assault. Fearing finding himself totally surrounded after the Allied gliders had landed, he reported to the military staff of the *21. Panzer-Division* before retreating. *Kampfgruppe Rauch* did likewise, withdrawing all its forces and re-establishing a position near Douvres-la-Délivrande.

20:00

– Six German tanks belonging to the *Panzer-Grenadier-Regiment 192*, commanded by Captain von Gottberg, make a breakthrough as far as Lion-sur-Mer, where they observe the landing operations before taking a u-turn.

The French commandos from the *1er Bataillon de Fusiliers Marins* reach the locality of Le Hauger.

20:15

– After bitter combat, the German position referred to as the Hillman Fortress is captured by men from the Suffolk Regiment and the 13th/18th Hussars tanks. At 06:45 the following day, Colonel Krug (commander of the *Grenadier-Regiment 736*) and around 70 of his men, still barricaded inside the underground command post (Bunker A), surrender to the British troops.

20:51

– The last remaining elements of the 6th Airborne Division land with 256 gliders on the landing zones in Ranville – LZ N – and to the north-west of Bénouville – LZ W (operation Mallard).

Handley Page Hamifax bombers, belonging to the Royal Air Force No. 38 Group, towing Hamilcar gliders with elements from the 6th Airlanding Brigade, 6th Airborne Division on board, during operation Mallard, shortly before 21:00 on the 6th of June 1944, just before flying over the warships HMS Warspite and HMS Ramillies, off Sword Beach. IWM (A 23924).

OPERATION MALLARD

Over 5,300 British and Canadian soldiers needed to be transported by the Royal Air Force groups 38 and 46. Since the two units had insufficient aircraft to transport the entire division to its respective target zones, the plan was split into two waves. The first (codenamed Tonga) comprised the operation's key missions, which were absolutely to be completed prior to the start of landing operations. The second (operation Mallard) comprised the plan's secondary missions. With this second airborne assault, scheduled at 21:00 on D-Day, the 6th Airborne hoped to reinforce two sectors: the east bank of the Orne (where units engaged during operation Tonga were isolated in enemy territory), by landing a share of its gliders on Landing Zone N to the east of Ranville, which had been cleared of any obstacles by sappers, and on the west bank, via the introduction of the new Landing Zone Z. The latter, located near the village of Saint-Aubin-d'Arquenay, between Ouistreham and Bénouville, had been identified via reconnaissance by commandos under the orders of the British 3rd Infantry Division, landed on Sword beach on the 6th of June.

Resources transported during operation Mallard comprised heavy equipment aimed at slightly increasing the firing power of the air-landed forces which, according to the Allies' tactical logic, had been issued with lighter-weight weapons during the initial assault. This time, the gliders were loaded with Tetrarch tanks, jeeps, trailers and antitank guns. A total of 142 planes (towing 112 Horsa gliders and 30 Hamilcar gliders) were designated to head for LZ N, a further 104 Horsa gliders being expected at LZ W. Mallard's 246 craft took off from England as from 18:40 on D-Day, with 216 Horsa and 30 Hamilcar gliders behind them. Four gliders were lost during the Channel crossing: one, belonging to the 12th Devons, crashed into the sea with its crew around 5 miles from the Normandy shores (five soldiers survived the crash and managed to swim to the coast at Merville, where they were taken prisoner by the Germans), the other crashed to the east of the landing zone and the last two made emergency landings back in England.

At 20:51, the first gliders reached the ground in LZ W. One section, commanded by Lieutenant Sneezum, was in charge of destroying – as soon as it landed – the railway line linking Cagny and Mézidon. The other elements immediately joined their defensive positions. The same applied to the units landing in LZ N near Ranville, where the Tetrarch tanks were headed: of a total of 30 vehicles, 11 were immobilised within 5 minutes of landing due to technical hitches. Indeed, the landing zone was scattered with parachutes which became caught inside the tracking, blocking the vehicles. The sector was also saturated with gliders which struggled even to find enough space to land.

Losses during the crossing were low considering the forces engaged: 242 of the 246 gliders successfully landed in Normandy. Skilled pilots, favourable weather conditions around the landing zones and prior work by sappers to clear as many obstacles as possible, such as the famous 'Rommel's asparagus', before the start of the operation, all enabled losses in the combat zone, in men and material, to be kept to a minimum. Operation Mallard deprived the German 21st Armoured Division of any further hope of succeeding its counter-attack before nightfall. The German staff was aware of the threatening possibility of further parachute jumps and glider landings behind their lines, over the night. In contrast, on the Allied side, the arrival of the 6th Airborne Division was known to all and considerably boosted morale among the troops in the sector as they prepared to spend their first night on French soil after a long day of combat.

OPERATIONS KEOKUK AND ELMIRA

The American airborne and air-landed troops were reinforced in men and material, offering precious relief to the parachutists who were isolated in Cotentin since the early hours of D-Day. Indeed, these men were in need of the heavy weapons, equipment and ammunition that had failed to be dropped, as initially planned, during the initial assault. These new air-landed reinforcements were scheduled to be dropped on LZ E and LZ W at 21:00 on the 6th of June. Zone E (operation Keokuk), on the north-western edge of Hiesville, was designated to reinforce the 101st Airborne Division. The zone was split into several fields and orchards, surrounded by the high hedges that are typical of the Normandy bocage and with lines of trees, some of which reached heights in the region of 50 feet. However, the fields in this sector were, on average, twice as large as in other zones in Cotentin. Zone W (operation Elmira) was assigned to the 82nd Airborne Division and was located on the RN13 trunk road in the region of Les Forges, just over a mile to the south of Sainte-Mère-Église. This landing zone covered an area of around 1.2 miles by 1 mile.

The first C-47s towing the Horsa gliders within the framework of operation Keokuk took off from the Aldermaston airfield in Great Britain at 18:30 on the 6th of June. The daunting formation of 64 flying craft formed the 101st Airborne Division's 29th serial. All of these elements then flew over the Isle of Portland before heading for the Îles Saint-Marcouf, in order to avoid the German anti-aircraft defence (the *Flak*) in the region of Cherbourg. The Dakotas released their gliders as from 20:53, seven minutes ahead of schedule, before swerving back towards England. When the first landed back at Aldermaston at 22:58, neither the *Flak* nor the German fighter planes had taken action.

The gliders, which were released at an altitude of 500 feet, landed on LZ E, which had been marked out by division pathfinders by means of green smoke and yellow markers placed to form the letter 'T'. They were covered by troops from the previous serial (serial 27, mission Chicago), by a section from the 501st Parachute Infantry Regiment's 3rd Battalion and by division artillerymen - all engaged under orders from Colonel Sherburne. A detachment of glider pilots, commanded by Lieutenant Victor Warriner, set to clearing the landing zone of its obstacles and to cutting down any trees likely to complicate landing. There were still very many Germans in the sector around LZ E when the gliders landed. German resistance was essentially concentrated in Turqueville and Saint-Côme-du-Mont, two villages respectively two miles to the north-east and the south-west of the landing zone. A counter-attack was underway against the American positions when the Horsa gliders touched the ground and certain craft found themselves isolated in the midst of the German soldiers, under heavy gunfire.

Operation Elmira was launched simultaneously. When serials 30 and 31 arrived, the Germans were still in control of a vast zone between Fauville and Turqueville, precisely under the gliders' approach route towards LZ W. General Ridgway consequently made the difficult decision to redirect all craft engaged in mission Elmira towards LZ O. This jump zone had been secured by the 505th Parachute Infantry Regiment (PIR) and its approach enabled the gliders to avoid the most dangerous zones. Ridgway tried in vain to make radio contact with General Collins, who was aboard *USS Bayfield* off Utah Beach, to ask him to relay information to the transport squadrons. He then ordered for LZ O to be marked out, in the hope that the Dakota pilots would, in turn, redirect to the north-west of Sainte-Mère-Église. However, the pilots had received orders to look for the landing zone located 2 miles from the village.

As the C-47s flew over Cotentin at an altitude of 500 feet, they prepared to release their gliders above LZ W, as per the initial plan. All was calm on the landing zone until the Horsa and Waco gliders came within firing range of the German guns. Combat on the ground was visible from the skies and several glider pilots decided to change sectors wherever possible. However, the vast share of serials 30 and 31 landed on LZ W. The same applied to the two following serials, which landed respectively as from 22:50 and 23:05. The Germans were still in large numbers to the north of LZ W when the gliders landed and they infiltrated the landing zone as from 21:00 in small groups ranging from a team to a section. Certain gliders found themselves isolated in the middle of the German troops, under violent gunfire, some of them even during their approach. Human losses were high with 157 of the 1,190 airlanded soldiers engaged killed or wounded during glider landing operations (15 aboard the Waco gliders and 142 aboard the Horsas).

20:53

– Start of operation Keokuk in the Hiesville sector, with the engagement of 32 CG-4A Waco gliders and as many Dakota C-47 planes from the 434th US Troop Carrier Group. They land in Cotentin, in Landing Zone E to bring reinforcements to the 101st Airborne Division.

21:00

–The attack by three *21. Panzer-Division* companies, commanded by General Feuchtinger, to the south of Juno Beach, meets with failure.

– Pointe du Hoc: 24 rangers, led by Lieutenant Charles Parker from Company A of the 5th Battalion, landed on Omaha Beach, reach the strongpoint. They take 20 prisoners along their way.

– Bombardments in Normandy: a new wave of aerial raids hits many Norman towns.

To the south of Sword Beach, these British artillerymen from the 3rd Infantry Division are watching parachute drops by the 6th Airborne Division at 21:00. IWM (B 5046).

CIVILIAN VICTIMS IN NORMANDY

The people of Normandy paid a heavy price for their liberation. Aerial bombardments, but also shellfire and artillery fire from land and sea led to 2,200 deaths among the civilian population within 48 hours of the launch of operation Overlord. The towns that suffered most were Lisieux and Coutances.

Although the logic of systematic bombardment was the main reason for these losses in human lives, their consequences were exacerbated by the extreme inaccuracy of aerial attacks. The Allies had preferred quantity over quality and it took them up to hundreds of bomber planes before they hit all their targets. Weather conditions contributed towards the increase in collateral damage: one layer of cloud was enough to render an aerial raid totally inaccurate. In addition to all these unfavourable conditions, the heavy bomber pilots needed to fly at very high altitude to escape attack from the German anti-aircraft batteries, hence further reducing their firing precision.

Throughout the Battle of Normandy, certain towns and villages were captured and recaptured, falling in turn in and out of enemy and Allied hands amidst repeated bombardments which left behind no more than piles of ruins. The civilians were left with two choices: to take to the road or to lock themselves up in their basements. Yet, even so, neither of the choices was to totally spare the local populations that found themselves amidst this cauldron of combat. Since Normandy was, and still is, a land of farm breeding, many animals were also among the victims of the fighting (around 80,000 cattle). At the time, the German army still used many horses within its horse-drawn units (to tow artillery pieces in particular). But they were equally affected by the ongoing battle with around 8,000 animals killed.

From the first preparations for operation Overlord in 1943 to the end of the Battle of Normandy in August 1944, no less than 1,572 localities were subjected to aerial bombardments and to land or naval artillery fire. The village of Aunay-sur-Odon, a strategic crossroads in Calvados, was entirely destroyed by the end of the battle. Tilly-la-Campagne and Vire suffered over 95% destruction, Villers-Bocage 88%, Le Havre 82%, Saint-Lô 77%, Falaise 76%, Caen and Lisieux 75%.

Civilian victims in Normandy during World War II:

– Calvados : 8,140 killed

– Eure : 900 killed

– Manche : 3,800 killed

– Orne : 2,200 killed

– Seine-Inférieure : 4,850 killed

Known total: 19,890 killed

Normans stricken and homeless: 300,000

21:10

– Landing on LZ W by the first American gliders engaged in operation Elmira, aimed at bringing reinforcements in men and material to the 82nd Airborne Division. A total of 36 Waco and 140 Horsa gliders are deployed.

21:30

– Portsmouth: General Montgomery boards the destroyer *HMS Faulknor* to travel to Normandy where he will supervise land-based operations.

– Field Marshal Rommel arrives at his command post after a 500-mile journey by car.

21:45

– Omaha Beach: artillery fire is reported from the south-east of the Maisy zone.

22:00

– The *12. SS Panzer Division Hitlerjugend*, commanded by *SS-Brigadeführer* Fritz Witt, reaches Evrecy. The unit has been held up by the Allied aviation and late-coming and contradictory orders (in particular due to misinformation created by operation Titanic which consisted in dropping 'Rupert' dummy parachutists near Lisieux).

In Caen, the many victims are recovered from their ruined homes, destroyed by incessant bombardments. The work of volunteers is complicated by fires that are difficult to contain. US National Archives.

ARROMANCHES AND PREPARATIONS FOR THE ARTIFICIAL HARBOUR

The beach at Arromanches-les-Bains (or simply Arromanches) has been famous since the 18th century for its calm waters. On old maps of the region, it is noted as being a prime location for mooring. Two centuries later, the Allies planned to install an artificial harbour there. It was to be built in England, towed across the Channel and assembled piece by piece. They planned to install two harbours - one off Saint-Laurent-sur-Mer (codenamed Mulberry A), the other off Arromanches-les-Bains (Mulberry B).

The village of Arromanches nestles between two cliffs and has a very narrow stretch of beach. The Allies did not want to reduce the village to ruins for the surrounding roads would become impracticable and transporting the supplies landed in the harbour towards the front lines would be delayed. Consequently, there were no landings off Arromanches and the Allies planned to take the village from the rear.

Although the village was placed within the Gold Beach sector, no unit landed directly at Arromanches-les-Bains on the 6th of June 1944. The regiment in charge of capturing the village, the 1st Battalion Hampshire Regiment, commanded by Lieutenant-Colonel David Nelson-Smith, landed at Asnelles before advancing westwards. The occupying Germans from the 1st Battalion of the 352nd Infantry Division's *Grenadier-Regiment 916*, steadfastly defended their position, succeeding in slowing down progression by the British troops. At around 19:00, the first Hampshire Regiment units reached Arromanches and succeeded in taking control of the *Kriegsmarine* radar station located on the top of the east plateau. At 22:30, all remaining pockets of resistance had been eradicated and the village was entirely liberated.

It was on the very evening of D-Day that the first ships to be used to create the breakwater arrived off Arromanches. They were scuttled over the following days. Construction of the Mulberry B artificial harbour began on the 7th of June and, in the village, a few houses were voluntarily destroyed to enable the convoys to move inland without unnecessary difficulty. The very first supplies were unloaded as from the 14th of June.

A violent storm, on the 19th of June, destroyed the harbour intended for use by the Americans on Omaha Beach (Mulberry A). Although the Arromanches harbour suffered great damage, it could easily be repaired. For the entire duration of the Battle of Normandy, for the two harbours combined, a total of 400,000 men, 500,000 vehicles and 4 million tonnes of material arrived in Normandy via Mulberries A and B. Over the last week in July, the volume reached its peak at a rate of 20,000 tonnes per day. Mulberry B in Arromanches was used up to the 19th of November 1944.

22:07

– Sunset.

22:30

– After fierce combat, liberation of the locality of Tailleville, defended by the 736th Grenadier Regiment.

– The men from the Royal Hampshire's 1st Battalion liberate Arromanches-les-Bains.

23:00

– Pointe du Hoc: a counter-attack by 40 German soldiers from the 1st and 914th Regiments - 352nd Infantry Division, is launched against the rangers.

– Omaha Beach: Major Tegtmeyer informs Colonel Ficchy by radio that nothing is in place to evacuate the wounded, and that something needs to be done.

23:30

– Pointe du Hoc: General Kraiss reports to General Marcks that, 'the counter-attack by the 1st Company - 914th Grenadier Regiment is still underway.'

A British soldier, wounded in combat, is evacuated towards the cruiser *HMS Frobisher*, positioned off the Normandy coast, 6th June 1944. IWM (A 24104).

SUMMARY OF ALLIED OBJECTIVES AND ACCOMPLISHMENTS ON D-DAY

On the evening of the 6th of June 1944, many of the initially planned objectives remained unaccomplished. Although the Allied bridgehead was, by now, solidly established in Normandy, it was still at risk of a large-scale German counter-attack with support from armoured divisions. The vast armada continued to land reinforcements and precious antitank guns on the barely secured beaches.

The liberation of Caen, initially expected by the evening of the 6th of June, was postponed, for the British tanks had progressed far quicker than the necessary infantry troops and, although just a few miles from the capital of Calvados, they had no choice but to retreat. Whilst results for the first day of combat were globally positive, the Germans had not for as much surrendered Normandy to the Allies. On the contrary, they continued to fight, putting up fierce resistance against the landed forces.

The situation at midnight on the 6th of June 1944 was as follows: 156,115 soldiers were engaged in combat in Normandy. The Allies had lost 10,500 men, 2,500 of whom had been killed - figures that were well under estimations. Indeed, prior to the launch of operation Overlord, Winston Churchill had forecast 20,000 losses. On the German side, early reports indicated 4,000 killed; however, in the early hours of the attack, certain reports varied by up to 100%.

The Atlantic Wall had been broken through and had only proven to be truly effective on the Omaha and Juno Beach sectors. But it was no longer any threat to the Allies, who now focused on enemy tank movements, for the German Tigers and Panthers were dreaded by the Allied divisions. To counter these armoured vehicles, the American and Anglo-Canadian troops literally filled the Normandy skies with incessant patrols by fighter planes. There was a striking comparison between the 10,000 Allied flights on the 6th of June and the meagre

These 'Phoenix' caissons are being towed across the English Channel towards their final destination off Saint-Laurent-sur-Mer and Arromanches-les-Bains. They will be used as breakwaters for the future artificial harbours, built piece by piece by the Allies. The caissons are surmounted with a gun for anti-aircraft defence around the harbour. US National Archives.

319 take-offs by German craft. General Rommel, Commander of Army Group B informed of his concern. He was one of the only German generals to realise that the battle had already been lost, for the Allies were now relatively solidly established in Normandy and the German tanks had failed to engage in time. However, the Normandy bocage was in favour of the defenders, for it was criss-crossed by several impassable hedges that rendered the tanks particularly vulnerable. Only the region around Caen was devoid of this type of vegetation with, on the contrary, vast stretches of plain.

Isolated on a narrow stretch of land, the Rangers at Pointe du Hoc are preparing to spend their first night on the front, with support from the guns of the Allied armada. US National Archives.

For the Allies, it was crucial that the bridgeheads be joined as quickly as possible for Juno and Gold were the only two sectors to have successfully joined forces on the evening of the 6th of June. The Anglo-Canadians attacked on the 7th, in an attempt to gain control of Caen, as per the plans of operation Perch; however, the German defences held out. The 2nd Battalion Gloucestershire Regiment liberated the town of Bayeux, located on the road from Caen to Isigny-sur-Mer and Carentan, whilst, to the north, the Canadian troops landed on Juno Beach and the British on Sword joined forces. The Americans also consolidated their bridgehead and advanced towards Carentan and Isigny-sur-Mer to meet with fellow US troops landed on Omaha. The day after D-Day, the Allied bridgehead measured 20 miles in length and 6 to 10 miles in depth. The Battle of Normandy had begun - to end 90 days later, after violent combat.

Focus on the Allied offensive at midnight on the 6th of June

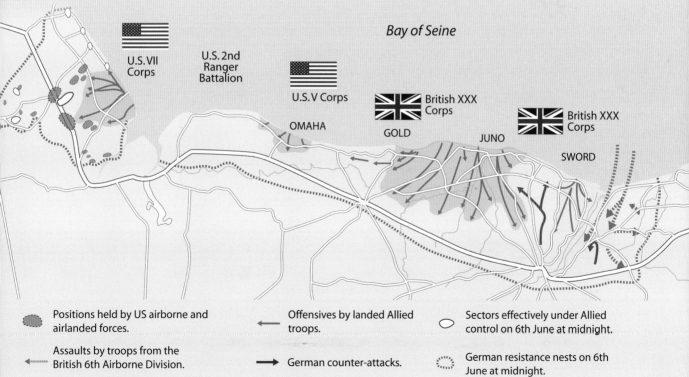

Positions held by US airborne and airlanded forces.

Offensives by landed Allied troops.

Sectors effectively under Allied control on 6th June at midnight.

Assaults by troops from the British 6th Airborne Division.

German counter-attacks.

German resistance nests on 6th June at midnight.

Landings of reinforcements intensify on Omaha Beach, where the Landing Ship Tank (LST) vessels unload their cargo without encountering any particular difficulty, in order to bring fresh men, ammunition, food and vehicles to the front. US National Archives

PART V:
The Key phases of the Battle of Normandy

ENLARGING THE BRIDGEHEAD

Immediately after D-Day, the Allies' priority was to reunite all the landing beaches within one single bridgehead, whilst ensuring the successful accomplishment of targets set during preparations for operation Overlord. The Anglo-Canadians attacked on the 7th of June, in an attempt to gain control of Caen, as per the plans of operation Perch; however, the German defences withstood after the surprise attack the previous day. The British 2nd Army in turn progressed southwards to liberate Bayeux, located on the road between Caen and Isigny-sur-Mer and Carentan, whilst Juno and Sword Beaches were reunited. The day after D-Day, the Allied bridgehead measured 20 miles in length and 6 to 10 miles in depth. In contrast, the American troops landed on Utah Beach in Cotentin were still isolated and had failed to join forces with those landed on Omaha.

On the 8th of June, further German reinforcements arrived in Normandy from Brittany in the form of the 3rd Parachute Division (from Brest), the 77th Division (from Saint-Malo) and the 353rd Division from Morlaix. The *17. Panzergrenadier Division*, placed on the alert on the 6th of June in Poitiers, only arrived with its first units on the 11th of June in the region around Caumont. Because of this delay, the German divisions had insufficient time to group together and to launch a collective offensive. They consequently engaged as and when they arrived and were never in sufficient numbers to truly pose a threat to the Allies, who clearly outnumbered them.

The two artificial harbours in Saint-Laurent-sur-Mer (photograph) and Arromanches-les-Bains, played an essential role in the logistics of the Battle of Normandy, compensating temporarily for the absence of a deep-water port. US National Archives.

On the 7th of June 1944, Mickaël Wittmann's Tiger tanks are making their way along the RN316 trunk road, towards Morgny. The Allied aviation made progress for the German reinforcements towards Normandy extremely difficult. Bundesarchiv Bild 101i-299-1804-07.

RESUPPLYING THE ALLIED FORCES

The landing beaches were devoid of any deep-water port such as Cherbourg or Le Havre, which are always particularly useful for wartime logistics. Pending the liberation of any such facility, the Allies needed to adapt. Hence, immediately after the D-Day Landings, they began to install their very own supply system.

The construction of the artificial harbours was part of operation Mulberry. The prefabricated pontoons, platforms and breakwaters were towed one by one across the English Channel and installed off the villages of Saint-Laurent-sur-Mer (for the American forces) and Arromanches (for the British troops). Their aim was to be able to unload up to 20,000 tonnes of material per day. In Port-en-Bessin and Sainte-Honorine-des-Pertes, in the sector between Omaha Beach and Gold Beach, the Allies implemented operation Pluto: networks of pipeline were installed to transport fuel to

several tanks. Finally, as from the 7th of June, the construction of airstrips (the famous Advanced Landing Grounds) began. The airstrip codenamed E1, then ALG, installed at the top of the Saint-Laurent-sur-Mer plateau was used to evacuate the wounded by air. The other strips were used to land or to rearm fighter planes. These supply solutions were nevertheless temporary: the Allies' key aim remained the capture of Cherbourg and its precious port facilities. The Americans who had landed on Utah headed west to cut the Cotentin peninsula in two and to isolate as many enemy troops as possible to the north of their lines. They then set off across the bocage hedges on their way to the famous deep-water port.

Meanwhile, combat to extend the bridgehead continued and it was only on the 10th of June that the Omaha and Utah sectors were finally reunited. On the 12th of June, the US 1st Infantry Division attacked towards the Caumont heights, just 20 miles south of the coast. The British troops attacked towards Villers-Bocage, on the road between Caen and Vire, only to be driven back after violent confrontations with the German Tiger tanks.

Thankfully for the Allies, they had command of the skies and their fighter plane formations terrified the German troops, be they in movement or in position. Hence, on the 12th of June, as the American soldiers from the 1st Infantry Division took control of Caumont, General Marcks, Commander of the German 84th Corps, was killed during an air raid as he was travelling in his car.

When the town of Carentan fell, the same day, into the hands of the parachutists from the US 101st Airborne Division, the Allied bridgehead had reached a length of 50 miles and a variable depth of 6 to 20 miles. The same day, 16 divisions, with a total of 326,547 men, 54,186 vehicles and 104,428 tonnes of material were landed in Normandy (9 American divisions and 7 British and Canadian divisions).).

In Port-en-Bessin, these oil pipelines are bringing fuel for the Allied forces, within the context of the logistics plan codenamed PLUTO (Pipe-Line Under The Ocean).
US National Archives.

CONSOLIDATING THE BRIDGEHEAD

The liberation of Caen was seriously behind schedule with regard to the initial plan, all the more so since Montgomery had decided to wait for sufficient reinforcement units before launching the offensive. At D-Day+17 (23rd of June), he planned to use the forces commanded by General Miles Dempsey, i.e. the 1st, 8th and 30th Army Corps (for a total of 60,000 men, 600 tanks and 700 guns). The operation was baptised Epsom. However, on the 23rd of June, a new storm was raging in the Channel and food, material and fuel supplies were blocked in ships or still in England, unable to be transported by sea in such deplorable weather conditions. Whereas the Allies suffered from their incapacity to advance, the Germans took advantage of this lull in the offensive to reinforce their front lines with a freshly arrived armoured division, the *Panzer Lehr*. In the sector around Caen, the Germans had a total of 228 tanks, 150 guns of a calibre of 88mm and several other guns of varying calibres at their disposal.

THE DIFFICULT CONQUEST OF CHERBOURG

Meanwhile, as from the 18th of June 1944, the Americans had reached the west coast of Cotentin at Barneville-sur-Mer, isolating around 40,000 German soldiers who retreated behind the first line of defence in Cherbourg, forming a semi-circle just over a mile outside the town. The set-up met with great criticism, even within the Reich army itself, for the Germans knew they were encircled and had no hope of retreating. General Farmbacher, chief of the 84th Army Corps was relieved of his command by Field Marshal Rommel, who criticised his opposition to the Führer's plans. The forces from the US VII Army Corps, commanded by Major General Joseph Lawton Collins, launched the assault, coming within reach of the German defences as from the 20th of June. Hence began the Battle of Val de Saire. On the 22nd of June, the American attack was launched according to plan: the aerial bombardment began at 12:40. A total of 562 fighter-bombers were engaged in successive waves every five minutes.

On the evening of the 26th of June, 10,000 German soldiers are taken prisoner in Cherbourg; however, the arsenal continues to resist the American troops, who only manage to seal control of the town the following day. US National Archives.

The Allies simultaneously engaged a naval force comprised of 18 warships taken from the existing armada positioned off the Normandy shores since the 6th of June. This fleet was aimed at reducing to silence the coastal batteries around 'Fortress Cherbourg', whilst providing support fire to the infantry. On the evening of the 26th of June, 10,000 German soldiers were taken prisoner, but the arsenal continued to resist. The Americans decided to wait till the following day before launching any further assaults. On the 27th of June, at 10:00, the surrender of the last remaining defences marked the end of combat operations to liberate Cherbourg. The battle had cost the lives of 2,800 American soldiers and around 7,500 Germans. General Collins' VII Corps also sustained heavy losses (5,700 dead and 13,500 wounded), whereas 39,000 Germans had been taken prisoner.

On the 26th of June 1944, day of the operation Epsom offensive, the Scottish soldiers from the 6th Battalion Royal Scots Fusiliers, 15th Scottish Division, support their section's progression. IWM (B 5959).

On the 7th of July 1944, Lieutenant General George S. Patton (3rd US Army, with his famous mother-of-pearl grip Colt at his belt), Lieutenant General Omar Bradley (1st US Army) and General Sir Bernard L. Montgomery (21st Army Group) meet in Normandy the day before the launch of operation Charnwood. US National Archives.

LIBERATION OF CAEN

Sunday 25th of June 1944 marked the start of the land-based offensive codenamed operation Epsom: 60,000 men and 600 tanks belonging to the British 2nd Army attacked to the west of Caen. Two days later, Scottish troops broke through the German front over a depth of around 6 miles which, although an impressive performance, was below Montgomery's expectations. From his headquarters established in Blay, he was concerned about the catastrophic reports on the British losses since the start of his offensive. On the 1st of July, operation Epsom was brought to a halt upon orders from the high command, yet Caen was still in enemy hands. The offensive had drawn several German armoured units within the vicinity of Caen, which had at least relieved the American front.

The town of Caen was encircled to the north and west by Anglo-Canadian positions along the River Odon. Some 2,500 tonnes of bombs were dropped to the north of Caen on the evening of the 7th of July. Two days later, the Canadian and the British 3rd Divisions succeeded in occupying the northern quarters of Caen, as the *12. SS Panzer-Division* withdrew to the south of the Orne.

BREAKING THROUGH THE FRONT

The war of the hedgerows

Although the Germans concentrated their defensive efforts for long weeks around the town of Caen, the situation was no less fluid for the Americans, who were making extremely slow progress and at a cost of heavy losses. The type of terrain in the Normandy bocage offered one explanation for this. Between La Haye-du-Puits and Lessay, they lost 1,000 men, put out of action, for every 1,000 yards gained, and the capture of Mont Castre alone cost them 5,000 men. The weather was appalling and prevented any aerial support for ground troops.

This was all to have a very negative effect on Allied troop morale.

The Americans developed a plan (operation Cobra) aimed at sustainably breaking through the front towards Brittany. They reunited four infantry divisions and two armoured divisions along a narrow 5-mile corridor. On the 25th of July, they launched the largest carpet bombing operation of the entire conflict: 1,500 planes dropped around 3,300 tonnes of bombs between Montreuil and Hébécrevon, to the north-west of Saint-Lô.

On the 9th of July, Privates Bernard Hoo, John MacCouville and J.R. Kostick from the Queen's Own Rifles of Canada, 8th Brigade, 3rd Canadian Infantry Division in front of the signpost to the west of Caen on the RN13 trunk road. US National Archives.

The US forces were confronted with a particularly dense landscape in the Normandy Bocage, seriously hindering their progression. The systematic use of support fire such as the aviation or artillery enabled them to finally overwhelm their adversaries. US National Archives.

These bombers were supported by a further 1,000 medium bombers and fighter-bombers: 60,000 incendiary bombs were dropped across a 4.6 square mile portion of bocage, i.e. over 13,000 bombs per square mile. Land-based artillery troops took over via massive bombing by 1,100 artillery pieces. Due to the bad weather conditions, the bombs killed 111 and wounded around 500 American soldiers. Killed during the operation, Lieutenant-General Lesley McNair was the highest-ranking American soldier to be killed in the European theatre of operations.

Yet, whilst the bombardments killed many American soldiers, they also proved disastrous for the German forces, who lost many soldiers (2,500 men) and vehicles – the *Panzer Lehr* only had seven remaining tanks fit for combat in the sector. On the evening of the 25th of July, the front line had progressed less than 2 miles to the south. The American generals, Bradley in particular, were concerned about this extremely slow progress, even if the German prisoners were still shocked by the intensity of the bombardments. The south Cotentin front was finally opened. The Germans chaotically withdrew and Bradley's tactics finally paid off: the tanks began to advance more easily with the infantry paving the way.

By the end of operation Cobra, the Allies progressed at startling speed, submerging the Germans who abandoned their positions to the US forces. The Pontaubault bridge, that opened the route to Brittany, was now under Allied control. General Patton, commander of the US 3rd Army, was duly proud of his men. The Allies could now safely say that despite terrible losses, Cobra had met with total success. The breakthrough towards Brittany nevertheless exposed a fragile flank to German resistance in the Avranches sector. On the 7th of August, the defenders launched operation Lüttich, aimed at isolating the US 1st and 23rd Armies. The offensive threw the American lines off balance during the first twelve hours of the attack. Yet, on the first day, the losses inflicted on the Germans were such that they were incapable of relaunching the operation. Of the 300 tanks they had deployed, around 150 were destroyed on the 7th and 8th of August. Allied supremacy in the airs brought a permanent end to the offensive. The Allies then succeeded in progressively encircling their adversaries. Indeed, the US 3rd Army took control of Le Mans on the 9th of August and General Bradley was quick to grasp that a noose was forming around the German 7th Army. The next few days of the Battle of Normandy were centred on closing the noose in the region of Falaise.

Two German *Panther Auf* A tanks (belonging to the 1st squadron of the *Panzer-Regiment 6.*) destroyed on the RD257 minor road in the Le Dézert sector during the counter-attack by the *Panzer Lehr* on the 11th of July 1944. US National Archives.

BREAKING THROUGH THE FRONT

General Bradley suggested to Eisenhower launching a pincer movement to encircle the enemy and to tighten the hold around Falaise. For the Allies, this was a unique opportunity to put an end to the German army's occupation in the north-west of France. Fierce combat was engaged around Alençon, which by evening was besieged by General Leclerc's *2e Division Blindée*, a French armoured division landed on Utah Beach on the 1st of August. The French troops penetrated inside the town, but it took them a few hours to totally clear the streets of its isolated German snipers. The German ranking officers were convinced that only a rapid retreat towards the Seine could save the majority of the Axis troops and vehicles engaged in Normandy. However, Hitler would have none of it and ordered for his generals to stick to their guns and to fight, till the death if necessary. General Crerar's Canadian 1st Army in turn hastened to the town of Falaise, in order to put a permanent end to any hopes of retreat for the German soldiers and vehicles in the sector. The operation was codenamed Totalize. By the evening of the 11th of August, the Canadians had advanced six miles in five days of operation.

To the south-west of Falaise, the US 15th Corps was heading north, despite several confrontations with *SS* armoured divisions. In one week, the US 1st and 3rd Armies had forced the German forces to retreat over 30 miles. Further north, the British 2nd Army and the Canadian 1st Army were also on the move. Between the two fronts, the Germans were closed in, with only one possible exit route - the region of Trun-Falaise. Several dozens of divisions were encircled by the Allies and the noose was tightening. The 7th Army, commanded by General Hausser, began to evacuate as many divisions as possible from the pocket, armoured units taking priority over the infantry. The Allied aviation relentlessly bombarded the pocket which had become a genuine firing range for the fighter-bombers.

On the 14th of August, the Canadians launched operation Tractable, aimed at taking control of the Germans' major escape route, located in the vicinity of Falaise. Despite the disastrous situation they were in, their withdrawal was extremely swift and, on the day of the 17th of August alone, around a third of encircled troops managed to break out of the cauldron. The 6-mile wide corridor in the area near Chambois, which enabled them to escape eastwards, was reduced little by little by the Allied armies. Since the start of troop evacuation towards the Seine, some 55,000 men had successfully retreated, i.e. around 40% of all troops threatened at the beginning of the encirclement manoeuvre. The pocket around the German forces was closed to the south-east of Falaise on the 21st of August 1944.

German soldiers surrendering to Company B of the Argyll and Sutherland Highlanders of Canada-Princess Louise's (4th Canadian Armoured Division) on the 19th of August 1944 in Saint-Lambert-sur-Dive. IWM (PA 116586).

In the Falaise pocket, German convoys become the targets of both the Allied artillery and the aviation: this column has been attacked by Allied fighter planes in an attempt to escape the 'cauldron' in the Chambois sector. US National Archives.

21st - 29th August 1944

THE RACE TO THE SEINE

Chaos in the Falaise pocket was indescribable: the smoking carcasses of vehicles, the bodies of soldiers and the horses that had been used for their evacuation were scattered along the roads and rivers, amidst terrible scenes of the routing army. Over 200 tanks, around 1,000 artillery pieces and as many vehicles had been destroyed. Nevertheless, several units still managed to escape eastwards, taking advantage of the morning mist to cross the Canadian, Polish and American lines: over 165,000 Germans finally reached the eastern bank of the Seine. A larger-scale encirclement was then envisaged, in order to trap all those who were fleeing Normandy and heading towards the east of France to reorganise their troops. During operation Paddle, the Allies immediately embarked on an expeditious thrust towards the Seine, which the Germans hurriedly crossed with whatever means at their disposal.

The Battle of Normandy had caused the death of over 36,000 Allied soldiers and around 50,000 Germans. On the 29th of August 1944, when the last German convoys crossed the Seine, the Allies had some 2,850,000 soldiers on the European continent.

Over the months to follow, France and its neighbouring countries were finally restored to peace. Germany capitulated without setting conditions and combat ceased in Europe on the 8th of May 1945, less than a year after D-Day. Around 100,000 soldiers of all nationalities are now laid to rest in war cemeteries across Normandy. They all remind us of the sad price of liberty: their blood.

In Saint-Lambert-sur-Dive on the 25th of August 1944, three young Normans pose in front of the imposing shell of a German Panther tank. IWM (B 9665).

ACKNOWLEDGMENTS

The author would like to thank his wife, Violette, for her unyielding support over many years, together with his family, thanks to whom he discovered Normandy from a very early age.

He also thanks Éditions OREP for the availability and the trust they have afforded him.

BIBLIOGRAPHY

Air: The Restless Shaper of the World, William BRYANT, W. W. Norton & Company, 2013.

Sword : Objectif Caen, Georges BERNAGE, Éditions Heimdal, 2010.

Omaha Beach, 6 juin 1944, Georges BERNAGE, Éditions Heimdal, 2001.

Utah Beach : Sainte-Mère-Église, Sainte-Marie-du-Mont, Georges BERNAGE, Éditions Heimdal, 2011.

Gold, Juno, Sword, Georges BERNAGE, Éditions Heimdal, 2003.

Pointe du Hoc : Énigme autour d'un point d'appui allemand, Helmut-Konrad VON KEUSGEN, Éditions Heimdal, 2006.

508th Parachute Infantry Regiment, Dominique FRANÇOIS, Éditions Heimdal, 2003.

Point d'appui WN 62 : Normandie 1942-1944 Omaha Beach, Helmut-Konrad VON KEUSGEN, Éditions Heimdal, 2004.

La 101st Airborne Division dans la Seconde Guerre mondiale, Vanguard of the Crusade, Mark A. BANDO, Éditions Heimdal, 2012.

Diables Rouges en Normandie, Georges BERNAGE, Éditions Heimdal, 2002.

J'ai débarqué le 6 juin 1944 : Commando de la France libre, Gwenn-Aël BOLLORÉ, Le Cherche-Midi, 2003.

It's a long way to Normandy, 6 juin 1944 : he D-Day Landings, as seen by one of the 177 men of the Kieffer commando, Maurice CHAUVET, Éditions Picollec, 2004.

Le Commando du pont Pégase, Norbert HUGEDÉ, Éditions France Empire, 2004.

Operation Overlord – D-day – Day by Day, Anthony HALL, Grange Books Ltd, 2003.

6 juin 1944, débarquement en Normandie, Jean COMPAGNON, Éditions Ouest-France, 1984.

Omaha Beach, C. PRIME, Éditions OREP, 2016.

Gold, Y. MAGDELAINE, Éditions OREP, 2012.

Pegasus Bridge, Y. MAGDELAINE, Éditions OREP, 2018.

Le Jour J et la bataille de Normandie, J. QUELLIEN, Éditions OREP, 2015.

Zone tertiaire de Nonant - 14400 BAYEUX
Tel.: 02 31 51 81 31 - Fax: 02 31 51 81 32
E-mail: info@orepeditions.com - Web: www.orepeditions.com

Editor: Grégory Pique - Editorial coordination: Sophie Lajoye
Graphic design: Éditions OREP - Layout: Laurent Sand
English translation: Heather Inglis

ISBN: 978-2-8151-0301-5 - Copyright OREP 2018
Legal deposit: 1st quarter 2019